STEINBECK
in VIETNAM

STEINBECK
in VIETNAM

DISPATCHES FROM THE WAR

Edited by Thomas E. Barden

University of Virginia Press | Charlottesville and London

University of Virginia Press

© 2012 by the Rector and Visitors of the University of Virginia

All rights reserved

Printed in the United States of America on acid-free paper

First published 2012

9 8 7 6 5 4 3 2 1

LIBRARY OF CONGRESS CATALOGING-IN-PUBLICATION DATA

Steinbeck, John, 1902–1968.

  [Selections. 2012]

  Steinbeck in Vietnam : dispatches from the war / John Steinbeck ; edited by Thomas E. Barden.

    p.   cm.

  Includes bibliographical references and index.

  ISBN 978-0-8139-3257-6 (cloth : acid-free paper)

  1. Steinbeck, John, 1902–1968—Political and social views. 2. Vietnam War, 1961–1975—Literature and the war. I. Barden, Thomas E. II. Title.

  PS3537.T3234A6 2012

  959.704′3373—dc23

2011026049

TITLE PAGE *Steinbeck in the door gunner seat of a UH-1 Huey helicopter wearing a headset to communicate with the pilot.* MARTHA HEASLEY COX CENTER, SAM GIPSON JR. BEQUEST. 1-538

CONTENTS

PREFACE

WHEN I MENTION that John Steinbeck went to Vietnam in the 1960s to cover the war as a roving newspaper reporter, most people respond with genuine surprise. Those who came of age after that turbulent time, along with many who lived through it and even some who were in Vietnam themselves, are usually unaware that Steinbeck was deeply and personally involved. Although his career continued for almost three decades after the 1939 publication of *The Grapes of Wrath*, he is still most closely associated with his Depression-era works of social struggle. But from Pearl Harbor on, he often wrote about America's wars from first-hand experience, and Vietnam was no exception.

Between December 1966 and May 1967 the sixty-four-year-old Steinbeck traveled throughout Southeast Asia, posting dispatches from South Vietnam, Thailand, Laos, and Indonesia as a war correspondent for the Long Island daily newspaper *Newsday*. This book makes all of those dispatches available for the first time since their publication over forty years ago.

The quarrels of those days are history now, but from a twenty-first century vantage point, it is easy to see how these essays, in which Steinbeck made his best argument for the necessity of the war and the Johnson Administration's execution of it, must have infuriated the doves and delighted the hawks of the late 1960s. But it is also interesting to consider from this distance how important the essays must have been to the large number of readers who were undecided and bewildered about the war and who considered John Steinbeck a reliable moral witness. He was an American voice readers had known and respected for decades. And unlike most of the other pundits and writers who were taking sides on Vietnam, he was actually willing to go to the combat zones and put himself in harm's way. His Vietnam essays offered his fellow Americans personalized accounts from a war that was splitting the country into increasingly angry factions and defying comprehension, much less resolution.

But these dispatches are significant beyond their value as historical documents. Even though they were written on the fly in hotel rooms and were often little more than field notes with off-hand political opinions thrown in, many of them still have the spell-casting power of Steinbeck's great works of fiction. They have immediacy and they have passion. And they are, after all, the last published writings of an American author of enduring national and international stature. It is important that Nobel laureate John Ernst Steinbeck's entire body of written work be available in print.

The introduction will provide basic background information and situate the dispatches in the context of Steinbeck's personal and writing life at the time. The tasks of analyzing, critiquing, and assessing the essays I have saved for an afterword. I want to avoid pressing my own ideas about the dispatches onto readers before they have had a chance to read them for themselves. I have also placed the individual notes on each essay at the back of the book to lighten the weight of annotation as readers encounter Steinbeck's original words.

There are some people and institutions I want to thank—the University of Toledo for giving me a sabbatical in the spring of 2010 to complete the research; the Princeton University Library staff for emailing me relevant portions of the Preston Beyer John Steinbeck collection; the staff of the Martha Heasley Cox Center for Steinbeck Studies at San Jose State University, especially Paul Douglass and Sstoz Tes, for their informed answers to my endless questions; the Manuscripts Division people at the Library of Congress; and the staff at the Pierpont Morgan Library.

My University of Toledo colleagues Jim Campbell and Joel Lipman helped me figure out how to tell this story, and fellow Steinbeck scholars Rich Hart and Michael Meyer helped me tell it better. Robert Harmon, Professor Emeritus of Library Science at San Jose State University, who worked this territory before me, was generous in sharing his knowledge. Llew Gibbons, my UT College of Law colleague, gave me good advice about copyright and permissions issues. Florence Eichen at Penguin Group and Rebecca Strauss at McIntosh and Otis were both very helpful in guiding me through the intricate process of gaining permission to reprint Steinbeck's work. Cathie Brettschneider, the humanities editor at the University of Virginia Press, helped tremendously by championing this book from the beginning. And Morgan

Myers, a project editor at the Press, gave the manuscript the tender, loving care of a true Steinbeck fan.

Joshua Mooney, my undergraduate research student, became a Steinbeck scholar in the course of our work together; in fact, he won the Louis Owen Award for Steinbeck Scholarship in 2009. Sean Odoms, University of Toledo student worker and keyboarder extraordinaire, provided good clerical support. My son Zacharias Barden, whose high writing standards make me proud, helped me fix many awkward sentences. And most of all, I thank Rayna Zacharias, my wife, music partner, dear companion, and intrepid research associate, for her knack for making research, and life in general, a great adventure.

Portions of the introduction appeared previously in Steinbeck Review *(vol. 5, no. 2, Spring 2008) as an essay titled "Steinbeck in Vietnam." Used with permission.*

INTRODUCTION

As everyone knows, John Steinbeck gained national prominence in the 1930s for books that focused on the plight of migrant workers, displaced Okies, political radicals, and the downtrodden in general. His novels *In Dubious Battle* (1936), *Of Mice and Men* (1937), and *The Grapes of Wrath* (1939) gained him a huge reading audience. They also gained him a reputation with conservatives, including some in the federal government and the military, as an extremist subversive—a dangerous figure. While Steinbeck was never formally investigated, the FBI kept a dossier on him, starting in the early 1940s (FBI Report #100-106224), that documented his political activities, his personal connections, and his writings. The army intelligence service, on the other hand, did formally investigate him in 1943 and filed a report (G-2 File: IX-O/S-1403c) that concluded, "In view of substantial doubt as to subject's loyalty and discretion, it is recommended that subject not be considered favorably for a commission in the Army of the United States." Thus, while he was in personal touch with, and personally advising, President Franklin Delano Roosevelt, Steinbeck was not allowed to join the army, even though he tried several times. His "association with elements" of the Communist Party, as the FBI dossier put it, and the fact that some of his writings appeared in Communist publications, were the bases for the army intelligence service's conclusion.

But Steinbeck was not a Communist, not in the 1930s, nor at any other point in his life. He was clear about this in an authorial aside he wrote in *East of Eden* in 1952: "And this I believe: that the free exploring mind of the individual human is the most valuable thing in the world. And this I would fight for: the freedom of the mind to take any direction it wishes, undirected. And this I must fight against: any idea or government that limits or destroys the individual. This is what I am and what I am about." Moreover, this emphatically anti-collectivist mindset was not a new position Steinbeck arrived at as the Cold War nuclear standoff with the Soviet Union blossomed in the 1950s. A close reading of his work in the thirties and forties shows that, even then, he was not the Communist revolutionary his enemies claimed him to be. After completing *In Dubious Battle,* he wrote in a letter to a friend, "I don't like communists either. I mean I dislike them as people" (*Life in Letters* 120). In *Of Mice and Men,* George and Lenny, his duo of working-class stiffs, do not dream of a proletarian revolution or the end of private ownership; they embrace the American dream of ownership in the form of a nice little house and a small plot of land. In *The Grapes of Wrath,* his protagonist Tom Joad is more concerned with getting food, wages, and protection from police brutality for his family and fellow Okies than he is in creating a utopian communal society. When he tells a camp operator he is a "bolshevisky," he is obviously being ironic. In short, any objective reader of Steinbeck must conclude that he was staunchly anti-Communist, basically an enthusiastic and liberal New Deal Democrat. John Ford's 1940 movie version of *The Grapes of Wrath,* of which Steinbeck wholly approved, made the New Deal association clear by casting an actor with a strong visual resemblance to FDR in the role of the federal migrant relief camp leader.

Despite his undeserved reputation as a subversive, Steinbeck's patriotism ran deep as World War II started. Even after being rejected by the army for his politics, he was determined to do his part in the war. He wrote to and spoke with President Roosevelt several times about the need to counter Nazi propaganda, which he felt was professionally done and often successful with nonaligned countries. He had seen this firsthand when he was in Mexico working on the script for the film *The Forgotten Village.* Roosevelt responded positively to his project proposals and directed him to William "Wild Bill" Donovan, who in 1942 was opening an office in the War Department called the Office of Strategic Services (OSS), the predecessor of the current CIA. Donovan, incidentally, was the basis for the Matt Damon character in the 2006 film *The Good Shepherd,* which depicts the birth of the CIA.

Working at the OSS without pay, Steinbeck wrote *The Moon Is Down,* a play-novelette about a Northern European country occupied by Teutonic invaders who are obviously thinly veiled Nazis following an infallible "Leader." The thesis of this work was that "herd" men, any group that gives over its individualism to a collectivist mentality, will always be bested by "free" men. While the book was about Nazis, the "herd versus free" dichotomy could apply as well to Communists as to fascists. The project did well as a novel, was staged as a Broadway play, and premiered as a popular 20th Century Fox film in March 1943. The work also depicted the difficulty an army has in sustaining its hold on an invaded people, and the toll this takes on the occupiers. A Nazi lieutenant who loses his sanity as the occupation wears on voices this by yelling to his commanders, "The flies have conquered the flypaper!" as he is taken away.

While at the OSS, Steinbeck also gained his first experience as a military field reporter. In the summer of 1942 he and an army photographer were flown 20,000 miles in various bomber aircraft around the country to see firsthand the life and camaraderie of trainees as they prepared for the extremely dangerous job of flying bombing missions in Europe and the Pacific. He ate in their mess halls, slept in the unit barracks, took the same tests the trainees took, and frequented the bars with them in the evenings. The result was *Bombs Away,* an intimate portrait of a bomber team that lionized the young airmen as "the best physical and mental specimens the country produces." The book stressed how the young men retained their individuality while at the same time they became part of a team that worked together seamlessly to accomplish its mission.

In 1943, realizing he would never be accepted into the military, Steinbeck applied for and got a paid overseas assignment for the *New York Herald Tribune* as a war correspondent. In over eighty dispatches, he wrote about the mundane aspects of the war that many journalists missed, such as daily life at a bomber station in England, the allure of the comedian Bob Hope, the popularity of the song "Lili Marlene," the exploits of a jeep driver named Big Train Mulligan, and a diversionary mission off the Italian coast. In this last assignment, he was actually in harm's way, having both ear drums ruptured by a close explosion. The columns were later collected in *Once There Was a War* (1958).

After the war, he went to the Soviet Union at the invitation of President Harry Truman's State Department to get a firsthand look at daily life there. The resulting book, *A Russian Journal,* is a scathing indictment of the USSR's oppression of its own people. He made his opinion of Soviet Communism unequivocally clear in an article for *Le Figaro:*

The Communists of our day are about as revolutionary as the Daughters of the American Revolution. Having accomplished their coup and established their empire, revolution is their nightmare. They have to hunt down and eliminate everyone with the slightest revolutionary tendency, even those who helped accomplish their own. Where they have absolute power they have established the most reactionary governments in the world, governments so fearful of revolt that they must make every man an informer against his fellows, and layer their society with secret police. ("One American in Paris" 12)

In the 1950s, Steinbeck avidly and actively supported Democratic presidential candidate Adlai Stevenson twice, in 1952 and again in 1956. He helped draft campaign speeches and wrote a sympathetic introduction to a collection of those speeches in which Steinbeck states that "Stevenson is durable socially, politically, and morally." His loyalty to the Democratic Party continued into the 1960s when John F. Kennedy took the White House back from the Republicans and when Lyndon Johnson became president after Kennedy's assassination. Both the Kennedy and Johnson administrations returned his allegiance, especially after he won the Nobel Prize for Literature in November 1962. It was a good fit with Kennedy's emphasis on art and culture to have such a celebrated writer in his circle, especially since, by the 1960s, Steinbeck's fame rested on his 1930s social activist phase that mirrored and reinforced Kennedy's civil rights emphasis. In fact, in the summer of 1963, Kennedy selected Steinbeck for the Medal of Freedom, although he didn't live to make the award.

That fell to Lyndon Johnson, who was happy to have the Nobel laureate at his side as he took over an administration that had actively courted and supported artists and writers. Kennedy's inner circle and his national supporters alike had considerable qualms about the burly, plain-spoken Texan who was suddenly their leader. He was as rough as Kennedy was smooth, both socially and culturally. And he was not part of the East Coast Ivy League establishment that dominated official Washington. For his part, Steinbeck was more comfortable with Johnson than he had been with JFK. As Jackson J. Benson points out in his biography *John Steinbeck, Writer*, Steinbeck and Johnson had a great deal in common, from a general discomfort with Harvard and Yale types and a hatred of communism, to their shared passion for social justice and FDR's vision of government assistance to the poor and disenfranchised. And they were both large rough-hewn men, both intelligent yet often portrayed as shallow thinkers, and both from "provincial," that is, non-eastern and non-elite, backgrounds. Benson points out that Steinbeck would often somewhat defensively bring up his time at Stanford University when the talk at White House events turned to educational backgrounds.

A personal relationship also existed between Steinbeck and Johnson through their wives. Lady Bird Johnson and Steinbeck's third wife, Elaine, had been friends since their college days together at the University of Texas, Austin. So it was reasonable for them to make sure that their famous husbands kept in close touch. It was not uncommon for the Steinbecks to spend entire weekends with the Johnsons at the White House. And Johnson worked diligently to solidify Steinbeck's friendship via his own formidable charm and skill at persuasion. He also utilized the dazzling power of the presidency. Benson writes how, when Steinbeck agreed to help Johnson with his 1964 party nomination speech, notes and materials were flown to his home on Long Island by a military airplane.

The Nobel laureate's support became increasingly important to Johnson, as more and more American intellectuals and celebrities began to turn against the war in South Vietnam after the 1965 bombing campaigns and the concurrent troop escalation. This combination of political and personal connections made Steinbeck's devotion to Johnson very strong. In a letter to Jack Valenti, a member of LBJ's inner circle (who later became president of the Motion Picture Association of America), Steinbeck wrote about his relationship with Johnson, "It would be perhaps well to say now what is true. Elaine and I do not give our allegiance readily, but once given, we do not withdraw it" (*Life in Letters*, 825). And in a letter to Johnson about a 1965 speech he gave to Congress, Steinbeck says, "I take great pride in the fact that you are my president" (ibid., 817).

Loyalty to "his" president was not the only emotional allegiance that made it difficult for Steinbeck to publicly criticize the Vietnam conflict, even after the major build-up of American troops. By late 1966, both his sons, Thom (who was twenty-two) and John IV (who was twenty), were in the army. John IV had been drafted and was in Vietnam; Thom, who had enlisted, was in basic training at Fort Ord, California, preparing to go. As readers of *The Winter of Our Discontent* know, Steinbeck became increasingly focused on what he saw as America's moral decay as he reflected on the culture of the 1950s. And this view only heightened as the 1960s antiwar movement developed and spread. He considered the young men of the military exemplars of all that was right about American youth—the opposite of the hippies, folksingers, and self-indulgent college students who opposed the war while hiding behind their 2-S draft deferments.

Given this web of factors, Steinbeck's support of the Vietnam War is not surprising. His affinity for the American military, his anti-Communist feelings, his life-long commitment to the Democratic Party, his personal and patriotic loyalty to Lyndon Johnson, and the presence of one of his own sons in the war made it almost inevitable. The essays in this book capture the time when he was putting that support in writing. They were controversial, coming as they did when American sentiment was beginning to swing against the war. The controversy did not move him to change his position, but, to an extent, his own experiences did. Beneath his continued public pro-war stance, his private opinions grew more and more conflicted as he explored the combat zones and returned home to synthesize and reflect on what he had seen. This is an important part of the story, but it remains unresolved because, after his return to the U.S. in late April 1967, his health deteriorated and, other than private letters, he wrote nothing about the Vietnam War, or anything else, ever again. He died December 20, 1968.

IN FEBRUARY 1965, the American military launched two bombing campaigns against targets in North Vietnam. Operations Rolling Thunder and Steel Tiger were massive carpet bombings of military, industrial, and supply sites in the areas of Hanoi and along the Ho Chi Minh Trail in North Vietnam. In March of the same year, the first large waves of American ground troops began to arrive "in country." Together these moves altered the mission from one of military advising and assistance to the South Vietnamese military to one of a full-fledged U.S.-led war. The Pentagon and Vietnam-based American military leadership took command and "Americanized" the war. In April 1965, Steinbeck wrote a letter to Valenti addressing various issues concerning the war, and particularly the bombing campaigns: "I wish the bombing weren't necessary, but I suspect our people on the ground know more about that than I do. I certainly hope so" (*Life in Letters*, 820).

He admitted that the war was "troublesome" to him and that various groups had asked him to sign petitions against the bombing campaign, although he did not. In another letter a few months later, he was even more explicit about his reservations.

> Well, I'm afraid bad days are coming. There is no way to make this Vietnamese war decent. There is no way of justifying sending troops to another man's country. And there is no way to do anything but praise the man who defends his own land. The real reasons for the war will never come to the surface and if they did most people would not see them. Unless the President makes some overt move toward peace, more and more Americans as well as Europeans are going to blame him for the mess, particularly since the government we are supporting is about as smelly as you can get. (ibid., 826)

Sometime before August 1965, Johnson personally asked Steinbeck to visit South Vietnam and report back to him on the American operations as Steinbeck saw them. We know this because his correspondence at the time frequently mentions substantial pressure from the White House. He resisted an official Vietnam visit, probably because he realized the propaganda value the president would garner from it for his increasingly embattled administration. In an August 1965 letter to Valenti about the proposed trip, he wrote, "I hope the Far Eastern thing is over as far as I am concerned. Certainly I have no wish to go, but the request had the force of an order, one which I hope is unnecessary. I do hope so" (ibid., 838). And he complained to his friend Howard Gossage that he would "probably have to go" (ibid.).

He did not end up having to go as Johnson's man. But, by the next year, things had changed in his personal and writing life and he was quite eager to make the trip, as a private citizen. The main change was that now his son was there. As Elaine put it, "The minute John, Jr. [as his parents usually called him] left for Vietnam, John was determined to go. But he didn't want to go as Lyndon's emissary or anything. It was important that he go independently" (Benson, 995). By then Steinbeck's older son Thom was in basic training and on his way to the war as well.

The second change came when his friend Harry F. Guggenheim offered to send him to Southeast Asia as a war correspondent for his daily newspaper, *Newsday*. Steinbeck had been writing for Guggenheim's paper since the fall of 1965, sending occasional columns as he and Elaine traveled in England, Ireland, and Israel. These pieces had been well received and Guggenheim, happy to keep the famous Steinbeck name associated with his paper, suggested that his next "beat" be Vietnam. Thus, a way opened for Steinbeck to see the war independent of Lyndon Johnson, one that allowed him to roam about freely (including visiting his son) and that cast him in a role he knew from past experience—war correspondent. The opportunity also assured him of a large readership, since *Newsday* had a circulation of over 400,000 readers and a syndication arrangement that placed his essays in twenty-nine American and ten foreign papers, including the *Washington Post*, the *Los Angeles Times*, and the *International Herald Tribune*.

Like his earlier columns, the new pieces were also titled Letters to Alicia. This was Steinbeck's idea and was meant as a tribute to Guggenheim's recently deceased wife, Alicia Patterson Guggenheim, who had been the paper's editor since 1940 and had overseen its rise to prominence. Here is how Guggenheim, acting as editor as well as publisher after Alicia's death, explained when the first essay of the first series appeared on November 20, 1965:

> As previously announced, John Steinbeck is leaving for Europe early next month on an extended trip as a reporter for *Newsday*. Any reports he sends back will appear in *Weekend With Newsday* as a column under the informal heading above. He will write some columns before his departure. The "Alicia" to whom these letters are inscribed is my late wife, Alicia Patterson Guggenheim, editor and publisher of *Newsday* from its founding in 1940 until her death in 1963. Mr. Steinbeck sent me this fond tribute to her. "When I told you I intended to write these letters to Alicia, I meant just that. It is not mawkish or sentimental. The letters should not be to someone who is dead, but rather to a living mind and a huge curiosity.

That is why she was such a great newspaper woman. She wanted to know—everything . . ." On this page is the first of Mr. Steinbeck's "Letters to Alicia."

Steinbeck wrote twenty-eight pieces for the first series, the last dated May 26, 1966. The second series began December 3, 1966, and was prefaced with this shorter explanation to *Newsday*'s readers: "This is the first in a series of columns from South Asia by John Steinbeck that will appear in this space, starting next week, under the title, 'Letters to Alicia.' The 'Alicia' referred to in the letters is the late Alicia Patterson, who was *Newsday*'s first editor and publisher and Steinbeck's good friend." There were fifty-eight essays in the second series. They constitute Steinbeck's formal body of writing about the Vietnam War and his last published work.

The role of correspondent called for Steinbeck to take a public stance on the war. He came out with gusto as a supporter, and he was backed vigorously by Guggenheim, who was also in favor of the war effort. In the first series, Steinbeck had written two pieces about the war that were dropped because they referred to specific news items that were "old news" to the copy editors at the time of submission. One was about the television images of an American soldier setting fire to a Vietnamese village and the other referred to pictures of draft card burners. Several war-related comments did make it into the published first-series columns, but only as asides. In a comic piece about the need for a U.S. Department of Nonsense, for instance, Steinbeck mentioned both hawks and doves as "opposing nonsensers." And in discussing Israeli youth in a piece from Tel Aviv, he praised their enthusiastic military service as opposed to the draft-dodgers and draft card burners at home.

But in the second series of Letters to Alicia, he focused directly on the war. His position was unequivocal. During a stopover in Hawaii on the way to Saigon, he was interviewed by the local press. And while he was reluctant to discuss his mission and chided reporters who pressed him, saying "I'm selling it, boys, not giving it away," he did eventually state his opinion of the war. He was clear, saying, "Yes, I'm in favor of it" (Fensch, 97). He saw his mission as one of observer, explorer, and reporter and he tried hard to maintain objectivity and independence from his handlers, but from the moment he and Elaine landed at Tan

Son Nhut airbase in the Republic of South Vietnam on December 10, 1966, until he was back in America, any reservations he had about the war basically disappeared from his writing.

ONCE THEY WERE in Vietnam, the couple, especially John, set a grueling pace. (He turned 65 in February 1967; Elaine was 52.) They saw John IV almost as soon as they landed, as he was stationed in Saigon and able to meet them at the airport and accompany them to the Caravelle Hotel. They visited with John IV and met some of his friends while Steinbeck received orientation briefings from numerous information and operations officers. He was given jungle fatigues, boots, and an M-16, and put through rudimentary rifle training on the weapon.

Then, after three days in Saigon, Steinbeck left Elaine at the Caravelle and started his first round of field observations. A marine officer named Major Sam M. Gipson Jr. was assigned to be his escort and guide. Since he traveled by helicopter, he could cover a lot of territory; he started with the areas around Saigon, and then went to the Mekong Delta and Da Nang. He was back at the Caravelle in time to celebrate Christmas with Elaine in their hotel room, complete with a small tree John IV bought from the Saigon market.

After Christmas Steinbeck was back at it, flying in "every kind of chopper we have save one," as he put it in one column (20). He went with river patrols in boats on the Mekong, got training on the M-79 grenade launcher, pulled the lanyard to fire a 105 mm howitzer, witnessed a B-52 bombing run, and flew missions as a fixed-wing forward observer. He would be out two or three days at a time, come back to the hotel, write from his notes, send the dispatches to *Newsday* via a Pan American Airlines special correspondence pouch, and then head back out. Elaine went with him on one of these sorties. They inspected Can Tho in the heart of the Mekong Delta, a secure village retaken from the Viet Cong that served as a model to show journalists what military and political success looked like.

Steinbeck quickly realized that the war in Vietnam was not a conventional one. In his January 14, 1967 dispatch, headlined "Vietnam War: No Front, No Rear," he wrote:

This war in Vietnam is very confusing not only to old war watchers like me but to people at home who read and try to understand. . . . It's a feeling war with no fronts and no rear. It is everywhere like a thin ever-present gas. I am writing this in a comfortable hotel room in Saigon. . . . And the war is here—in the street below, on the roofs, always present. When I leave my wife here and go out to the hard-bitten sandbag redoubts in the countryside, she is in as much danger as I am. (30)

He described a restaurant bombing by the Viet Cong in the January 21, 1967 dispatch, headlined simply "Terrorism":

At about ten o'clock in the evening two strolling young men paused in front of a crowded restaurant and suddenly threw two grenades in at the wide-open door. One was a dud. The other exploded and tore up the people and their children. There were no soldiers in the restaurant either American or Vietnamese. . . . The children who had been playing on the floor of the restaurant were the worst hit by the low-exploding grenade. The doctors and nurses of the brutal, aggressive, imperialist American force worked most of the night on the products of this noble defense of the homeland. (40–41)

Steinbeck's writing displayed an admiration of the weaponry of the war that was close to awe. In his February 25, 1967 dispatch, "Puff, the Magic Dragon," he described a Puff—a Douglas C-47 military transport modified for gunship duty—and its use in precise detail:

It is armed with three six-barreled Gatling guns. . . . And these three guns can spray 2,800 rounds a minute—that's right, 2,800. In one quarter turn, these guns fine-tooth an area bigger than a football field and so completely that not even a tuft of crabgrass would remain alive. . . . The pilot fires them by rolling up on his side. There are cross hairs on his side glass. When the cross hairs are on the target, he presses a button and a waterfall of fire pours on the target, a Niagara of steel. (101–2)

Steinbeck addressed the question of when the war would end:

The question comes from home so often—when will it be over? I can only guess, Alicia, but at least I am guessing on a base of observation from one end of this country to the other. I guess that a cease-fire is not too far in the future because we and our allies can meet and defeat any military foe that will face us. But a cease-fire is only the beginning. . . . The trained, professional hardcore V.C.s in their cells of three infest the country. They must be rooted out one by one until the villages and hamlets are able to defend themselves. And that may take a generation. (42)

He also railed against the war protesters in several pieces.

I must believe that the plodding protest marchers who spend their days across from the UN and around the White House hate war. I think I have more reason than most of them to hate it. But would they enlist for medical service? They could be trained quickly and would not be required to kill anyone. If they love people so much, why are they not willing to help save them? . . . It might be dangerous to see this method of protest, and besides, if they left the country, their relief checks might stop. But in return they might gain a little pride in themselves as being for something instead of only against. (41–42)

After five weeks at a punishing pace, with thirty-two columns written or under way, John and Elaine left South Vietnam in late January 1967 and continued their tour of the Far East, visiting Thailand and Laos before heading back to the United States in late April. In Bangkok, in his first extended period away from the war since he arrived, Steinbeck was able to spend time "deskbound," as he termed it in a letter to his agent, Elizabeth Otis. This gave him time to expand his field notes into columns and to write some pieces that were more editorial in tone. But when the couple went into the north of Thailand, where an active insurgency was building, and Laos, where the Pathet Lao were operating freely, the on the scene, close to the action style reemerged.

In fact, according to Benson, Steinbeck was extremely close to the action several times in Laos. He went on several combat missions; visited an agricultural station near the Plain of Jars, where enemy activity was high; and accompanied a group of Baptist missionaries to a village to deliver medical supplies. At one point, Elaine got close as well. When they went together to visit an agricultural area in Laos, it was overrun by two battalions of Viet Cong crossing over from safe havens in Cambodia. They had to be evacuated to safety by a supply helicopter.

From Vientiane, Laos, they tried unsuccessfully to get visas to visit North Vietnam, Cambodia, and China. In late February, they returned to Bangkok where they met the Thai king and queen. Then they traveled by train down the Malay Peninsula and by boat to Penang, Malaysia. In this island setting, John spent another session at his desk, writing up his latest field experiences. The final legs of the tour were Indonesia, Hong Kong, and Japan. The two columns written in Indonesia returned to the Bangkok mood and were specifically about the change of regimes, from Sukarno to Suharto, in that country.

From Indonesia, they traveled to Hong Kong where John suffered a severe back injury while helping a stranger move cases of beer up a narrow stairwell with a hand truck. The last Letter to Alicia was written and datelined from Tokyo. It was an effort to summarize and draw conclusions from his five months of whirlwind experience. The Steinbecks were also able to see John IV again because he was in Tokyo on R&R (Rest and Rehabilitation) from the war. They returned to New York toward the end of April 1967.

Rather than discussing the essays further here, I think it is best to turn to the writings themselves. Since the order of their appearance in *Newsday* was not always the order in which Steinbeck wrote them, I have sequenced them using either his own numbering, which was erratic, or internal evidence. The dates given are those of publication, not composition. The essays as presented here are based on Steinbeck's original handwritten versions rather than the edited published texts. In a December 19, 1965 letter to Guggenheim as he was submitting the first Letters to Alicia to *Newsday*, Steinbeck wrote, "The stuff I'm sending you is very rough I know, but that's the way it comes out." In cases in which his *Newsday* editors changed his texts substantially in their efforts to smooth out that roughness, I have described the changes in the notes section at the back of the book. The few editorial glosses I have made appear in square brackets.

STEINBECK
in VIETNAM

DISPATCHES FROM THE WAR

December 3, 1966 / New York

Dear Alicia,

To me, very exciting news. *Newsday* wants my wife and me to wander about East Asia, all of it we can get to, to see what we can see.

At 64, does this seem foolish? They say there's no fool like an old fool, but when I see some of the long haired young protesting against a life they have yet to live, I don't think we aged have a monopoly on folly. It doesn't make us less foolish. We just have more company.

What makes this new journey electric to me is that it is a great part of the world and a majority of the world's people that I have never seen. Furthermore, it seems to me that we are going to be increasingly related to what used to be called the "Far East." It's not so far any more.

Another excitement lies in the fact that I don't much trust what I've read about it. The only way I've ever learned about anything has been by seeing, hearing, smelling, touching. I never get over excited curiosity. I feel as I once did when as a child I would be going from Salinas to San Francisco, a whole hell of a hundred miles away.

Anyway, Alicia, I'll let you know what I find. It may not be any more accurate than the others, but the errors will be mine own.

And do you know the best thing? We hope to see our boy in Vietnam. Wouldn't that be a joy? I'll write you about it all, if you want to hear. And meanwhile, I'm almost jumping out of my skin. I can't wait. I might miss something.

December 10, 1966 / New York

Dear Alicia,

You must have seen a crowd of bloodthirsty but cowardly people urging two others to fight. It's been a little like that in a small way since my friend the Russian poet [Yevgeny] Yevtushenko has been visiting in this country.

You remember, Alicia, the recent nonlethal thing we had. He wrote a public letter to me setting forth his views based on what information he had. And I answered him using what information I had. You know, I get an awful lot of mail. A part of the letters want something. Then there are a goodly number of screwballs, some compliments, and finally there is the hard core of those who use the mails to defile, to injure, to destroy. This vicious filth makes me very sad for those who must hide in distance and anonymity to spew their hatefulness. I've had a large number of such letters since my open letter to Yevtushenko.

I would not have answered him if he had not been my friend and had I not known him to be a good and honorable man as well as a good poet. I had no quarrel with him or him with me. It was a discussion— two views based on different information.

And now too often during his visit here, he has been badgered and prodded and taunted by those people who thought it was a fight and wanted nothing more than to see it go on.

I must say Zhenia [Yevtushenko's nickname] has fielded their wild pitches with skill and adroitness. His message is peace and he is not about to be drawn to battle as an argument. On the other hand, he has never backed down. He believes just as he did when he wrote his first poem, and so do I. And both our stands are based on information not entirely pure. I suspect some of my information and all of his—and perhaps, although I do not know this, he has the same problem.

And because I feel half informed, I am going to South Vietnam to see with my own eyes and to hear with my own ears. And if it were permitted I would go to the north and to China to look and to listen. And wouldn't it be a good thing if Yevtushenko could come with me to South Vietnam, could meet and talk with our soldiers. And wouldn't it be good if we could go north together. That would be wonderful because both of us would be looking not for arguments but for truth. And this is one man I would trust to know a truth when he saw one. We still might not agree, but at least our point of reference would be what is rather than what we have been told.

You know, Alicia, armies haven't changed in one respect since Roman times. They have never liked nor trusted news. Given their druthers, army commands would announce victories and deny defeats and nothing more. Only civilian demand allows what news we have.

Then there are government and political men. They are either running for something or trying to hold their own, with the result that they tend to warp reality gently in their favor.

The ordinary news media are mostly interested in selling papers, and unless they can get exciting or violent news they don't think they are doing this job of promotion.

But a poet, at least one not on the make, has only one purpose—to see and to communicate what he sees in the most effective way he can. You will remember that I do not want poets either dictating foreign policy or rewriting the rules of good manners, but I do believe that poets might be the best reporters in the world. Ernie Pyle was a poet, so was Walt Whitman—so for that matter was Homer.

I know that governments are not about to let the two of us, Yevtushenko and me, just look around and write what we see. The south might let me and the north let him. And there we are, right back where we started. I'm convinced that this idea is so impossible that I haven't even suggested it to Yevtushenko, but I am also convinced that he would approve of it. We both want peace and, you know, we're never going to have it until we bring in truth as a mediator.

Does this sound silly? I don't think it is.

December 17, 1966 / [No dateline]

Dear Alicia,

Every year about this time we have China season at the United Nations. This is a signal and open season for every amateur to get in the foreign policy act. I hope you didn't think I would miss out on such a chance.

This year we get a choice of one China or two Chinas—and I'll bet a good many diplomats could find it in their hearts to wish that there weren't any Chinas.

The whole thing gets pretty silly, as you know. We have always maintained that we have had commitments to Nationalist China and therefore we have voted against admitting Red China to the UN. On the other hand Red China demands that Nationalist China must be kicked out before she will accept membership.

This year we—I mean the U.S.—for the first time are admitting that there is such a thing as Red China so we now are a two China country. The Chinas have not gone that far. Neither China admits that the other China exists. This state of utter confusion might well continue for years, giving UN delegates of variegated Chineseness a chance to make the same speeches they have been making for years. There's nothing nicer than a good foolishment, Alicia. I feel as mean as a kicker-over of sand castles when I am moved to suggest that the problem should be taken out and inspected as though it were a new and shiny nonsense rather than the mildewed mess it really is. I don't for a moment believe that foolishness in either logic or in semantics has ever been a deterrent in human history. But inspection is sometimes amusing in a horrid kind of way.

Since we now have two Chinas (in the second grade it was always two apples) would it be cheating to ask—what is a China? It seems to me that a China is a big hunk of geography inhabited and controlled by Chinese. Well one of our two makes the grade but our other China is a very small island inhabited by Formosans and controlled by an old people's home whose stock went off the board. Once there was a fair-sized army of Chinese escapees from the mainland but most of those retired or died of old age so that even the army is mostly made up of Formosans. The only Chinese are on the reviewing stand.

This is Nationalist China and this is the China with which we have unbreakable treaties. It's funny how we have changed. In 150 years we never kept a single treaty with the Indians, but there was a good reason for that. The Indians were broke. The Nationalist Chinese had one universally admired characteristic. When they lost the war and jumped the mainland, they took everything they could fold, melt down or pack flat—all of it negotiable. This made them acceptable, except perhaps to the Formosans who thought at first they were the hosts, just as the Injuns did when we first landed. We had a firm treaty with these talented refugees which they kept alive by using their loot to hire the most effective lobby in Washington. And we even go along with the fairy tale that these old people will one day take back the mainland and again set up the enlightened form of government that wrecked them before.

The other China, the existence of which has escaped us, is by all reports a bloody mess but it does have two things we should think about. It is Chinese and it has China and that's pretty tough to argue away.

Where have we got so far, Alicia, with logic—that of the two Chinas, one isn't by definition Chinese at all. But you know very well how we humans are. When logic lets us down we switch to something else.

I think perhaps semantics is the solution. Everybody is very sensitive about wanting to be the "real-true China," and facts don't seem to change anything. Years ago in Salinas I knew a boy named Mabel. When he was born, his mother was confused and his father worked on the railroad and by the time they discovered that he wasn't of the Mabel gender, they had not only got used to it but were even a little proud of it. After all, he was the only boy in the world named Mabel.

It's somewhat the same situation at the UN in China season. The name is very important. If for instance the island of Formosa should have a paper revolution and announce that they had become the People's Oligarchy of Taiwan, why we would break our necks recognizing them and they could have their seat in the UN. And the Red Chinese could sit down with the Taiwanian delegation in peace and dignity with an interpreter.

You see, Alicia, that would solve it and nobody would get hurt. Of course we would have to give up China season but we could take that. But we're not going to do it and you know it. We're not going to get trapped by something as simple and unhuman as that.

December 25, 1966 / [No dateline]

Dear Alicia,

The bugs are in again in Vietnam, according to news reports, and so the war follows the usual pattern, and I don't mean bugs simply as a discomfort and a misfortune. Sooner or later in any conflict, our minds turn to bugs as combatants.

Remember in the First World War the reports of typhus-infected lice enclosed by the Russians in letters to Germany? Remember how in the cold war we were charged with dropping potato bugs on Czechoslovakia?

Somebody is always using bugs in warfare and as we become more civilized and sophisticated the bugs have to become more civilized and sophisticated too.

Not long ago I read how we were experimenting with bedbugs. It was top secret, of course. Even private and domestic bugs we don't advertise. But, between us, we were giving highly trained elite bedbugs a dash of radiation which would register on instruments and then sending these agents out to live on the enemy and incidentally to show us where he was.

I don't know what happened—maybe the bedbugs were double agents, or maybe they defected, or maybe the Viet Cong bug washed them. Anyway, the news says we would like to forget the whole thing.

But now the Viet Cong have a bug corps, at least according to their reports—hornets, fierce and indoctrinated hornets, to swarm out and sting the hell out of American soldiers. It is a horrifying thought. I wonder how they (the hornets) can tell us from them.

Maybe it's the deodorant or the advertised hair gook that drives girls crazy with love. That non greasy kid stuff might well drive hornets to battle fury.

Actually the tactic will simply add to the burden of the soldier. In the future he will have to go into combat with a smoker and a beekeeper's hat in addition to everything else. And he'll look silly with a fly swatter hanging from his belt.

You know, if we're looking for sophisticated and humane weapons, we have a beauty. It incapacitates half of the undergraduates at examination time. It wipes out the business community at income tax time. It house-binds just about all employable Americans during a World Series. It's the common cold. If we could put it on the enemy we would have them.

But so far in our earnest attempts to draft bugs, we have always tried to send them against humans. Maybe that's where we've made our mistake. How about bugs against bugs? Our opponents could recruit an army of ants, all volunteers of course, and we could draft two or three divisions of a different species. Then each side could relax while the ants were locked in mortal combat. Might pick up a bet here and there. A whole new kind of professional military man might arise—ant trainers, spider handlers, scorpion experts. But if this kind of warfare should catch on and become popular, it would be inevitable that some groups would be against it. In a free society you can't tear the placards out of the hands of natural-born protesters. They have to march—otherwise thousands of people would be out of work. I can see them now trudging in front of the White House with their signs. "Mothers for bugs," "Drop-outs for bugs." Perhaps even "Bugs for bugs," "President Johnson is a Bugacide." Sooner or later we would split into two groups, Bugs and Moths.

Well, Alicia, I guess if you are just naturally born bad, you'll find a way. If bugs were forced against their will to give up war and spend their time fighting their own kind, we might move on to plants. We could turn loose a devastation of crabgrass against the enemy. We could with satanic cleverness develop a new strain of left-handed bindweed, backed up by heavy and diabolical fungi. You see anything is possible to us warmongers.

But meanwhile, Alicia, what do you suppose went haywire with those special force bedbugs—the Gray Berets. I thought they showed a lot of promise.

December 9, 1966 / Honolulu

Dear Alicia,

We stopped here to be briefed by the Pacific Command and it is not brief. For two days a tidal wave of the figures and facts of life and death have been given me by Army, Navy, Marine Corps and Air Force. Let me say now that if the size and complication of our East Asian operation have been printed in home newspapers, I must not have read very carefully because I had no idea of the magnitude of the job. And I wonder how many people at home know what is being done. It will take me some time to get the mass of information sorted out in my own mind, the distances, the difficulties, and the differences of this job. It is beyond my past experience or reading. I will try to tell you about it as I go along and as I am able or not to match information with personal observation.

The first surprise to me has been the comparative absence of se-crets. You will remember how in World War II practically everything was classified including what you would have for breakfast. This does not seem to hold true anymore. Any questions I have asked have been answered with candor and even eagerness, and how is this for a switch? When an answer was unknown, that too was stated fully. In my past experience with the military I have never before heard an admission of ignorance. It is refreshing and a little frightening.

Don't worry, Alicia. I am not about to swamp you with statistics. I will just have to feel my way into a new and strange world.

We fly out tonight and will arrive in Saigon tomorrow. This morning I get my last shots for plague and a new smallpox scratch. We have an absolutely minimum amount of equipment and only a few light garments—no typewriter, no tape recorder. We do have a cheap Instamatic camera, which if lost or banged up is expendable. Anything else needed will have to be acquired as we go along. We do have confirmed quarters at the Hotel Caravelle in Saigon. I don't know what I will find there and I'm doing my best not to anticipate because such guessing is usually wrong.

There is always a kind of breathless lost feeling when you take off for a completely new world. It is like a mixture of anxiety and anticipation, an under the skin excitement. And as you know, a small, last minute reluctance, a what the hell am I doing here when I could be living in quietly desperate comfort at home, bitching about taxes and foreign policy, fighting city hall and the subway, sweetly torn to pieces by traffic and martinis for lunch. And we are turning our backs on that heavenly existence for heat and bugs and occasional gunfire. But now the boundaries of decision are passed, and we are gone before we leave.

I drove up to the beautiful Tripler Army Medical Center for my last shots—smallpox and plague. If I were a junkie I couldn't be more punctured. Theoretically I am armed against the small and bitter enemies. If only there were inoculations against weariness and fear, against laziness and stupidity I would rush to get them, but there is no immunity against these. We have to live with them.

Isn't it strange, Alicia, how things work out? No one of my family had ever been to East Asia and now my youngest son is in Vietnam. My older son is at Fort Ord training to go and my wife and I are on our way there and that's all of us, a kind of family migration. At home we can abuse and outrage our country. That is our right and perhaps our duty. But when we are away we become proud and protective. If that is sentimental, make the most of it. The truth is that we walk tall all of us—and I'll tell you more about that when I write to you from Saigon.

December 31, 1966 / Saigon

Dear Alicia,

Remember how the lordly jet cuts its engines at 35,000 feet and floats gently toward the earth like Mark Twain's polyhedron on lonely pinion? Well, that's not the way you land in Saigon. Your friendly pilot pulls the plug and scuttles down like Walter Kerr leaving the theater or water making an exit from a bathtub. I guess he figures that the quicker he gets in, the less chance he has of taking a hit from a VC crossbow.

Anyway, we made a sea-gull landing with our feet spread and there waiting for us in fatigues and muddy boots, the carbine he is married to slung from his shoulder, looking lean and brown from lack of sleep, was our son and heir John.

At some future time, Alicia, when he is no longer available for court-martial or Viet civil action, I intend to write the life and oriental times of my son John. Right now I'll pass it by saying that he knows his way around, and has the kind of friends you make the hard way.

You wouldn't be proud of me. I've been here two days going on three and I haven't got a tailored bush jacket, a blue shirt and makeup pot for television, and I am not an authority on this war. A lot of things have happened which will take some time to sort out—kind of crazy things.

For instance, yesterday we took a chopper out to the 23rd Artillery Group, which guards one approach to the city. These are 105-mm. howitzers and they airlift them around the way Santa Claus delivers packages. Anyway, their air spotter called in some activity and they honored me by letting me fire the first round from the No. 4 tube. It was a proud moment and they gave me the shell casing to take home. That will be a logistical problem but I'll manage it.

But my military and murdering instincts were not the reasons for the visit. I've warned you that you are going to hear some crazy things. I went to this area to attend the opening of Gadsden Village, 30 new, white, hand-made cement brick houses for 30 families who have been living in mud, having been driven from their homes by the liberating activities of the Viet Cong. These families built the houses themselves, pretty much by womanpower because not one of the 30 families has a living adult male.

But this story gets crazier. The money for the cement was sent as a present by the people of Gadsden, Alabama—not much money. It didn't need much. Now these housed people will start 30 more houses, and so on and so on. Doors, frames and furniture are made from ammunition boxes.

I don't know whether communications are open to [J. William] Fulbright or Wayne Morse country, but wouldn't it be nice if one or two of their constituent towns would revolt and be for something for a change. The enormous energy that goes into painting and carrying protest posters could get one hell of a lot of poor beat-up people out of the mud. Gadsden Village has a dispensary, a trained native midwife and the services of a doctor. And you should see those women throw their might on the lever of the hand-powered brick compressor. Anyway, it was a big day for me and I met a lot of the new kind of do-it-yourself soldiers. They make me very proud. It's a whole new concept of soldiering and I'll tell you more about it later.

Things happen too fast. I'll never get them down.

Tomorrow I'm moving out and will be out of touch for something over a week. I'm going north to the mountains and the D.M.Z. I'm going to be with the 1st Cav and the Marines. To Pleiku and Da Nang and to Hue, all new and strange to me. I'm having to learn to pronounce them.

But this afternoon I'm going out on the range to check out in small arms, grenade launchers and mortars. A lot of this weaponry I've never seen, let alone fired. I don't want to be dead weight. And I've never had much sympathy for the innocent bystander. I want to be a guilty bystander, if necessary. Peaceful though I am there's a great difference between a dove and a pigeon.

You would be delighted with my uniform. I love my oversize fatigues . . . only garment I ever had with enough pockets. In fact, fatigues are nothing but a lot of pockets strung together by a little cloth. I have never made a smart military appearance, but this is ridiculous. I look like a green plum pudding that has been struck by soggy lightning. Might be a secret weapon, though. I think a sniper couldn't put a sight on me for laughing.

Anyway, I should have quite a bit to tell you when I get back.

December 24, 1966 / Saigon

Dear Alicia,

I must say I'm glad to be getting out of town at this time, I mean near the jolly yuletide season. There are upward of 100 correspondents here and nearly all of them on orders from their papers all scurrying about trying to dig up a Christmas gimmick. For the next little while, it isn't going to be safe in Saigon. Some of them from a national news magazine are going to put Tiny Tim on a crutch if they have to break his leg themselves.

Yes, Virginia, there is a Santa Claus even in this baroque Pearl of the Orient. The tiger lady who runs the Fanny Bar and Ladies Improvement Society appears nightly in white whiskers and her faithful Saigon tea hustlers are wearing antlers and practicing their prancing. The tiger lady got the idea from the bunny clubs of America. You can see how our civilizing influence is spreading. Stick around and you'll wear tinsel.

Already the mess halls are beginning to wear festoons of hand-made paper chains. You would be surprised at the Christmas ornaments you can make out of the cellophane from a package of cigarettes.

But these are standard stories. The worried correspondents are being prodded toward new angles. And this is a tough assignment. The Defense Department is not to be caught short. Tinsel is being issued cut to the proper length to gay up an M-14.

I haven't been here long, but already I am able to advise relatives and friends of servicemen about presents. First, make sure your present is large, bulky and breakable. Second, choose for your loved one something he can't possibly use. A cut-glass woolen muffler would be a nice present. Fluids in fragile bottles will remind the soldier of home.

When you have chosen your present, wrap it in a lumpy package and tie it with grocery string. Next and most important is the label. It should have inadequate glue so it can fall off, but if by some chance it does not your soldier's serial number and APO number should be either illegible or wrong. Two false digits should do the trick. If you want to go way out, enclose some American currency in the package. This will assure him that you love him while he is in the stockade for having it.

When all of these arrangements are made mail your package as near to Christmas as possible. Thus assuring your soldier a happy Fourth of July.

For a time I thought of cornering the Tiny Tim market. This would enrich my stable of little boys and they would like that. An inspired boy on a homemade crutch charging 50 p. a snapshot could retire by New Year's.

For myself, I hope to get back to Saigon before the Christmas truce. I'm told it gets very dangerous when the fighting stops.

December 31, 1966 / Saigon

Dear Alicia,

The Christmas truce is over and we are counting our dead and wounded products of the Viet Cong's violations of the truce. They knew we would keep the truce. And they knew they would not. There is a mutter of anger from our soldiers and the soldiers of our allies. The Pope asked for peace and we gave it and did not receive it. In addition we know about the rush of troops and supplies southward from Hanoi. They knew we would keep the truce. And they knew they would not.

There is a building hatred of the hypocrisy which we go along with. The D Z [Demilitarized Zone] is an example; it is nothing of the sort. It's a staging area for enemy troops and supplies. It's like the little kid in the schoolyard who punches another in the nose and steps back yelling, "King's X." Defeated enemy troops cross the line and are safe and free to regroup and re-equip. And we observe this nonsense. And by observing it our so-called "image" gets worse and worse. But the anger is growing and the New Year truce is coming up.

If I had the ear of authority, Alicia, and by this letter I am trying to get it, I would suggest with all conviction that the commands of our soldiers, of our allied soldiers and of the Vietnamese soldiers, should publish, broadcast, and by leaflet-drop proclaim the following and mean it—that we intend to keep the New Year's truce, but if there is one violation, even one, we will instantly throw the works at them as they have never seen it thrown. We have the capacity. We have leaned backward to be fair and decent, and today we are sending home the bodies of our men murdered while they kept the truce.

Let's face it; it hasn't worked. The enemy forces and the VC have no respect for honor or decency. They consider these matters stupid and weak. So let us try another truth and keep our word to the letter. Our statement should not be a warning. It should be inevitability. We will keep the New Year's truce, but with the first violation we will clobber them.

Maybe it's like the old story of the cavalry mule trainer who spoke softly and was obeyed. Asked to demonstrate his method, he picked up a piece of lead pipe and knocked the new mule to its knees. The committee protested, "but we thought you used kindness," to which the sergeant replied, "I do, but first I have to get their attention."

For myself, I think it is time to get their attention.

January 5, 1967 / Saigon

Dear Alicia,

Strange happenings are becoming commonplace here in South Vietnam. Yesterday United Press International gave me a piece from the Soviet youth newspaper *Komsomolskaya Pravda* in which I was accused as "an accomplice in a murder" because I rode in a U.S. helicopter during a mission in Vietnam. This is a staggering charge and an even more staggering piece of reasoning. It out-Joes McCarthy. It creates a new crime—guilt by observation.

Alicia, I know it is silly to answer because my answer would not be printed. Editorial comment is a one-way street in Moscow. The *Komsomolskaya Pravda* piece went on to say that a writer "must not remain a passive observer but must take a certain position." Well, Alicia, I have taken a certain position but I don't think it is the one the *Komsomol* paper had in mind. However, the Soviet newspaper is in a superior position to take "a certain position," because it has no observers here to mess up its preconceptions.

I want to make an offer to *Komsomolskaya Pravda,* and I'll bet its readers never hear of my offer and my suggestion. I suggest that one or more good Russian writers, good but honest observers, brave men and true Russian patriots, not likely to defect to the corrupt West (I know at least a dozen such men personally)—I beg that some of these men be sent as observers to South Vietnam. I am quite sure they would be admitted and allowed to move about freely, even in booby-trap and ambush country. I can promise that their observations and copy would be neither censored nor read at least until it came to your editorial desk.

Such men might find this war more shocking than they had thought. They might see new hospitals where none were before, houses for refugees from the harassment of the Viet Cong. They might see, if they looked, revolutionary development developing in the villages, paddy peasants beginning to learn to defend themselves after 20 years of being pushed around. It's not all good, nor far along, but it is a start. Your representatives might see some blood shed, even possibly some of their own, but they would not see women and children as U.S. or ARVN [Army of the Republic of South Vietnam] military objectives.

Anyway, this is my suggestion, *Komsomolskaya Pravda,* and since "Pravda" means truth, you should be delighted to have access to some of it. And please don't think your representatives would be led through a set piece. The Potemkin village is not an American invention.

I promise to try to get your writers admitted here and I have every hope of success. But in return I would like to ask that you get me admitted on the same terms to North Vietnam, so that I can observe the other side. Turnabout is fair play.

By the way, *Komsomolskaya Pravda,* do you have an observer in Hanoi? Can you get one there? If so, does his copy come to you uncensored? It would be interesting to know whether or not you base your "certain position" on what you have seen or only on what you have been told.

I know very well that you will see this letter, *Komsomolskaya Pravda,* but I'll bet 10–1 you will not pass it on to your readers. They must continue to think of me as a murderer—because you have said so. It is truly a dialectic dementia.

[No date] / [No dateline]

Dear Alicia,

Just back from a field trip of eight days covering just about all of Vietnam north of Saigon and that's an awful lot of country. Enclosed is a map on which I've marked the route, in case you're interested. [No map was found in any of the files for this dispatch.] It's going to take me several days and a number of letters to tell you even a part of what I've seen and heard. I know perfectly well that the war or any war is largely dull and listless—99% sitting around waiting. Well by accident every place I have gone I have landed just in time for an action. This is nothing but pure luck and I'll get back to the action little by little, because to me the detail is the major interest, so I'll do a quick whirl for you and then come back to the spots.

Remember how when we go to a new or rather a strange city, we take the grand tour—the #11 bus in London, the boat trip around Manhattan? That way you spot places you want to go back to to stay a while. That's what I've done here. I've seen one whole hell of a lot of country, and I've noted a number of places to return to to sit still until the pattern of life becomes clear.

Time stretches and snaps like a rubber band. The eight days I've been out have been eight lifetimes, all different and all fascination. I was right to be unhappy about the reporting of this country and this war, only such is the complication and magnitude of the thing that I wonder whether I can do any better.

It seems to me that the best thing I can do is to keep the field of vision small and the generalities as few and far between as possible.

Whereupon I am about to fire a salvo of generalities consisting of things I didn't know about Vietnam and perhaps you don't understand. I've flown over it end to end and side to side (north, that is, of Saigon) and it is a much larger country than I could have imagined. Also it is of a beauty almost dream-like and of staggering variety. Again, I had thought of it as a densely populated country only to find and to see that up to 90% of the people live on the coastal fringe and the Mekong delta. The plateau and the mountains are sparsely peopled and many areas have no people at all except tigers and snakes and little deer and many monkeys. In fact, there is more game here of all kinds than I thought existed in the world. The variety of scenes would put an itch in the palm of any normal travel agent, the miles of golden beach on a green and blue sea, the winding rivers, peopled with boats of all kinds and edged with bathing children. When you fly over, the rice paddies are irregularly square like a coarse lace, and surely rice with its sturdy green is one of the prettiest of crops.

Then comes the rising upland, deep wooded and mysterious and then the high plateau which, particularly around Pleiku looks and feels and smells like the upper panhandle of Texas or southeastern New Mexico, the air sharp and clean, the plain low brushed and undulant, parceled by the cuts of waterways. It is just waiting for herds of Brahmas, or wide ranging white face Herefords. There's rain enough to keep the grass coming and space enough for herds to feed eastern Asia. And finally the mountains, with jungle so dense that the earth is dark at midday, peopled with giants of the most precious hardwoods and movable on the rivers which everywhere cream down the steep mountainsides in the kind of waterfalls we dream of and then slither like serpents to the sea.

This is surely one of the most beautiful countries I have ever seen. It is also potentially the richest country for its area I have ever seen. All tropical and subtropical fruits grow in profusion. Every stream is edged with rice paddies. There is gold in the mountains and many kinds of precious woods and stones. More game animals and birds live here than I have ever seen congregated. And finally the Mekong Delta to the south of Saigon where the Mekong River splits to many as the Nile does, could feed all of East Asia from China to New Zealand. It could, if required, bring in three crops of rice a year with never any chance of a crop failure. And this, of course is one of the main reasons for war. However Hanoi may speak of liberating the south from its beastly inhabitants and from the brutal Americans, the real prize which China must have to survive as a communist state, or whatever it is just at the moment, is an ever full and overflowing dinner pail.

But there is another promise for the future. The great Mekong River—look at it on the map, how it rises far up in China, wanders down the borders between Burma and Laos, between Thailand and Laos, cuts across the center of Cambodia before it enters Vietnam to enrich and water the delta region. This is a very great river, shared by six nations or at least bordering them. Some dams have been built and more are in process and in plan. When even part of this river control is completed it will be a super East Asian Tennessee Valley Authority, delivering an enormous potential of electric power to five of the six nations. The self interest involved will bring these nations together in peaceful cooperation. You don't fight against your own interest. Only China refuses to share. It wants it all.

But in addition, the Mekong River Authority, or whatever it is called, owned and built by the five bordering nations, is a deep and desperate threat to the whole Red China concept. If it succeeds, then the tottering economy, the inept and mismanaged agriculture and production of China might be re-inspected by those Chinese who have not been completely snowed by Mao's thinking, because just as nothing succeeds like success so nothing fails so resoundingly as failure. This letter has been a kind of a lecture, Alicia. "Sorry about that." But I wanted to fill in the background as it came to me. Now I'll get off the podium and down to the little stuff.

[No date] / [No dateline]

Dear Alicia,

If I had any ambition toward a journalistic future, I would dateline these letters from the field, drip a little sweat and blood on them (it's in good supply) and write pantingly to give an impression of immediacy. Actually I did no writing in the field except for notes of names, units and places. I tend to forget these things, but I do have total recall, a photographic memory, for the look and sound and feel of things if only I fix them with notes in time and place.

I think I told you I had checked out in weaponry short of artillery and did surprisingly well with them from the carbines through the automatic weapons and the machine guns. I did not fire the 50-calibre because it is the same gun I knew in World War II. I couldn't come by a grenade launcher until the Marines east of Da Nang let me use one in V.C. country. My son John swears by this weapon and I must say I agree. Even I was able to place three grenades in a very small area at 300 meters. However, I think a large part of my proficiency lies in the excellence of the new weapons: The M16 is a beautiful thing when you need it, light, fast, accurate and a man can carry twice as much ammunition as he could for the old M1. This just about doubles his fire power and that's a comforting thing in a fire fight. Most of this indoctrination was done at the Saigon airport where a sergeant of Military Police put me through it kindly but firmly on the shooting range.

Our first jump was to Pleiku in the central highlands. Things start early but they don't necessarily continue early. Military impulse is to get you out on some kind of line in the first dawn where you may remain until noon. But having got a bunch of men out early seems to satisfy a basic brass appetite.

The alarm went off in our pleasure dome in the Caravelle hotel and I put on my newly acquired army fatigues. These are the ones I told you about with so many pockets in pants and jacket that I have put pencils and small notebooks away and never found them again. The double and triple entrances of those pockets are as tricky as the hidey holes of the V.C. Anyway you get the pants and the thick socks on and tie the draw strings at the bottom. This is to keep out leeches from below. Then the boots. They lace over the draw strung pants bottoms. The laces do not have stiff ends. Even now, lacing those boots in the morning leaves me exhausted and covered with sweat. Under mortar attack when you find a sense of security in a bunker, you get there barefooted. Getting those boots laced is a ten minute job. There is a zipper you can lace in and I'm getting one immediately. I will not lace those damned things again. In the bottom of the boot is a plastic insole with the texture of a nutmeg grater. I'm sure it serves some purpose. Mine rolled up and crippled me until I took them out and shot them.

Anyway there I was, rumpled and sweaty and it wasn't even daylight yet. My cap was too big. I had to hold it on in even a light breeze. I said a quick warrior's farewell to my weeping wife, brushed a tear aside and strode like Hector down the marble steps of the Caravelle to the lobby. In the dim light I could see every chair, couch and lounge occupied by sleeping staff. The glass front doors were locked. The curfew wasn't over. I couldn't even get out in the street. Hector grounded his spear and collapsed on his shield and waited for somebody to open the door.

Did you know that the airport at Saigon is the busiest in the world, that it has more traffic than O'Hare field in Chicago and much more than Kennedy in New York?—Well it's true. We stood around—maybe ten thousand of us all looking like overdone biscuits until our plane was called. It was not a pretty ship this USAF C-130. Its rear end opens and it looks like an anopheles mosquito but into this huge anal orifice can be loaded anything smaller than a church and even that would go in if it had a folding steeple. For passengers, the C-130 lacks a hominess. Four rows of bucket seats extending lengthwise into infinity. You lean back against cargo slings and tangle your feet in a maze of cordage and cables.

Before we took off a towering sergeant (I guess) whipped us with a loud speaker. First he told us the dismal things that could happen to our new home by ground fire, lightning or just bad luck. He said that if any of these things did happen he would tell us later what to do about it. Finally he came to the subject nearest his heart. He said there was dreadful weather ahead. He asked each of us to reach down the paper bag above and put it in our laps and if we felt queasy for God's sake not to miss the bag because he had to clean it up and the hundred plus of us could make him unhappy. After a few more intimations of disaster he signed off on the loud speaker and the monster ship took off in a series of leaps like a Calaveras County frog.

Once airborne, I got invited to the cockpit where I had a fine view of the country and merciful cup of black scalding coffee. They gave me earphones so I could hear directions for avoiding ground fire and the even more dangerous hazard of our own artillery. The flight was as smooth as an unruffled pond. And when we landed at Pleiku I asked the God-like sergeant why he had talked about rough weather.

"Well, it's the Viets," he said. "They have delicate stomachs and some of them are first flights. If I tell them to expect the worst and it isn't, they're so relieved that they don't get sick. And you know I do have to clean up and sometimes it's just awful."

Anyway we landed in the perfectly huge installation at Pleiku, a giant sitting astride Route 14—the main road across the waist of the country from Cambodia to the sea. But I'll leave to tell you about that in my next letter.

January 7, 1967 / Pleiku

Dear Alicia,

Where do we get our impressions of places we have never seen? I had no idea that the central highlands of South Vietnam would look like the Texas panhandle, that the air would be clear and brisk, that a blanket at night would be desirable.

It was in the area around Pleiku that Hanoi and the V.C. tried to cut the country in half. Here we met them head on and drove them back and they have not been able to mount an offensive in force since.

Pleiku is like many other places here—a small, old tree-shaded village, then rings of slapped up temporary shelters for refugees, then the beginnings of permanent housing. The military and air installations are enormous, supplies, munitions, vehicles and aircraft of all types deployed all over the landscape to the horizon.

The soil is a good sticky clay, fairly stable now, but I have seen photographs of tanks and half tracks and howitzers almost disappearing in the mud, a gooey sticky mud.

Private enterprise lurks near the surface in the Vietnamese. Given the incentive of troops, business sprouts like mushrooms, laundries, bars, little stores that sell a staggering variety of things, very pretty and largely useless. Near to the river there stand many platforms of varying sizes. Here you can have a tank or a truck washed clean of its gathered muck. There are car washes and even bicycle washes. The cost is small and the vehicle laundries are heavily patronized. The clothing laundries also do a land-office business. Barbed-wire perimeters are literally covered with clean and drying Army fatigues. It is a giant festival of cleanliness and at the end of a day tramping through mud and dust and sometimes both at the same time, you soon see why. Toward evening my fatigues doubled their weight with accumulated crud and my boots were so weighted that I walked in slow motion like a half-speed film.

In my opinion the chopper is the greatest invention since the wheel. In eight days I have covered areas and put down in places it would have taken many months to visit on foot and that would be the only way to travel since there are few roads, and many of these are impassible, and what railroads there once were are cut and mangled by the fighting. I think I have traveled in every kind of chopper we have save one, or rather two. There is a single-place bubble I've missed because I can't fly the thing, and I haven't been on the giant Sky Crane, which looks like a huge dragonfly or praying mantis and which can take in its arms anything it can grip. It has transported a complete operating room with surgery continuing during flight. Eventually, when we have enough of them, the Crane will be of major logistical importance.

Right off I was invited to have tea with Maj. Gen. Vinh Loc, commanding the Second Corps area ARVN, pronounced "Arvin" like Marvin and meaning the Army of Vietnam. Vinh Loc is a titular prince, I believe the highest ranking officer of the ARVN and an expert on the history, culture, etc. of the Montagnards, locally called Mountain Yards, which I like better. His house or headquarters is palatial and very beautiful and I don't think I will ever taste tea as exquisite as that he served me. He gave me two books he had written about the Mountain Yards in an English as delicately flavored as was his tea. Since I have become fascinated by the Mountain Yards also, I'll tell you more about them later. They are unique and interesting people who look very like American Indians.

From tea with the charming and, I am told, very efficient ARVN Gen. Vinh Loc, I went in an H23, a bubble three-place chopper, to the base camp of the U.S. Army Fourth Division, the Ivy division, and had lunch with Maj. General Collins, commander of the Fourth Division. Wherever I have gone, the command has very kindly allowed me to sit in on a briefing of the immediate local situation. Gen. Collins' briefing was particularly interesting because of ARVN Lt. Col. Nghia of G2 or intelligence of the Second Corps area, the largest, incidentally, of the four corps areas. A tough, tight-rawhide small man, he spoke in an accented but meticulous English of the distribution of enemy forces in the Second Corps area. You will remember that the Fourth Division backed up with the 23rd Group Artillery plus B-52 strikes, scattered the Hanoi forces over to the Cambodian border and took away their initiative. Col. Nghia reported what intelligence he had on where they had gone and what forces they were trying to regroup. I won't try to tell you the unit numbers because you would forget them as quickly as I do. But he reported their heavy losses in dead and wounded.

Both the V.C. and the Hanoi regulars do their best to take out their dead and wounded in order to keep us from knowing what damage they have suffered. Their hopelessly wounded they shoot and other wounded they carry out on improvised stretchers or piggyback. I asked whether this violence of transportation might not suggest an increased death rate of the wounded and Col. Nghia said this was so not only because of the roughness of the country but also because of an increasing shortage of medicines.

Many graves have been found after their retreat and prisoners and defectors have repeatedly reported a lack of medical supplies. One prisoner of rank had agreed to fly over his former outfit in a loudspeaker airplane, calling his comrades by name and urging them to surrender, because contrary to what they had been told, they would be well treated by our forces and the ARVN.

I won't go on at much length about military matters, Alicia, but I did want to tell you about this process. On visiting a unit or a command, I have been briefed on the immediate situation and the planned future. The futures of course are off the record for obvious reasons unless they are likely to be finished before you get the account. This briefing process happened at every stop so I won't go into it again. At the front of the room is a map of the area with troop dispositions marked in and also suggested concentrations of enemy forces. The briefing officer takes out his weapon, which looks like a steel pen with a pocket clip. This he pulls out like a telescope, whereupon it becomes a pointer like a baton, with which he points out the map indications. I am interested in this side arm of the briefing officer, and suggested that if it had a ball-point pen at the tip, it would be available for even more complex attack, and I was told that some of the pointers have just that.

I am very anxious to get my hands on one of these instruments. It would be useful in pointing out girls or calling waiters, but so far I have not acquired one, not even by the last resort of theft. Believe me, Alicia, I would steal one in a moment, but I have yet to see a briefing officer put one down. He snaps it shut and puts it in his pocket. And I am a lousy pickpocket.

That's all for now, my dear. Perhaps next time I'll tell you about going into the hills or the jungle trails you've heard so much about.

January 7, 1967 / Pleiku

Dear Alicia,

I would like more than anything to be able to plug in so that this letter might carry the feel and sight of things but more the deep throbbing glory-feeling of being alive in a world of living things. And I suppose part of this exquisite aliveness grows in the steady reminder that at any moment you may not be.

Let you be aware of these statistics. Michael Shaughnessy, commander (Shamrock Flight), D Troop, First Squadron, 10th Cavalry, from Tacoma, Wash., a major of very un-Irish gaiety, perhaps because he has never been to Ireland. The Huey choppers of his flight are painted with bright green shamrocks, the result of a can of green paint sent by Michael's wife. News, or rather a feel, of this man precedes him, so that when his chopper dips down on the pad like a skipped stone and he leans out saying, "I hear you want to go hunting leprechauns," I reply:

"That I do sir."

"Well it just happens we found a fairy ring in the hills. Hop in!"

Hopping in for me in fatigues and field boots is more like clambering, but I manage and pull the buckle straps tight near the door seat, which I like because you can look straight down. I nod to the door gunner on my side and pat the twin handles of his weapon, now down-pointed and unloaded. Airborne, he will swivel up the muzzle, flip up the breech block and lead the first shell up the belt into the chamber, slam the cover down, move the gun up and down and from side to side and then settle back to watch for any movement on the ground. It is a joy to have him there. His potential burst of tracered fire may well be a deterrent to the casual part-time sniper who can take it or let it alone.

I know about the leprechauns. In this case they are called Charley and high in the jungley hills, D troop has found their crock of gold, this time an extensive cache of rice, and we are going up to look at it.

Shaughnessy lifts the Huey from the pad, backs up in a kind of curtsey, wags it like a tail and off we go. We go fast and low, taking cover in water canyons, and when we breast a ridge we graze the trees and instantly drop down on the other side. You can either fly high above the range of small-arms fire or you can cut low and tricky like a snipe. We drop into a forward supply camp (I am not supposed to mention places or units if an operation is still in process. This sits fine with me and my faulty, this time gifty, tendency never to remember a name or a date or to forget a face or a place).

Settling in, our rotors kick up a smog of fine red dust so that our faces seem to have a sunlamp pleasure burn. We are to move to the Huey of Maj. James Patrick Thomas of whom it is said that he has changed the classic sophist's question to how many choppers could Thomas sit on the point of a pin.

Alicia, I wish I could tell you about these pilots. They make me sick with envy. They ride their vehicles the way a man controls a fine, well-trained quarter horse. They weave along stream beds, rise like swallows to clear trees, they turn and twist and dip like swifts in the evening. I watch their hands and their feet on the controls, the delicacy of the coordination reminds me of the sure and seeming slow hands of [Pablo] Casals on the cello. They are truly musician's hands and they play their controls like music and they dance them like ballerinas and they make me jealous because I want so much to do it. Remember your child night dream of perfect flight free and wonderful? It's like that and sadly I know I never can. My hands are too old and forgetful to take orders from the command center, which speaks of updrafts and side winds, of drift and shift, or ground fire only indicated by a tiny puff and flash, or a hit and all of these commands must be obeyed by the musician's hands instantly and automatically. I must take my longing out in admiration and the joy of seeing it.

Sorry about that leak of ecstasy, Alicia, but I had to get it out, or burst.

You will gather that we are now in V.C. country, where every tree may open fire and often does. Maj. Thomas dips into a stream bed cascading down a twisting canyon and you realize that that low green cover you saw from high up is towering screaming jungle so dense that noonday light fails to reach the ground. The stream bed twists like a snake and we snake over it, now and then lofting like a tipped fly ball to miss an obstruction or cutting around a tree the way a good cow horse cuts out a single calf from a loose herd.

Low as we are flying, we are gaining altitude rapidly because the mountains are steep and high and our stream is cascade and waterfall. I wonder how the pilots find their way. On the hillsides are little fields chopped out of the jungle by Montagnards farmed for a season or two and left to overgrow. And these cleared places are not close together but separated and random with dense growth between.

Suddenly, up and ahead there is a burst of purple smoke, our landing signal, and we loop over to a chopped out clearing so small that our rotor blades barely clear the giant bamboo. Out of the undergrowth, thicker than any I have ever seen, faces, or really only eyes, appear. Mottled helmets and fatigues disappear against the background. Faces black or white from sweat and dirt have become a kind of universal reddish gray. Only the eyes are alive and lively. And when we settle and the rotor stops, their mouths open and they are men, and what men. Can you understand the quick glow of pride one feels in just belonging to the same species as these men? I suppose it is the opposite of the shiver of shame I sometimes feel at home when I see the dirty clothes, dirty minds, sour smelling wastelings and their ill-favored and barren pad mates. Their shuffling, drag-ass protests that they are conscience-bound not to kill people are a little silly. They're not in danger of that. Hell, they couldn't hit anybody. I think their main concern is that a one-armed half blind 12-year-old V.C. could knock them off with a bunch of ripe bananas.

I didn't mean to get off on that. I guess D troop set me off. They smelled of sweat, hard-working sweat. On the back of every helmet, under the strap, was a plastic spray bottle of insect repellent. I went into a V.C. trail so deep and covered with jungle that you are in perpetual steaming dusk. It was one of the V.C. transport trails over which they force the local people to carry their supplies. The rice cache was fairly large, a stilted structure deeply screened and disguised. The weary men were sacking unhulled rice to be air-lifted to the refugee centers, a good haul, 300 or 400 bags. Once it would have been destroyed. Now if possible at all it is saved and distributed sometimes to the very people from whom the V.C. have taken it.

I started down the dark cave of a trail and a sergeant quite a bit bigger than a breadbox called, "Don't go far. It's booby trapped." P.S. I didn't go far.

January 7, 1967 / Saigon

Dear Alicia,

Do you remember my telling you that any mistakes might be beauties but they would be my own? Well, I've only been two weeks in Vietnam but of that time I have spent 10 days out of 14 in the field from base camp to forward position, to patrol, to assault operation. I've covered a lot of country and have seen many things ugly and/or beautiful with my own eyes. I haven't been to the Delta yet. I go there next week.

Anyway I'm cocked and set to make some generalities which the home guard commandos can shoot down if they wish. In New York, in other places and in those full-page paid advertisements in the *New York Times* as well as in political speeches aimed at U.S. foreign policy, I have heard and read that we are interfering with the internal affairs of a foreign country—that this is essentially a civil war and that the Vietnamese people should be allowed to settle it for themselves, that the V.C. is an organized army of Boy Scouts, selling their lives to free their people from the intolerable pressure of a ruling class backed up by the brutal and imperialist soldiery which delights to kill and maim women and children.

My first generality item is that this is pure horse manure, and I base this on what I myself have seen. I wish my friend Yevtushenko could be with me. He is a fair-minded man with a good eye and a deep-seated love for people.

The V.C. has much the same selfless impulse, the same gentle democratic direction and uses the same methods for gaining his ends as the Mafia does in Sicily. The parallel is very close. Terror and torture are his weapons. He bleeds the people he is saving of everything movable, kidnaps whole villages for forced labor, recruits the young men and holds the parents hostage. He murders any opposition noisily or secretly.

He impales living bodies on sharpened stakes, slashes stomachs so that a man drags his intestines on the ground before he dies. He tosses grenades in markets where poor people gather to buy food. If a village refuses to pay his tax (the Mafia or Cosa Nostra would call it protection) he burns the houses. And lately he has a refinement. A man suspected of communicating, only suspected, is taken to a village center. His neighbors are forced to look on while he is taken apart little by little, starting with fingers and toes but carefully so that bleeding will not give him quick release, and when they have finished, he is a ghastly mound of butcher's meat. You don't believe it? I could show you photographs but no American paper would dare print them for fear of disturbing the comfortable self-satisfaction of its readers. I wish I could take the people who have written me hate-letters calling me murderer through some of the sweet and tender activities of the National Liberation Front which is what Charley calls himself. But I suspect their stomachs couldn't stand it. They prefer to make up their minds like spreading up beds that haven't been slept in.

I would like them to see the refugee camps we help to build and help to maintain. These people did not run from us. They ran to us. Doesn't it make any impression that there are no reverse refugees? Nobody runs north to escape the brutality of the South Vietnamese and the brutal Americans. Why is that?

Of course this is a most complicated situation. The new party-line word in so many of my hate-letters is simplistic. Well if this is simplistic, comrades, make the most of it. Charley is a pure son of a bitch. His purpose is domination of the land and the minds of poor people and he will stop at no horror, no lie, no trick to achieve it.

This is a simplistic generalization, Alicia. I can go into its complicative opposite if you wish, but meanwhile, if you hear someone celebrating the misunderstood and mistreated V.C., just punch him in the nose for me, will you?

Last week I went through the booby trap school near Da Nang. The course is about 400 yards long, winds through thick cover, and on the path and in the houses is every kind of booby trap that has been found. When you trip one a loud blank cap goes off. I set off three and it makes you feel foolish because you are looking for the trip wires and the traps. The instructor told me that since our men have gone through the course casualties have gone way down, and I can understand that. For several days after, I looked very carefully at the ground before I stepped.

I enclose some drawing of the beastly things [see gallery]. They're pretty savage. But this is not a pretty war and Charley sets the pace. Our kids are learning to fight back. But how I would like to run a protest parade down a V.C. trail. Charley puts paddy peasants over a suspected path before he goes in. Maybe the Peace Marchers might like to serve in this capacity. Sorry to be so vehement but I've seen a boy with punji (sharpened bamboo stakes) wounds.

January 12, 1967 / Saigon

Dear Alicia,

Here in Vietnam, people give me presents, small mementos left in the box at my hotel, letters I can't read nor easily have translated. One young and respected writer has written an open letter to both Yevtushenko and to me. It is in Vietnamese but I will have it translated and send it on to you.

Meanwhile I have been given a poem addressed to me which even in translation I find so sharp and moving that I can't resist sending it to you. There is a fury in it and at the same time a trust. I hope you will find it as meaningful as I have.

These are lovely people, Alicia.

Yours, John

To the Novelist John Steinbeck
Nguyen Quang-Hien (Dec. 1966)
translated by Thach-Chuong

Hail to John Steinbeck's visit to Vietnam
Hail to the author of *The Grapes of Wrath*
I am not clear which motive has brought you to this
place where force shall prevail
where powder red fire
tears blood sweat and conspiracy muddily interlace
where also the air is filled with heroic songs
in the light of the day or the dark of the night
Maybe you come to Vietnam from chivalry
desiring to participate in this antiviolence combat
(anyone could remember how oppressed the Dust Bowl people
   were)
Maybe you come here from curiosity
searching for stories to tell or maybe you come to Vietnam

as an ordinary tourist in spare time
going to contemplate the wonders of the world
But for whatever reasons unknown to me
in my name, an ordinary Vietnamese youth
who writes verses for the country for love of life
I welcome you, John Steinbeck to Vietnam
even as a tourist going to contemplate wonders
I will introduce to you Vietnam as a wonder
of suffering and forbearing
But if you come to Vietnam
to see where truth and reason are hiding
then I will tell you Vietnam has many truths
which cannot be understood and reason
Please find it anywhere in this portion of land (so stretching yet
    not so fertile)
Find it in the populated cities
or in the isolated muddy fields
Maybe it's in the middle of a blood gushing battle deep in the
    woods
Maybe it's in the airstrikes
of the enemy's concentration camps
Maybe it's in the shabby looking hotel of a small province
in the Saigon drinking bars with the deceiving light
Maybe it's in the shelter trenches
of a woman with her young children
whose father has regrouped (to the North)
or was dead in some night when the shells were crackling in the
    air
Maybe the reason is among us
but we cannot find it together.
Welcome you to Vietnam John Steinbeck
the author of *The Grapes of Wrath*
a man who's not concerned with the luxury of successes
regarding them as other haughty skyscrapers
which with time will be reduced to nothing
You will find Vietnam has thousands of Mother Joads
hundreds of thousands of Rose of Sharons

hundreds of thousands of Oklahoma plays
ten times more tragic
but also ten times more heroic
Please visit Vietnam everywhere
not by her four thousand years on the worn out papers
but by her thousand years of rebellion
and when in some evening she stood
watching the sky
the earth the clouds
the rain the wind the sun the moon
longing for the feet to harden and the rocks to soften
for the sky to be tranquil and the sea to be calm
only then could she be in peace
but how long more will the sea be calm
and the sky tranquil with the life in front
Welcome John Steinbeck to Vietnam
even when you see morals are being sold on the street
and truth is made of imported nylon
still Vietnam is not the five gates to the suburbs
the Perfume River or the Saigon traffic
Please register the voice of the docile people
whom suffering cannot beat
whom immoral oppression and violence
can never persuade

Welcome John Steinbeck to Vietnam
when going back please relate
to the freedom-loving people of America
Please tell it with the sincerity of writers
people who love to fight for freedom justice fraternity
Hail to John Steinbeck's visit to Vietnam
even as a tourist in spare time
going to contemplate the wonders of the world
I introduce to you once more
Vietnam a wonder
Of enduring suffering
And insubordination

January 14, 1967 / Saigon

Dear Alicia,

This war in Vietnam is very confusing not only to old war watchers but to people at home who read and try to understand. It is mainly difficult because of our preconceptions accumulated over several thousand years. This war is not like any we have ever been involved in. I'll try to tell you some of the points of difference as I have observed them.

It was easy to report wars of movement, places taken and held or lost, lines established and clear, troops confronting each other in force and fighting until one side or the other lost. Big battles are conceivable, can be reported like a bullfight. You could see if only on a map all previous wars—on one side of a line our friends, on the other our enemies. Vietnam is not like that at all and I wonder whether it can be described. Maybe the inability to communicate its quality is the reason for the discontent and frustration of the press corps here. Many of the fine reporters here understand this war, but their readers don't and often their editors demand the kind of war they are used to and comfortable with.

Maybe I can't tell you what it is like, Alicia, but I'm going to try so you can feel it. It's a feeling war with no fronts and no rear. It is everywhere like a thin ever-present gas. I am writing this in a comfortable hotel room in Saigon, which was once a beautiful city and now has a worn and sagging look like a worn-out suit that once was well tailored. And the war is here—in the street below, on the roofs, always present. When I leave my wife here and go out to the hard-bitten sandbag redoubts in the countryside, she is in as much danger as I am and perhaps in more because I am armed with alertness while she, walking in a civilized street to post a letter, may run into a murderous exchange of fire.

At night when we have drinks and dinner on the roof we can see the flares and hear the thunder of artillery all night long, and very often the quick-sharp rattle of automatic small arms fire. Both she and I know the sound of mortar fire and we are conditioned, if it comes close, to roll off the beds pulling the mattresses over us with one motion to veer off fragments and flying glass. This city is heavily fortified, but the bridge you cross to go to a small restaurant may be blown up before you return. The smiling man in the street selling colored etchings from a bulging briefcase may have a gummy lump of high explosive under the pictures—and he may not. There is the problem—he may be simply a smiling man selling pictures. That is the feeling all over the city. Any person, any place may suddenly erupt into violence and destruction. You have it with you every minute. You avoid clots of people in the streets and are prepared almost automatically to fall to the sidewalk or the street and to be perfectly still. Bob Capa's first instruction to me years ago was, "Don't move. If they haven't hit you they haven't seen you." No better advice was ever given.

I realize that this account makes it seem that we are surrounded by thousands of enemies and that is just not true. The armed forces radio and television station was riddled with about 200 rounds from automatic rifles, by just two men. The airport, the largest in the world and surely the most guarded, was penetrated recently by 15 heavily armed teenage boys, and they would have done great damage if the guard dogs had not smelled them out. You see, it isn't that the enemies are many but that you don't know which ones they are. And three with modern weapons can do the destruction of a hundred. One man, sauntering slowly past with a basket of fruit on his head, can slaughter half the peasants in a village market with one grenade and he does not hesitate to do it. In many areas, we completely control the place by day, but no one moves about by night. Then the secured road is mined. Then a dreadful claymore mine is aimed to be exploded by the first man who opens the village gate.

On Christmas Day General [William] Westmoreland took me with him to visit the farthest outposts. The 101st Airborne has not been to its base camp for nearly a year. The Special Forces, Green Berets, are dug in in redoubts far in the hills. They range the countryside day and night like casting setters [hunting dogs] and very gradually they clear out the snakes. We called on the Special Forces at Plei Mrong and Polei Klong, elements of the 25th Division and the Eighth Infantry at Pleiku, the airborne and three battalions of infantry at Kontum and the First Cavalry at An Khe. The General must have rabbit blood. I had to run to keep up with him. The finest Army we have ever had, he said, the best trained, most experienced soldiers in our history and with a morale that clanged through the valleys like a struck gong.

Does it make you feel hopeless that these wonderful troops plus the equally fine allied troops cannot bring this thing to a quick victory? I find I am very hopeful but not for a quick victory. It is a large subject and I'll try to tell you more about it in my next. There is far too much to try to get in one letter.

January 14, 1967 / [No dateline]

Dear Alicia,

Tomorrow I'm going south to the Delta country, to look at what has to be the next phase of this war, but now I want to speak of our troops, the U.S. soldier or marine. And don't forget I have known him intimately in other wars. The present soldier is a new breed of cat. Bill Mauldin or Norman Mailer wouldn't recognize him. And he is different because his training, his orientation, his enemy and his mission are different from anything we have ever known.

I've seen the training and I'm impressed. Remember the old days when if a soldier began a sentence with "I think" he was told to forget thinking for the duration and simply to obey.

Now in this drifting phantasm of a war, we have found that the individual and his judgment and his initiative are not only valuable but essential. The day of the big battalions is over perhaps forever. This war is and must be conducted by small units, mobile and self-sufficient to a large extent and at the same time coordinated with the whole. Leadership grows out of the squad level. The soldier must think for himself, must exercise judgment to survive and often enough when casualties indicate, must assume command.

This new Army does not sit on a line endlessly. This is a war of movement, of advance and retirement as shifting and feinting as is a good boxer. When you come to think of it, this is the first kind of warfare Americans ever knew. We learned it from the Indians and used it successfully in the war for our freedom. It would be strange if we could not relearn what every frontiersman once knew.

There is a pattern in this action as far as soldiery goes, which is completely unique. In other wars, the generals sat back and made the plans and drew up the orders. It was a rare thing for a soldier to see his commanding general except at a parade.

The chopper, the helicopter, has changed all that. The commander can be and is almost every place at the same time. We remember the paintings of Napoleon watching a battle from a hilltop while messengers galloped about, often arriving with orders after the engagement was over. Now it is no unusual thing for the commander to hover over the field, observing every change and having his orders instantly received by the men on the ground. He knows his men intimately and personally to an extent that has never been true before. He is there with the result that the once impassable gulf between soldier and high brass has almost disappeared. There is an old Mexican agricultural saying to the effect that the best fertilizer is the shadow of the boss. To my mind the best morale builder for a forward position soldier is not only the shadow but the presence of the commander. It makes him feel that they are in it together.

I want to tell you about another thing that changes the attitude of the American soldier in Vietnam. From the moment he arrives, he knows that one year to the day, he will go home. I remember troops in World War II who hadn't seen their families in three to four years and who were sunk in a kind of desolate hopelessness. But this open end is the greatest morale builder we have. An increasing percentage of men elect to extend their overseas service on the promise of a month at home. And as far as the nation is concerned, the rotation guarantees an ever-increasing reservoir of highly trained and battle tempered soldiers.

Because my son Tom is in training I've looked in on the methods of the new Army and have seen that the drill instructors, D.I.s, are not the hard and cynical professional martinets they once were, but battle tested veterans who know what they are talking about and whom the kids can trust. And that's a big switch too.

In the short time I have been here I have moved about in every direction due to the unbelievable mobility the chopper provides. And I am certain of one thing. If we were fighting this war in the way all previous wars in history have been fought, we would lose regardless of our incalculable strength and fire power. We would be wilted and nibbled, wearied, and slowly destroyed by a thousand small wounds and frustrations.

If I am hopeful, Alicia, and I am, it is because there is a new thing in the world, a new kind of warfare and thank heaven our Army and those of our allies are learning it. The iron-bound and final dictum of [Carl] von Clausewitz is dying if not dead. He said, you remember, "War is an extension of politics." Now it is amended and this is our great and only hope. "Politics is an extension of war." For the first time in history, an army has undertaken a twofold mission—to defeat the enemy and by help, instruction and example to give a hard-pressed, defeated and often double-crossed people, the courage, the pride, the economy and the ability to defend themselves. That this has been spearheaded by the Army, backed up by the civilian agencies is the new thing, the hopeful thing and the only thing that can possibly succeed.

Sun Tzu, who wrote of *The Art of War* nearly 3,000 years ago, has this wise and permanent thing to say: There are three military objectives and in the following importance—the mind, the land and the economy. If one wins the mind, the other two will fall without a fight. After the failures of war that we know of since recorded history we are at last beginning to learn that the techniques of peace must be not only an extension but an integral part of war. We will make many false starts and have many failures, but I feel and many others feel that this is the light at the end of the long dark tunnel.

I guess I have flang [sic] a lot of generalities at you in this letter, Alicia. In the future I will try to tell you how this Revolutionary Development is being tried and tested. I'll go into it on the rice paddy level and on the village level, in terms of people, of women and children, of food and medicine and self-defense. And I will try to tell you how this is not stupid generosity but a matter of self-interest to the United States. It will take a very long time and it is absolutely essential to our future peace and security. Finally, if it succeeds, and it must, Revolutionary Development, or whatever name it is given, is the fluid wall that can melt the hungry imperialist pressure from the north and west which is miscalled communism. Anyway, that's my opinion and in future letters I'll try to back it up with exact detail.

January 19, 1967 / [No dateline]

Dear Alicia,

I have to tell you about the massive nature of this strange Vietnam action, but small and shining things come through that kind of illuminate the picture and make it feelable and personal.

When recently a hard core unit of Viet Cong crept in the dark to the Saigon airport, cut the wire and slithered silently through toward the revetments where the aircraft lay, they might have succeeded if the

THE DISPATCHES | 35

guard dogs had not detected and attacked them. And such is the fear the V.C. have of these dogs that their first mission was to try to kill the dogs and they succeeded in killing two of them with automatic rifles.

Since then I've seen the dogs and talked with their trainers. They are of two services—the guard dogs and the scout dogs, and their training is completely different. The guard dog, usually an Alsatian or German Shepherd we call a police dog, is a trained and conditioned piece of ferocity. He is handled and directed by only one man who is his master and friend, the only human in the world he trusts. He will attack instantly any other human. So fierce are these dogs that they often break their teeth biting wood or iron and wear stainless steel teeth instead. If the dog's handler is killed or returned home, the dog must in most cases be destroyed. The guard dog is used to protect supplies and closed perimeters at night in areas where anything that moves or breathes can be presumed to be hostile. The dog's nose, suspicion and fierceness are essential in this secret and murderous kind of war, where every shadow may be your death, a tiny movement of the elephant grass may flare with devastating mortar fire. The guard dog knows whether it is a shadow or an enemy, a breeze or a mortar crew. He tells his master and instantly attacks. Sad as his lot may be, he saved many lives and much equipment and his very presence is a powerful determent to the infiltrator.

The scout dog is an entirely different animal with a different mission. He may be a police dog but several other breeds are used, Labradors, poodles, even some kinds of hound. These scout dogs go on leash ahead of a patrol both day and night. They are trained to move silently, sifting the air with their noses, smelling for the ambush hidden and waiting beside the patrols. Attack is no part of the scout dog's duty. When his nose picks out a suspicious odor, he stops, stands stiffly with his head aimed at the point of suspicion. Sometimes two scout dogs separated go forward in parallel. The wind may fool one which the second picks up and if both get the same object, the angles of their heads triangulate to pinpoint the suspicious place.

When the scout dog stops, the handler signals the patrol moving behind. The men then fan out and move on the suspected place alert and ready. These scout dogs have detected a great many ambushes and they are greatly loved by the troops. The V.C. have tried many methods to eliminate them, usually poisoned meat left in the trail, but the dogs are trained to eat only what their handlers give them and to drink only from their special vessels.

I asked a handler and trainer why it is not possible to let the dogs cast and range the way a bird dog does. "We couldn't do that," he said. "They might range out of sight. I keep my dog on a lead. I know him so well that I can practically read his mind. I know from the set and trim of him whether he is only suspicious or whether he is damn well sure there's someone hiding in the brush. He can even tell me if he is only uneasy, but if he warns—we take his advice. Even if he's wrong he knows more than we do."

I asked how the Labradors were shaping up, because I had heard that a large new shipment had come in.

"Very well," the trainer said. "They're obedient, have good noses and they don't get sick and besides, they are absolutely tireless. Nothing stops them—water, mud, heat, nothing. But sometimes we have to put boots on them because of the punji (bamboo) sticks. But, you know," he said, "the dogs can even smell those out because the points are smeared with filth. And they're great for finding the deadfall or a trip wire to a booby trap."

"Have you used dogs to smell out the tunnels?" I asked.

"Not yet, not trained for that, but we will. That's in the plans. And you know they're great for morale," he said. "First the V.C. are scared to death of dogs and besides the scout dog gives a man a lot of confidence. I hope we get a lot more of them."

And I hope they do too, don't you?

January 21, 1967 / Can Tho,
70 miles Southwest of Saigon

Dear Alicia,

By chopper to Delta region of Vietnam, a vast level plain much bigger than Kansas and just as flat. It is a watery plain through which the great Mekong River, split into many sinuous silver snakes, winds in looping curves to the sea.

In this respect it is like the Nile delta, but only in this. From 3,000 feet up this enormous rice bowl of Asia stretches from horizon to horizon a checkerboard of irregular-shaped rice paddies, some rich green, some harvested and some flooded for planting, for the growing season is the whole year and if the five and a half million people who live here wished they could grow three crops a year. That they do not is because for 1,000 years they have had it taken away from them.

The potential of the Delta is staggering. It is crossed and recrossed by thousands of waterways, some natural and some man-made but all of them navigable by some kind of craft. The main channels of the river take seagoing traffic far up into Cambodia, but even the smallest water paths swarm with traffic. The V.C. are everywhere for the very good reason that here is the richest source of rice and money in all of Vietnam. The Viet Cong tax collectors roam through the countryside almost at will.

I came down to the Delta to go with the patrol boats which inspect the river traffic for contraband arms supplies and V.C. personnel. It is a long and frustrating job and the best it can hope for now is to inhibit and to make difficult the movement of supplies.

Two boats make up a patrol. When the leader intercepts and inspects, the second stands by covering against surprise attack.

I went on River Patrol Boat 37 (PBR) to cover a 10-mile stretch of the Bassac River. These are 31-foot craft with water jet propulsion. The hull is not armored but the steersman is protected by a steel box, and two plates aft give some protection against shore fire. She is armed with twin 50-calibre machine guns forward and a single 50 aft. She also carries an M-70 machine gun with two M-16 automatic rifles and two M-79 rocket launchers. On the 37, the boat captain was Harold Chase, engineman first class of New Bedford, Mass., a quiet red-haired man with restless eyes. In addition to the gunners and crew, we had aboard a Vietnamese river policeman to do the interrogation and inspection.

We put out shortly after noon under a flaring sun. The river banks are surprising. From the air the flat country seems to be nothing but endless rice paddies but now I could see that the waterways are edged with high and dense fringes of palm, of bananas and of all manner of fruit trees with little thatched houses nestled among them. The banks are pierced with many small canals and half-concealed entrances. A boat attempting to escape inspection, if it has time, can literally disappear into what appears to be solid riverside.

As our two-boat patrol moved down river there was little river traffic under the noonday sun. The junks and sampans were tied up near to the bank in the shade of overhanging trees. In the middle of the river a black tube about six inches in diameter bobbed up and down in the water. Mines are not practical in the main river course because of the current but booby traps are often encountered.

Our boat circled the canister warily keeping well clear. Then making sure of a clear field of fire one of our gunners opened on it with his M-16 and sank it with his first burst. Whatever it was it did not explode.

Now the river traffic began to move up and down river but staying close to the bank and I saw everywhere an engine new to me. It is a one-cylinder Briggs gas engine of the kind and power we use on lawn mowers. Extending from its drive shaft is a piece of pipe about eight feet long housing a propeller shaft and ending with a small two-blade screw. The whole affair is socketed in a hole bored in the stern of the boat and it can be turned 360 degrees or lifted out of the water. At right angles to the boat it can push the thing sideways. When clogged with eel grass, it is simply raised out of the water to spin in the air. It is the simplest contraption I have ever seen and it pushes even fairly large riverboats along at surprising speed. It would be ideal for trolling in the weedy inland waters of Long Island. The cheap little air cooled engine uses very little fuel. I'm going to make one for myself when I get home.

Now we began the job of stopping and inspecting boats. The procedure is always the same—a shrill whistle and a waving hat and if the called boat does not turn outward at once, a few shots ahead of it. When the boat comes alongside, two riflemen stand ready. The Vietnamese river policeman scrambles aboard, collects identity cards and manifest papers, which he inspects closely. The cards with photographs and fingerprints are passed to our boat captain, who checks them against lists of violators or known V.C. The piles of loose rice are probed for weapons, baskets and packages opened and unwrapped. And in the poorest raggediest boats strange things come to light—transistor radios, painted vases, sets of hinges, a china doll, bits of tin and metal. Our policeman must have a decent approach. When the boats first came alongside the people, the women and children were worried and apprehensive, and why not? The V.C. tell them that we enslave them and steal their children. But in a few moments, even while probing through their effects, our policeman had them laughing and relieved. I watched the faces closely. These are very poor people, their clothing ragged, their possessions pitifully few.

Most of the shallow draft boats are roofed with thatch or corrugated iron against rain and sun. Some were so poor and old and leaky that the women could not pause in bailing and others were beautifully trim and well built and one in particular I admired because its deckhouse was completely shingled with flattened Hills Brothers Coffee cans, the printing and colors still bright. In the distance the thing seemed to be made of stained glass.

And I remember one poor boat that came alongside. A father with one eye, a wife tiny and shriveled and three little boys. I can't forget the pain of worry on the faces, the eyes haunted and the little boys' faces wounded with fear. They looked over the side into our boat, at the guns and the ammunition belts and all the gadgetry with which we surrounded ourselves. And nothing happened to the boys, no one pounced or shouted at them and I saw the fear slide away and the eyes brighten with normal curiosity. And then one, the biggest, put out a timid hand and touched the fiber glass of our siding and then he looked up and laughed and his brothers laughed because he had touched a snake and had not been bitten. And his tiny mother laughed and the one-eyed father laughed. And maybe it's over hopeful but I like to think that a bit of carefully planted poison got flushed away in that laughter.

In all we stopped and inspected 80 boats of all sizes and with every kind of cargo, but mostly rice and fruits, stems of bananas, piles of mottled papayas and lots of produce I have not yet learned to identify. After inspections our policeman would report. "They say the V.C. are out collecting. They are moving the rice to save it." Charley is pushing them harder than ever, taking more and more. The afternoon waned into evening and the tree-clustered banks were black and threw even blacker shadows on the water and from the little hidden houses—glimmers of yellow light like fireflies. The slow-moving boats pulled near to the shore to anchor for the night for with the darkness comes the curfew when no sampan can legally move. This is the time when the V.C. move on the waters, creep stealthily across with their sacks of stolen rice and their wads of crumpled small bills collected by threat and terror.

In the black night we moved quietly on the river, showing no lights, watching the soft glowing radar screen for anything moving. Sometimes we stopped our engines and listened for the sound of a putt-putt or the dip of oars. But there was nothing, or if there was, we didn't know it, just the quiet and unshiny blackness of the hooded shores and faint stars reflected in the steel gray river. Now and then small islands of lily pads floated by detached from someplace far upriver. Any place on that dark tangle can belch fire and it often does from bunkers hidden in the undergrowth. But this night—quiet—quiet.

I've only been in country a few weeks but everywhere I've gone there has been the intimacy of the war. I went in with the lead ship of an assault team of the First Cav [First Air Cavalry Division, a helicopter-assault division]. In the north I've seen the volcano of a B-52 strike from a chopper five or six kilometers away. And I've been with the Marines in their forward positions, burning up in helmet and steel vest and glad to be so burning. The heavy drum of artillery and the lazy floating flares and the quick tearing of rockets have become almost commonplace. Perhaps that is why the dark quiet of the night river with faint stars and squinty yellow hut lights made such a deep impression on me.

When our time was up our two-boat river patrol went back to base to report no action, no activity—but it didn't last. I'll have to tell you about that when I can write again.

January 21, 1967 / Can Tho

Dear Alicia,

I wrote to you about the quiet patrol on the river, the silent shores and the stars doubly twinkly because of the damp atmosphere. We came into dock a little before 9 o'clock. Part of Operation Game Warden is based on Can Tho, the largest city in the Delta region. There are a few small restaurants in Can Tho where Viet people, always with their children, go to eat and talk in their language, which sounds like singing. The lights are not bright in such places. Because of power shortages most of them are lighted with flickering lamps.

At about 10 o'clock in the evening two strolling young men paused in front of a crowded restaurant and suddenly threw two grenades in at the wide open door. One was a dud. The other exploded and tore up the people and their children. There were no soldiers in the restaurant either American or Vietnamese. There was no possible military advantage to be gained. An American captain ran in and carried out a little girl of 7. He was weeping when he got her to the hospital and she was dead. Ambulances carried the broken bodies to the long building, once a French hospital and now ours. Then the amputations, and the probing for pieces of jagged metal began and the smell of ether filled the building. Some of the tattered people were dead on arrival and some died soon after but those who survived were treated and splinted and bandaged. They lay on the wooden beds with a glazed questioning in their eyes. Plasma needles were taped to the backs of their hands, if they had hands, to their ankles if they had none. The children who had been playing about on the floor of the restaurant were the worst hit by the low-exploding grenade. The doctors and nurses of the brutal, aggressive, imperialist American force worked most of the night on the products of this noble defense of the homeland.

Meanwhile the grenade throwers had been caught and they proudly admitted the act, in fact boasted of it.

I find I have no access to the thinking of the wanton terrorist. Why do they destroy their own people, their own poor people whose freedom is their verbal concern? That hospital with all its useless pain is like a cloud of sorrow. Can anyone believe that the V.C., who can do this kind of thing to their own people, would be concerned for their welfare if they had complete control? I find I can't. We and our allies too often kill and injure innocent people in carrying out a military operation. The V.C. invariably wash themselves with innocents. They set up a machine gun in the doorway of a peasant's house and herd the children close around it knowing our reluctance to return fire at the cost of people. They build their bunkers in thickly populated areas for the same reason. And people do get hurt. I've seen the care we take to avoid it, and instant care when it cannot be helped.

One wing of the old French hospital at Can Tho is for V.C. casualties. The doors and windows are barred, of course, but inside the treatment is the same we give our own. But in the eyes of the injured prisoners I saw another atrocity, the long conditioning of these minds to expect only torture and death from us and their uneasy suspicion when it did not come. These minds are crippled by the same plan which plants the satchel charge in a market or throws a grenade into a crowded theater.

I must believe that the plodding protest marchers who spend their days across from the UN and around the White House hate war. I think I have more reason than most of them to hate it. But would they enlist for medical service? They could be trained quickly and would not be required to kill anyone. If they love people so much, why are they not willing to help to save them? This country is woefully short of medical help. Couldn't some of the energy that goes into carrying placards be diverted to emptying bed pans or cleaning infected wounds? This would be a real protest against war. They would have to be told of course that their V.C. heroes do not respect peaceful intentions. They bomb hospitals and set mines for ambulances. It might be dangerous to use this method of protest, and besides, if they left the country, their relief checks might stop. But in return they might gain a little pride in themselves as being for something instead of only against.

The question comes from home so often—when will it be over? I can only guess, Alicia, but at least I am guessing on a base of observation from one end of this country to the other. I guess that a cease-fire is not too far in the future because we and our allies can meet and defeat any military foe that will face us. But a cease-fire is only the beginning. During the Christmas truce, which amounts to a cease-fire, there were over a hundred violations of the truce and not one by us. But that is not the finality of this war. The trained, professional hardcore V.C.s in their cells of three infest the country. They must be rooted out one by one until the villages and hamlets are able to defend themselves. And that may take a generation. But anyone who doubts that it can be done should look at South Korea. In one generation that is a changed people, proud, efficient and self-reliant. Their troops here in Vietnam are as fine as any in the world. And what happened to them can happen here—and must. If we are too quick to pull out or too stupid to understand the price, we may win the battle and lose the war.

[No date] / Dateline—All over the place

Dear Alicia,

Want to hear some pure James Bond, 007½ scuttlebutt? I've stumbled on the thing in a number of places and in bits and pieces, a kind of jigsaw puzzle that comes in broken down. When you fit the pieces together, this is the story that emerges—

In many more than a few cases, V.C. snipers have been found in their holes or on the ground beside their hiding trees. Their heads were terribly torn, in some cases practically blown off. What makes the story strange is that their weapons were found beside them and that in each case the whole breech area was literally blown to pieces. In other words—the man was killed by his own weapon exploding as he fired it. Only snipers have been found. It is argued that if this happened in a group, both the weapon and the body would have been taken away.

If such a discovery happens once, it is an accident and you forget it, but if it is repeated again and again, interest becomes engaged. A weapon could only explode this way if the cartridge were loaded with high explosive, something like TNT or even dynamite. These exert their explosive force in the direction of the maximum pressure, in this case the chamber and breech mechanism of the weapon. And such a load would do just what I have described, would destroy the head of the man firing the weapon.

The switch from powder to high explosive is quite easy to do. You simply draw the bullet, pour out the powder or most of it, fill the cartridge case with the substitute and replace the head. Carefully done, it would be practically impossible to detect the doctored cartridge except by firing it, in which case your knowledge would go with your head. The weapons found have been of Chinese manufacture or their Hanoi counterparts and the loads the standard Chinese ammunitions, which is made in both places.

The inference, of course, is that someone, or some group, is inserting these deadly additives in the ammunition supply, not many, perhaps one in a hundred. And the whisper comes in, I am told with defectors that the V.C. are beginning to be afraid to fire their own weapons, and that a kind of panic is seeping through the cells and cadres.

Now the questions begin, where, by whom and why? Are these little bombs being made in Chinese factories or are they introduced somewhere along the line of supply? Is it being done by those dissidents in China against whom the red guards are deployed or could there be secret opposition in Hanoi or even a faction within the V.C. organization itself? It is well known that both Hanoi and the V.C. are puzzled and split by being caught in the middle in the Russo-Chinese support particularly since China has refused to allow Russian supplies to cross her territory. All of this is naturally speculation and speculation about a rumor at that.

The rumors continue that whatever the source of the booby-trapped ammo, the V.C. are growing uneasy, even panicky about their weapons. Some of them are said to insist on non Chinese supplies. It is also said that increasing defections are stimulated by fear of this undercover activity.

As I said at first, Alicia, I can't prove any of this. Our intelligence and psychological warfare people have given me the fish eye treatment. I have heard that orders have gone out to our front line and outpost troops that they are not to fire that either. I have heard, and this is the veriest scuttlebutt, that *Life Magazine* has pictures of the exploded weapons and bodies but that the editors have not dared to print them or have been asked not to. I heard it both ways.

Well there it is—as crazy and improbable a story as you could wish—a beautiful example of the spy chiller-diller fad in fiction. As I said, I have got nowhere asking our authorities. They get a blue lipped and bleak-eyed look when asked.

But I will tell you why I am writing you this romance. I have seen some of the exploded weapons. And anyone who asks where I have seen them will get the same fish eye that has been turned on me.

January 28, 1967 / Pussi Mountain
near Pleiku in the Central Highlands

Dear Alicia,

I came up here to visit the Pussi Mountain Garden Club, as motley a crew of talent as ever got shook out of a dice box. Officially it is a big brown self-contained combat television van—Armed Forces TV Detachment No. 3, Channel 11, Pleiku. Officer in charge—Navy Chief Chuck Brown of Tacoma, Wash. The electronics engineer is Cpl. and Witch Doctor John Rooney of St. Paul, Minn., a dark-eyed mystic with the mind of a computer. He needs a haircut. Says he can't find a bowl that fits.

When the history of A.F.R.T. is written, no one is going to believe this outfit. For instance, Sp. 4 Tom Tucker, of Pacific Grove, Calif., Lance Cpl. Dan Ziegler of Eagle Pass, Tex., and my own son John who is generally called "Hemingway," were drinking beer in Pleiku when a wayfaring soldier joined them.

"What's your name?" he asked, pointing.

"Tommy Tucker."

"And what's yours?"

"John Steinbeck."

He turned to Dan Ziegler and said, "If you tell me you're Little Bo Peep, I won't be surprised, but I'll be pretty mad."

There are 12 men in Detachment No. 3, or rather 11 men and a little tailless yellow dog named Pfc. Dragon after what this mountain used to be named. But I might as well go over the roster—let's see, there's Pfc. "Stormin'" Norman Dunlap of Rock Island, Illinois. Then there's Sp. 4 Bob Nitzburg of Baltimore, a real time fiend. He has two Accutron singing wristwatches and would like as many more as he can get. It is said that he has watches in his nose. Next are Sp. 4 Darrell Dalton of Salt Lake City, an engineer in full bud, and Sp. 4 Keith Turcotte of St. Louis, the supply man and that explains a lot. And last there's Ol' Sarge Flanagan of Hollywood, Fla., who hates snakes and is proud of it. He also has a distaste for firearms, due no doubt to a childhood experience of some kind.

The vanguard of Detachment No. 3 straggled up the left flank of Pussi Mountain in the driving rain on Oct. 28. They pitched tents but didn't get dry until Christmas. Their mission was to receive a new television van due in from the States with which they were prepared to spread news and culture throughout southeast Asia.

Well, you know how such things go, Alicia. First the van, a vehicle about the size of a highway transport truck, got lost, that's right—mislaid. No one could find it. It seemed to have been landed but then it disappeared. Sometime in early December it was found but it was also found that it had been injured either in crossing or in unloading which is probably why it was lost in the first place. Now it had to come overland from Da Nang to Pleiku over a road that even now is about as secure as a snake farm.

Meanwhile on Pussi Mountain, Dai Vi (that's Viet for Captain) Luckey governed Detachment No. 3 with a delicate hand and a wrist of iron. Once the concrete pad was ready and the thick jungle roached back to a decent perimeter, the Dai Vi was faced with the fact that his detachment was an incipient but very sophisticated bomb. Every man was an expert in his field and his field was not policing the left flank of Pussi Mountain. I am told that philosophy was studied and the early-English plain song explored.

Late in December the van was on its way but now the tower was lost. A kind of hopelessness set in and I am told that the Dai Vi, an ex-paratrooper, began giving lessons in free fall from an embankment. The jungle up there is full of monkeys but you never see them. However, they chatter a lot when disturbed and they were disturbed.

This was the situation when I arrived to visit Detachment No. 3 and my son Hemingway. Not having gone through the long wait, my interest and exuberance brought a breath of fresh nausea to the electronic mountain yards.

You remember in an earlier letter, Alicia, I mentioned with pride and some cowardice that everywhere I have gone on this junket, I have drawn fire. Quiet sectors have erupted on my arrival. Attack orders were issued almost as though I had brought them. I have begun to feel a certain coldness toward the promise of a visit by me.

When I climbed out of the sweat-dripping jeep at the Garden Club center and was introduced around by Hemingway, I sensed a certain lack of enthusiasm, an unspoken "as if we didn't have enough trouble already" sort of feeling.

I tried to overcome a boring hostility by arguing, "Look. Wherever I go, there's action. Now what action is likely here? I tell you I am magic. The van will arrive." There was some grumbling. "If the witch doctor (Rooney) can't get it here, what do you think you can do?"

"I can pour a libation on the ground to the Gods, and I have the whisky to do it too."

Dai Vi Luckey threw in with me. "Breakfast Clubbers, listen to me," he said. "The van is coming in to Pleiku and here are two professional magicians working on it. But I will go even farther. If the van gets up the hill tomorrow, I will burn my draft card."

And will you believe it, Alicia? At 2 o'clock on Jan. 7 the huge brown thing, big as a boxcar, came grumbling up the narrow twisting road preceded by a caterpillar in case of trouble. And to make it perfect it was followed by a truck piled high with the disassembled and crated antenna. It was a glorious moment—a modern triumph for necromancy. The night of the 7th we poured libations. The night was bright with flares, rockets poured down in the mysterious west toward Cambodia and a Puff the Magic Dragon ship poured waterfalls of tracers on suspected areas. And in the mystic light the Dai Vi kept his promise. While the detachment stood at as near to attention as possible, the captain whipped out his draft card and handed me his lighter.

I said, "You know, sir, this could get you five years at hard labor, by act of Congress."

"I know," he said happily. "Light her up." So I did and do you know— a draft card is nearly fireproof, but finally it caught flame. But halfway through I beat out the flames. I wanted the charred half as a remembrance. And I have it.

That was a night to remember but the next night . . . But that I'll have to save for another letter, because it was kind of different.

January 28, 1967 / Pussi Mountain Culture and
Rest Center Central Highlands, South Vietnam

Dear Alicia,

In my last, I told you about the triumphant arrival of Detachment No. 3 Combat TV Van, and the night of disciplined joy that followed. Well the next morning the witch doctor, Rooney, disappeared into the van and was not expected to come out until it goes on the air about Feb. 1. It was a bright day, fresh and cool in the highlands. The big air and artillery installations in the Pleiku area, which spread out like a sand table model below our high outpost, were singularly quiet. There was no artillery fire and while the chopper traffic was as heavy as usual, the whole complex lay under a baleful quiet. And I don't think this is an impression after the fact. We had C rations for lunch and after the food at the Hotel Caravelle in Saigon, the meat balls and beans were a delight. We were dangling the C ration cans on wire nooses in the boiling water of immersion heaters when the field radio began to splutter nervously. It reported V.C. activity widespread—small groups, probably mortar crews but very active. We were given an alert.

Then about 2:30 in the afternoon, the road between our mountain and Pleiku went up with a land mine and the route was closed to traffic. And the radio got that cold and detached tone of voice that comes when it is very serious.

The situation was hairy, it indicated and if we knew which side our bread was buttered on we would look to our defenses.

Well, we did look to them and we didn't have any: Oh! There were weapons enough, but nothing to get behind. The cultural nerve center to be called Detachment No. 3 AFRT isn't out of anything. It never had anything. A Quonset hut, two tents, and $100,000 worth of new-come TV station on the pad, and no sandbags. There weren't any sandbags, hadn't been any. There wasn't any detergent or toothpaste or sunburn lotion but that afternoon what we craved was sandbags. One mortar hit and Detachment No. 3 would go back to waiting for a new van. I don't know why there were no sandbags. They had been ordered over and over. The hill is loose red earth that crumbles like cookies when dry and runs like syrup when wet. Without sandbags to hold it up, a dug bunker disappears as fast as you dig it, kind of like the sand funnel an ant lion digs. And that big damned van standing out against the sky with nothing to protect it even from rifle fire—I hope my cry is heard clear to the Pentagon building. For heaven's sake, get some sandbags to Pussi Mountain if you have to weave the jute yourselves. I promise you, Alicia, if we had had thread, we would have started weaving gunny sacks.

Now the field radio became a little incoherent. There were reports of satchel charges and mortar rounds but where and how much was garbled.

You don't have to be told that a good officer is a good officer. You know it instantly. Capt. Luckey and Chief Brown went quietly to work, assigning posts and weapons, one station to cover for another. Weapons and ammunition we had in great plenty—grenade launchers, machine guns, automatic rifles, hand grenades, claymores and an unspecifiable number of 75-mm. recoilless rifles. You understand, Alicia, that I'm a civilian and observer, a noncombatant. But I long ago discovered that I can observe much better if I have some means of self-defense handy, and real handy.

Of course you understand that we thought the V.C. were getting ready to overrun our mountain and destroy the van before it ever set up business. Maybe it was vanity but that's what we thought. And we had nothing to protect it except fire power.

It came on evening and the radio increased the alert, if that were possible. We were set up like a trip-wire claymore mine. That was one of the strangest nights I ever spent, Alicia. The darkness came and Haloway below us was hit by mortar fire; a little later the town of Pleiku came under fairly heavy attack. We couldn't see that because the upper thigh of the mountain hid the town from us but we could see the explosions reflected on the clouds and hear the thud of the charges.

I don't know and didn't know what was happening. Last night was bright with gun ships and artillery fire, with flares and zip lines of tracers. Tonight was dark, a velvety crumbling dark, no firing, no earth-lighting flares swinging from their parachutes. No, it was dark and it was quiet. Once in a while a searchlight would stab through, waggle and go out. Once below us there was a kind of bungling of headlights where they shouldn't be. We called artillery but discovered in time it was one of our tanks that had got lost, poor thing. There are always lights on a dark night even if our eyes have to invent them. But out on that upland thick with small trees and elephant grass taller than a man, there really were lights, perhaps the glow of a family lantern. When you look at such a light steadily it begins to move erratically, it makes spirals and little dives and sometimes disappears entirely.

The Dai Vi had been very specific about posts. Mine was high and unprotected but I had a helmet and a vest and I can get down real flat if I have to. I knew where my son's station was below me, but I heard him say softly as someone walked by, "Who in the world could imagine that on a night like this, my dad would be up above me with an M-79 covering me?"

And who in the world would!

A night without action, with only waiting and listening to sounds that aren't there and seeing shapes that aren't there—such a night is a very long night. The dew was heavy and very cold. And there was no attack—not then. Maybe they hadn't been after us at all. Or maybe they had word of our armament. But we were glad of the dawn, very glad. I had a wire cut on the right leg and the cold made it ache. Come to think of it, I ached all over.

I hope I haven't made you ache.

February 2, 1967 / Saigon

Dear Alicia,

Soon after I arrived in South Vietnam, I became aware of the constant presence of slow, low-flying, fixed wing, single engine airplanes that coast and cruise about, circling and quartering. And it wasn't long before I began to hear about the F.A.C. or Forward Air Controllers. They are among the bravest and the most trusted and admired men in this shattered country, and to the enemy, the F.A.C. must be about the most feared. I had heard many stories of their duties and their accomplishments and just a day ago I was allowed to fly with one on three separate and different missions, and it was an experience I will not soon forget. I'll try to tell you about it in detail, Alicia, while it is still clear and tingling in my memory.

As usual it was an early trip through the roiling traffic of Saigon to the 120th Helicopter Operations at Tan Son Nhut Airport. It gets light late this time of year. At 0710 it was still dawn. Then there was the quick and businesslike chopper trip to My Tho in the Delta district. At breakfast I met my pilot, Maj. William E. Masterson, called "Bat" of course, the Forward Air Controller for the Seventh ARVN Division, a strong good looking officer with a very knowing and humorous eye. He was a B-52 pilot who volunteered for FAC. Indeed, I may be wrong, but I believe all FAC pilots are volunteers.

Our aircraft was an O-1 "Bird Dog," a single-engine, propeller driven, fixed wing Cessna which moves at 90 to 100 knots and has two seats, one behind the other. It is the same aircraft you see all over America, a slow, dependable job with fixed landing gear, fairly safe if its single engine is properly maintained. Our craft carried four rockets on the wing tips, two M-16 carbines, hand operated and mainly for self-defense in case of a forced landing, and a number of smoke bombs for signaling and marking.

We had no parachutes. They would take up too much room and flying as low as the FAC fly—anywhere from 200 to 2,000 feet, you couldn't get out in time anyway. We did wear the armored vests which are said to take the sting out of small arms fire.

Major Masterson, Bat, said, "They don't shoot at us much because we can call in an air strike in a few minutes and snipers just don't want to take the chance. But if we should get hit, I'll set down easy if I can and then we pile out and hit for cover with the M-16s and wait for rescue."

I was pretty clumsy getting into the back seat with the thick vest on, and butter-fingered getting the belt and shoulder straps tight. There was no fooling around. The prop soared and brought the oil up to pressure. On the edge of the airstrip a ground man pulled out the pins from the rockets arming them and passed the pins in to me.

The little ship danced down the runway and jumped into the air. I had earphones and a mouthpiece for communication. Our first mission was visual reconnaissance, called naturally VR, and it is unique and fascinating work. Each FAC man has a sizable piece of real estate for which he is responsible. He flies over it every day and sometimes several times a day. He gets to know his spread like the back of his hand and he looks at it so closely that he is aware of any change, even the smallest.

I asked what Bat looked for. "Anything," he said, "absolutely anything." We were flying at about 500 feet. "See that little house down there? The one right on the river edge."

"I see it."

"Well, I know four people live there. If there were six pairs of pants drying on the bushes, I'd know they had visitors, and maybe V.C. visitors. Look at the next place—see those two big crockery pots against the wall? I know those pots. If there were three or four, I'd investigate. Oh! Oh!" he said and swung suddenly in over the paddies away from the river. About ten water buffalo were grazing, standing in the watery field. Our bird dog swung low and the beasts raised their heads at us.

"V.C. transport," said Bat. "See, how thin they are? They're working them hard at night." He made notes on the detailed map on his lap. "We'll flare tonight and maybe catch them moving."

"Tell me some other things you look for," I asked.

"Well, there are so many things I don't know where to start. Too many water plants torn loose. Lines in the mud on the canals or the riverside where boats have landed, trails through the grass that have been used since yesterday. Too many people in one place or not enough people where they should be. We spotted a flock of Charleys because one pair of blue jeans was hanging on a peg in a house where there shouldn't be blue jeans. Sometimes it's too much smoke coming from a house at the wrong time. That means they're cooking for strangers. I can't begin to tell you all we look for. But sometimes I don't even know what it is I'm seeing. I just get a nervous feeling, and I have to circle and circle until I work out what it is that's wrong. You know how your mind warns you and you don't quite know how."

"Like extrasensory perception?"

"Yes, I guess something like that," he said.

We followed the river down to the sea and then moved along the beach south and eastward to where the Marines had recently landed. Their beachhead was manned and we turned inland and swept right and left until we found the advance force moving painfully through the flooded muddy country, all mangrove swamp and nastiness. Masterson talked to the ground. "I can't see anything up ahead," he told the weary command. "But don't take my word. You know how they can hide."

"Don't we just!" said the ground. We swung back toward the river quartering the country like the bird dog we are named for. On a canal ahead, a line of low houses deep in the trees was slowly burning, almost burned out. "Ammunition dump," said Bat. "We got it yesterday. Must have been quite a lot from the secondary explosion we got. Have to go back to refuel now. We'll have a bite of lunch and then we've got a target, I think a real good one."

Not very long afterwards we dipped down on the little airstrip as daintily as a leaf and taxied in. I handed the pins out the window and the ground man stuck them into the holes that disarmed the rockets. And then we drifted to a fueling place and I edged my way out of my seat. The ground was a little wavy under my feet.

We went in to have lunch. And I'll have to tell you about the rest of the day later, that is if you're interested. My hand is tired with writing now.

February 3, 1967 / [No dateline]

Dear Alicia,

As I told you in my last letter flying with the O-1 Bird Dog of the Forward Air Control is a very personal matter. The survey of areas is rather like that of a Fuller Brush Man, knocking on every door. The afternoon mission of Maj. William E. (Bat) Masterson was to direct an air strike on a grenade factory.

I am interested always in how information develops. In this case, the first knowledge of the existence of the concealed factory came from an informer and that is all I know or want to know about him. He described the exact position of the target. His information was then submitted to scrutiny of air photographs. (I enclose a picture of the target. This picture is not classified because the place is cut off and also the mission is completed.)

An expert goes over the photographs with a magnifying glass. Some things would be obvious to you but many more are apparent to the trained eye. The place is in a dense cover of palm trees. It is available for transport by way of a small canal which connects with a larger canal.

The plantations nearby of trees are arranged in lines but the paddies in the area have been untended for some time. The tops of the trees over the target itself seem to be drawn inward, perhaps by ropes, to cover whatever structure is below from air observation. A good analyst of photography can read the ground with a large degree of accuracy. The strike on this target is to be carried out by the Vietnamese Air Force flying A-1-E Skyraiders. They have been called to rendezvous at altitude not far from the target area.

We had a last cup of coffee and again I clambered into the rear seat of the tiny O-1 Bird Dog, and this time I pulled the shoulder straps straight, because from the ground I had watched these little birds swoop and dive. Our rockets were unpinned again and we bounced into the air again flying at about 800 feet. I had the (enclosed) picture in my lap and the earphones close adjusted. In a very few minutes I could make out by angled fields and the steep curve of trees the place which was to be our target.

"Bat" Masterson talked to the Skyraiders gathering far overhead, and when they were in position, he said, "I'm going to put a rocket on the target. Shoot at the smoke, napalm first, and then bombs." The Bird Dog swung down to 500 feet, circled and then upended and put its nose on the target, and a rocket screeched from the wingtip, burst and put up a column of smoke to the left of the target. "Bad shot!" the major called. "Come in six meters to the right of the smoke." He rolled up on edge and away from the area. And looking sideways from my window which was in fact straight up, I could see the formation of Skyraiders peel off and dive on the target. The first cluster of napalm smothered the grove in brilliant red flame which while we watched revealed some large structure beneath the cover. The Skyraiders climbed almost straight up and fanned back to position.

"Now bring in the bombs!" And they peeled and dived again. The first bombs exploded in a series of puff bursts but the second plane struck pay dirt. As he roared up there was a huge explosion on the ground and white smoke towered into the air and our little ship jumped sideways like a blown feather.

The next run brought another secondary explosion but this time the smoke was a brownish yellow, thick and greasy looking. "Good shooting," Masterson called to the bombers. I know that the size, shape and color of the secondary explosion tells a great deal about the nature of the objective—what kind of explosive he is using and for what purpose. By now the dense little grove of trees in the picture had disappeared and a black smoking area had taken its place. We flew low over it. From the size of the craters, it must have been a fairly large operation. Even at this altitude we could see no movement on the ground. No boats moved in the canal, no people were dotted about the fields: the flat, wet landscape stretching to a round horizon might have been a planet deserted by its people. It was like the silence in the grass when a hunting hawk flies over.

Evaluation comes always and in a war evaluation is a sadness. Perhaps 20 or 30 people were killed by the secondary explosions, but they were killed while making the weapons to kill us. But the people who were assembling the grenades in what is now a black and smoking hole—were they involved with the use of those ugly little murdering tools? Who is guilty and who innocent? I have seen the work of these grenades in the markets of the villages, in small eating places, even on crowded boats.

To me all war is bad. There are no good wars, and I can find no soldier to disagree with me. But I do not understand those who think that by turning their backs and looking away, they have become innocent, for those who look away have found one kind of war bad and the other good. Masterson, and the Marine private wading in the leech swarming swamps, and the paddy family huddled and frightened in a mined hut at the end of a booby-trapped path, and I who have looked at this war up close—all of us would agree—it is all bad, but it must be all removed at the same time, else it will continue as it always has.

February 4, 1967 / Saigon

Dear Alicia,

Ev Martin, who is bureau chief here for *Newsweek*, is to my mind a war correspondent in the great tradition; in other words, he gets his information in the field rather than from bars and official handouts. A couple of days ago he took me to an outfit he has followed so long and faithfully that he is practically a part of it—the Fourth Battalion, Ninth Infantry, 25th Division, called the Manchus from the time of the Boxer uprising in China.

Lt. Col. Robert A. Hyatt, 39, of Fairfax, Va., is battalion commanding officer and he took us to Bravo Company working the hamlets and paddies. Capt. Nicholas Turchiano, something well under 30, has Bravo Company. He is from Valley Stream, Long Island and that's pretty close to home. Furthermore, the town of Farmingdale, L.I., has adopted the outfit as its own.

The operation in progress is the slow careful day and night occupation, inspection and patrol of an area as hairy and difficult as any in the country. It is miles of small square rice paddies, deep flooded with water, each one bounded by a narrow embankment which is also the pathway, deep with mud and slick and slippery as a greased pig. Scattered about the flat country are houses and hamlets sitting each on its own island or platform of earth. These islands have been built up over the centuries by dredging up mud in baskets and patting it in place to dry. The result is that each house or collection of houses is surrounded by a fairly deep moat from which the mud was taken to make the island. The houses are of thatch and woven palm with floors of packed earth, and each island has its coconut palms, its bananas, papayas and many fruits I haven't yet learned about.

To get to Bravo Company we took a chopper, which landed us in a rice paddy. I knew it was going to be wet when I jumped out but I didn't realize that I would be nearly waist deep finding bottom and that from there I would begin to sink slowly in very sticky gluey mud. To pull one boot free drove the other one deeper. I managed to half scramble and half stumble to the edging bank without dropping equipment or drowning but I pulled out making sounds like a big old cow in a swamp.

We slipped and slithered along the narrow path greasy with mud and we kept a decent distance apart. This is prime sniper country and it doesn't pay to bunch up. Ev Martin was behind me, and looking back, I saw his plan. His camera was ready and he was waiting for me to slip on the path and go sprawling into the watery muck. He wanted a picture of that and maybe I should have obliged him, but my mean streak made me extra careful, moving along with little mincing steps while Ev, maneuvering for a good camera angle, slipped and went in himself. It is interesting to see professional instinct. He went in holding his camera high over his head.

Col. Hyatt was inspecting his companies. The men were pretty tired. They had been out for many hours searching the houses for explosives and slowly wading the ditches and paddies probing for weapons. The

V.C. often sink their weapons in the muddy water and also their ammo sealed in pottery jars. Then they can retrieve it any time they wish. In the miles of ditch and paddy it is remarkable that any of this stuff is found. But yesterday they came on a large cache of guns and ammunition and this morning stumbled on a few weapons, but not many. The difficulty is that you may see something in the water that looks suspiciously like a rifle barrel and on trying to dislodge it, set off the booby trap it is tied to.

We straggled to an island on the narrow path, stepped over a low pig gate and came on a thatched house in a grove of lush and fruitful trees. The interrogation was under way, translated by the Vietnamese Army interpreters into a kind of universal pidgin. There was an ancient man with a long and thin white beard and a white moustache that wilted around his mouth corners like rootlets reaching for soil. His eyes were wide and cautious—completely noncommittal. The woman was old and rumpled and the bare feet of both were as wide as they were long, the toes splayed and spread apart, much better for getting a grip on the mud, than were our field boots. A sick man lay with closed eyes in a woven hammock strung between house posts.

At one end of the house was a large pile of unhulled rice and behind the pile at least 10 big sacks of rice. These sacks leaned against a structure that is in every house, low parallel walls of brick or mud on top of which are planks of hard wood at least three inches thick and on top of that a mound of hard dried mud. It is the house shelter, mortar proof. The ends are open. They crawl in these at night to sleep in some kind of safety.

Hanging overhead was a large and very fancy mantle lamp with a huge glass shade, quite beautiful in design. Everything is incongruous in these houses. There are two very heavy carved dining tables with claw and ball feet and legs carved in reverse curves, looking far more Spanish than oriental and strangely out of place in this thatched house with its packed mud floor.

"You see the damnedest things in these houses," said Capt. Turchiano. "No telling where they got them or when."

A sergeant in helmet and steel vest questioned the old people. "Where are the young men and women? Where are the children?"

A burst of questions and answers in language like a song, then:

"He say they go away. They afraid."

"Where did they go?"

"He say he don't know."

"Ask him who is harvesting the rice?" The singing exchange.

"He say he do it."

"Nonsense. He couldn't. There's too much of it."

"He say other people help."

The sergeant sighs with frustration. "What's the matter with the man in the hammock?"

"Sick."

"We'll send a doctor."

"He say 'good.'"

"Do the V.C. come often?"

The old wide eyes veil themselves without closing.

"Sometimes."

"What do they do? Do they give you lectures?"

"Sometimes. They make us cook for them."

"How often do they come?"

"He say not possible to know."

"What time do they come?"

"He say late in the dark. They go away before morning. Not see again."

The sergeant said bitterly, "Some of them are probably lying under water out there right now, breathing through reeds. They can stay down for hours."

I asked, "Don't the leeches get them?"

"Sure. Everything gets them—leeches, snakes, malaria, pneumonia, tuberculosis. They're nearly all sick."

"How do they survive?"

"They don't. They die young."

"But there are old people."

"Two," said the sergeant, "in a house built for 20."

During the interrogation the search went on, peering into the thatched walls, feeling in the piled rice, probing the sacks with steel rods. A corporal made his report.

"Clean as far as I can tell, and you know how much I can tell."

We moved outside into the shaded place where chickens and ducks sat in mid-day quiet. A Vietnamese soldier came from an outhouse strumming experimentally on a guitar. Col. Hyatt said, "Where did you get that?" The man grinned and gestured at the outhouse with his head. "Well you put it back where you got it," the colonel said. "You know damned well we're not here to rob these people."

The soldier turned back reluctantly, almost sullenly. "I wonder if we'll ever get through to them," said Hyatt. "We have to if we're ever to get any place."

Two soldiers, Americans, were wading in the moat that surrounds the little square island. The muddy water was over their waists. They felt about with hands and reaching boots.

"Find anything?" Capt. Turchiano called.

"Joe found a punji stick with his hand. He went back to have it treated."

Suddenly I remembered something. I said, "Out at Sag Harbor I have a five pound magnet on my dock. I bought it war surplus. It will pick up 75 pounds under water. I tie a line to it and drag it on the bottom when anything goes overboard. I've picked up everything from a pair of pliers to an outboard motor in nine feet of water. Why wouldn't that kind of thing work here? Two men could walk the banks and swing it between them. It should locate anything made of iron or steel."

Col. Hyatt looked excited. "I never heard of that," he said. "It sure might. But where am I going to get a magnet?" I said, "I'll see if I can find one in Saigon, and if I can't, I'll try to get one flown out from home for a test."

"If it works, I can put in an order," the colonel said. "We could string three in series and cover a ditch with one pass."

And that's the way it is. I've asked some very knowledgeable people to try to find a magnet here. If they can't, maybe you can get one or two in the U.S. and air freight them out. It's worth a try anyway. Every weapon found probably saves one or more lives. Surely it's worth a try, don't you think, Alicia?

Yours,

John

P.S. The life it saves might be Ev Martin's or mine. It gets kind of personal out here.

February 4, 1967 / [No dateline]

Dear Alicia,

Very often you read in the papers that there has been a leaflet drop over V.C. country or over North Vietnam. But have you ever seen these leaflets? And would you be interested? Some of them are news bulletins designed to overcome propaganda misinformation. Some are instructions for coming over to the other side; some are warnings issued to help people to save their lives and finally some are instructions to evacuate for safety areas which are coming under attack.

Because some of these leaflet drops have been very effective, I think you would be interested in seeing them. Perhaps the most effective have been the ones mentioning names and places. Many from the N.V.N. [North Vietnamese] coming over have said they have been influenced by these drops.

Anyway, here are a few for your inspection. I find the approaches very interesting.

Yours,
John

[Enclosed note to *Newsday* editors]

I don't know whether you will find these informative and interesting enough to use. One thing they do accomplish. They show that we do not bomb innocent people without giving them a chance to escape. This in itself is a refutation of the Ho Chi Minh charges of our savagery against civilians.

But you will have to decide whether you wish to use these examples of psywar [psychological warfare]. Actually they are very effective and it seems to me that they should be given some currency. There is no security involved.

TARGET: South Vietnamese Civilians

Warning to Villagers

Your hamlets are completely surrounded by United States and Vietnamese Forces who will shortly advance to destroy the Viet Cong who oppress and endanger you and your families. In order to protect you from danger during this operation, we urge you to quickly leave your homes and move to the area directed by our loudspeakers. You will be transported to a civilian collecting point where medical attention, food and temporary shelter will be provided for the duration of the operation, after which time, you will be quickly returned to your homes. For your own safety, please cooperate with us. Act immediately, as we advance in a few minutes.

Victory for the Government Is Inevitable

You have seen for yourselves the enormous strength and power which the government has at its disposal to crush the opposition of the VC and frustrate the efforts of their Communist masters. These resources are inexhaustible. The government, with the support of its Free World allies, including the Americans, the Koreans, the Australians, New Zealanders, Filipinos, and others, can withstand and turn back any assault its enemies can mount. WITH THE SUPPORT OF MANY OF THE MOST POWERFUL NATIONS IN THE WORLD COMBINED WITH THE IRON WILL OF THE VIETNAMESE PEOPLE TO DEFEND THEIR FREEDOM, THE VICTORY OF THE GOVERNMENT IS INEVITABLE.

The Government Wants to Protect People

The VC are misusing your land and your homes for hostile activities against the people. The government must destroy the VC. It will destroy them unless they see the light and come to the cause of justice of the government. Because the VC are hiding in your homes and your land, you might be affected by the government effort to destroy the VC. The government does not want to hurt you. As best you can stay away from the VC, do not shelter them or help them, so you will not be hurt when the government destroys the VC. Protect yourselves. Support the just and winning cause.

TARGET: COMMUNIST TROOPS

How to Return to the Just Cause

Follow these instructions to return to the National Just Cause. You may report to any official at any government outpost, or you may come in to any allied soldiers. They will readily welcome you. In any case, follow these instructions for security reasons: 1. Hide your weapons. Later you can lead RVNF soldiers to the weapons and receive your reward. 2. When reporting to any unit or official whom you can expect to be armed, report only in the daytime; you should hold up your hands to show your good will and display a safe conduct pass or any other leaflet if you have one. 3. Even if you do not have a leaflet, you still can rally. When you come to report, just hold both hands upright to help the government and Allied troops understand that you intend to return to the Just Cause. On your return to the National Just Cause, the government of the Republic of Vietnam promises you a warm welcome and good treatment. You will have the opportunity to return to your family, and if you or your family need medical care or other special treatment this will be provided.

Friends in the Viet Cong Ranks

This is our family picture taken in front of our comfortable house which I abandoned three years ago to join the Viet Cong. I did not return until recently. I had a happy reunion with my aging mother, frail wife, and two young children. I have dreamed of this occasion for three years. And now my dream has come true! I feel so thrilled and happy, as if I had been reborn. However, I cannot help feeling sad when thinking of you who are still engaged in aimless adventures, day and night working for the Viet Cong in inhospitable jungles, away from your families and loved ones. You live as fugitives in the obscure mountain areas, deprived of love.

The Fatherland and the people are waiting the return of the misled children to the warm, loving embraces of the Nation! Goodbye now, friends! I wish you lots of luck so that you can defect from the Viet Cong ranks soon and rally under the banner of Chieu Hoi. I hope to meet all of you again in the land of freedom, happiness and prosperity.

(signed) Returnee Troung Van Trieu, former VC Instructor

Are These Your Enemies

Before you came south, you were told that you would fight Americans, to save the nation, that you would liberate the rest of the land that is occupied by the American invaders. But what did you see here? Everywhere people are determined to fight the Communists, and you yourselves are forced to kill innocent Vietnamese, including women and children. Now your enemies are the VN people in hamlets, villages, districts, etc. They don't need your "liberation" because they are living peacefully and happily without you. That is why they do not "welcome" you, but are determined to fight against all Northern troops to the end. With the strong support from powerful Allied Nations, not only Americans, but Australians, New Zealanders, Koreans, and Filipinos, they will certainly defeat you. Your cause has been lost, and the Northern troops don't have enough strength to resist the people's forces assisted by the inexhaustible resources of their powerful allies. Your cause is hopeless!

TARGET: NORTH VIETNAM

Civilians Warned

Bombing is not directed against you. Don't risk your life. Stay away from all military targets such as: Oil tanks and other petroleum storage areas: Bridges, highways, railroads and water ways used to carry military supplies and troops, barracks, gun emplacements, all military installations, electrical power stations, military port facilities.

Why are Northern Soldiers Being Sent South?

Because over 40,000 soldiers and cadres of the Liberation Front of South Vietnam have rallied to the SVN Government. Over 1,000 continue to rally each month. Soldiers of North Vietnam, why don't you follow their example? They know the situation in South Vietnam, they know that the mighty forces of the Republic of Vietnam and its allies are winning the war. Why should you fight when your southern comrades are quitting? Why die needlessly when you can lead a peaceful constructive life under the Chieu Hoi program? Here are some of the 40,000 of your former southern comrades who have rallied under the Chieu Hoi program. Your cadres will deny what this leaflet says. Look around you in the south and see how your cadres have lied to you about everything.

Compatriots Beware

Compatriots who are forced to repair bridges and roads, beware! Roads and bridges will continue to be bombed to prevent the Lao Dong party from sending troops and weapons to attack the south. The quicker they are repaired the sooner they will be bombed again. Compatriots, try to avoid working on roads and bridges, you will save yourselves from a needless death.

THE DISPATCHES | 63

Northern Soldiers Killed in the South

Already thousands of North Vietnamese soldiers have been killed in the south. Here are a few of them: (list of dead Communist soldiers). Do you want news of your loved ones fighting in the south? Every day the Voice of Freedom broadcasts names of Northern soldiers who have been killed, wounded, captured, or listed as missing. Listen every day at 5:25 AM, 5:35 PM and 8:35 PM Hanoi time to the "Family News Announcements."

What Is the Future?

More Bombs More dead Sons and Brothers Or Honorable Negotiations The South Vietnamese and the Americans are ready to negotiate . . . but Hanoi authorities refuse.

Vote Proves South Loves Freedom

"The so-called candidates must withdraw their names immediately from the list of candidates."—"Liberation" Radio, 21 August 1966

"The Liberation Armed Forces in Saigon-Gia Dinh will smash the election farce of the U.S. aggressors and their henchmen in Saigon."—Radio Hanoi, 25 August 1966

Dear Compatriots,

Why did Hanoi and its so-called "Liberation Front" fear the September 11 elections? Why did the Viet Cong kill 30 innocent people and wound 167 others in trying to frighten people away from the polls? Because they knew that the elections would prove that the Viet Cong do not control ¾ of the people. In all South Vietnam 5,298,561 people representing 75 percent of the eligible voters were registered. On election day 4,274,812 actually voted. They represented 82 per cent of the registered voters. All were free to vote or not to vote. Despite Viet Cong threats only 8 of 640 candidates withdrew. Even Radio Hanoi and Nhan Dan (Sept. 8) pointed out that the candidates were not afraid to criticize the government. The September 11 elections prove that the masses in the south prefer freedom to Communism. Your Southern compatriots love their freedom and want to be left in peace. Your sons sent south will see the truth. Tell them to leave the ranks of the aggressors and enjoy our freedom.

Young Men of North Vietnam

1. Be ready to leave your unit when you are sent south. 2. Be ready to enjoy good treatment by the armed forces of the Republic of Vietnam and allied forces. 3. Be ready to live to enjoy life in free Vietnam or return home some day. You Can Help End This Cruel and Senseless War. For several weeks there was no bombing in the North as the Republic of Vietnam and other nations throughout the world sought ways to end the war and bring peace to our land. Your Lao Dong rulers foolishly rejected these sincere efforts to restore peace. Instead, they continued to force increasing numbers of your loved ones to go south and kill your compatriots. They do this completely disregarding the disastrous consequences for you.

Compatriots, workers, peasants, intellectuals, you and your families can help prevent further sufferings. Peace will come with the collapse of the Lao Dong aggression in the South. Before your husbands, sons, brothers, and loved ones are sent South, tell them not to attack their southern brothers but seek and use safe conduct passes to leave the aggressor forces. They will be well-treated. They will live to return to their homes. This will help end the war.

Happy New Year! The people of South Vietnam wish the people of North Vietnam a happy and prosperous New Year. All the Vietnamese people can enjoy such happiness and prosperity if the Communist rulers of the North will cease their aggression against the peace loving people of the Republic of Vietnam.

February 4, 1967 / Saigon

Dear Alicia,

Very often since I have been "in country" I have fervently wished for the company of good writers of any nationality. Men like Edward Albee or John Updike or Truman Capote, sharp observers who could expose themselves to this scene unblinded by preconceptions with minds as yet unfixed in amber. Surely there are good reporters here and some of them, a few at least, even get out into combat areas, or rather what are called unsecured areas. But the hard news men are limited to the immediate and the dramatic and often the copy they send in is tailored and hollandarized [blended] by the established policies of their papers or magazines.

There are many reasons why this very real war has not been communicated to the reader at home. I had to come here to find what some of these reasons are. In all the wars of our experience, we have been able to put pins in a map—to move them ahead or back as the armies advanced or retreated. This is no longer possible. The enemy is in front of us, behind us and often among us. The battalions of north or south we can and have met and defeated until they now rarely make a stand. Rather they strike, retreat, disperse and regroup. Their losses in men and equipment they conceal to the best of their ability.

And this makes statistics, at least those I have read, rather meaningless. For example, I read recently that in spite of our bombing of the lines of communication, 8,000 North Viet troops a month are moving to the south. On the surface this sounds like a slow and overwhelming buildup. It is only when you talk to prisoners or read their statements that the picture wavers. According to many prisoners, the Northern divisions have suffered such losses from bombing, combat and particularly from disease that their strength is down in some cases as much as 80 per cent. In addition he has lost 50,000 killed and over 20,000 have come over to our side during the last year. The number of defectors increases constantly. In the light of these very conservative figures, 8,000 new troops a month would fall far short of keeping the units up to strength.

There are so many uninspected statements which we print and absorb as truth. One is that in spite of our bombing of roads, bridges, trucks and oil and military supply depots, the flow continues uninterrupted. This is nonsense. A line of men and women with back loads, moving only at night, cannot by any wishful thinking supply the nine divisions, seven of the North Vietnamese Army, with food, medicine and military hardware. The first thing prisoners discuss is an appalling shortage of medical supplies. It is true that they can exist on rice and some fish but it still takes a great tonnage to feed an estimated 280,000 men. One man can carry only one 81-mm. mortar shell on his back and often it must be carried in excess of 200 miles over the roughest trails and at night. The people in transport must outnumber the combatants in excess of 10 to 1, and, since noncombatants are never given the care of active troops, these logistical ants have a higher disease rate than do the troops they supply.

I have seen the desperate terrain where the V.C. and their Northern friends must live month after month, wet most of the time, in forests alive with poisonous snakes, and the water underfoot crawling with leeches. They are not immune to these nor to the mosquito, which has no ideological friends. With medical shortages, some units are reported to have a malaria incidence of 97 per cent. The oriental insides are not immune to the deadly invasions of amoebae, tapeworms, pinworms and the many little creatures that cause nausea and dysentery and all of those things make deep inroads where the food supply is inadequate. Finally, these people are highly susceptible to tuberculosis. Some villages have a 50 per cent incidence, which must increase among the soldiery and the transport people.

You see, Alicia, the figures of men and supplies do not give a really true picture. Nor does the steady report that the general run of Communist is a single-track, devoted, uncomplicated animal who follows orders unquestioningly and fights his way to a hero's death.

The truth is, and this is from interrogation of defectors and prisoners of war, that the Communist world is split down the middle by the ideological civil war between Peking and Moscow. Hanoi, under the iron hand of Ho Chi Minh, is on the surface in the Chinese camp, as opposed to the Russian. In this area there was wide if quiet difference of opinion. But now China is split apart also in a separate internal struggle for power. It is not beyond thinking that in the near future parallel factional splits will open the seams of the once iron-bound North.

It is perfectly true that large parts of South Vietnam are still dominated and terrorized by the V.C. This is said to be Charley country and surely it is very dangerous. But this also is to be inspected.

Many of the villages and hamlets have gone along with the V.C. because they had no choice. But now the pressure is on and it becomes apparent that the hard-core V.C. cadres have little interest in the villager except to dominate him. As the pressure increases, Charley seems to lose his head, to rely on terror and torture and murder to keep his power. And he bites deeper and deeper into the peasants' rice. In some parts of the Delta the V.C. tax collectors are demanding 60 per cent of the produce and absolutely all of the money. And as the pressure on the V.C. continues to increase, so also does his brutality increase toward his own people. And it does not take many Charleys to dominate a peaceful and unarmed village. Three men with automatic weapons can by consistent pressure and the murder of any rising opposition, keep a village of 2,000 people in subjection until outside help comes in.

You see, don't you, why I wish for calm and inspective [sic] writers here. Sometimes when I read reports in American papers and magazines, together with political speeches of contenders for office, in the light of what I have seen with my own eyes, I think I am going nuts. Here history is being written but in transmission, it is being so rewritten as to be unintelligible.

There—I have made quite a few generalities. Soon I'll write you about [the] exactness from which some of these conclusions have been drawn.

[No date] / [No dateline]

Dear Alicia:

As you are well aware, wars and rumors of wars do not change very much. After a time of conflict, it is natural that an interested or perhaps nervous government should think of the changes that have taken place in its soldier sons. Then it is natural for a form-letter to be drafted and sent to the Nears and Dears of young heroes about to return home from a foreign clime. It is just as natural for someone along the line to write a parody of the "be careful with our boys" letter.

I just came upon one such here. If I knew who wrote it, I would give him credit, but he is anonymous. It is interesting, I think as well as amusing. Every war has constants but each one develops a vocabulary. But mainly this parody is a documentation of a dark and dangerous and frustrating year. That a man can jeer at it is all to the good.

Dear _____:

As a service to American personnel departing the Republic of Vietnam, the Command here issues to you the following briefing containing some helpful hints that may make the readjustment easier for _____, and is most certain to make your reunion a more enjoyable experience.

As of ___, after serving in the "Gardenspot of Southeast Asia" for the past ___ months, _____ will be returning to the Continental United States.

This, as we are well aware, will be an anxious moment for you as it will be for him. However, we feel it is our duty, being totally responsible for the absence, to warn you of certain changes in his mannerisms and behavior that are likely to make these moments more anxious than you might normally expect.

Therefore, we forward in the interest of all concerned some "dos" and "don'ts" that should be strictly observed.

1. Prepare yourself for the initial shock of that first meeting because the man stepping off of the airplane, though he may bear a striking physical resemblance to the man you waved good-by to long ago, will appear out of place, nervous, and prone to look at everyone with suspicion. You may, if you are carrying a handbag or sack, have to empty the contents of same on the ground for a routine inspection. Avoid crowds and if you should celebrate the homecoming with a drink or two, don't question him if he prefers to sit at the table in the rear of the bar. Also, when the waitress takes your order, it would be wise for you to do ALL of the talking as he may make some embarrassing comment such as "Get loose or I don't buy you any drinks!"

2. Explain to him that taxi fares are slightly higher in the States than in Vietnam because when he reads the meter, he may slug the driver. Don't be shocked—this is standard procedure in Vietnam. If he tells the driver to "Toi" he isn't talking baby-talk. Don't question him—just politely tell the driver to stop. If he says "dee-dee" take it in stride and ask the driver if he would kindly go a little bit faster. If he rolls down the window and starts flapping his arm, explain to him that the taxi has turn signals.

3. For the first few weeks, or until you are sure an adjustment has been made, don't ask him to go to the store and buy hairspray for you. Other items that should be left off the shopping list are Dove soap, Hershey bars, perfume, apples, oranges, Tide soap, bleach, starch, and in general, all cosmetics. Also, you may find that on his first few trips to the store he may fumble around looking for his PX card.

4. His eating habits may be somewhat changed. He will probably want his steaks well-done and may shove milk aside and ask for a beer. If he gets into your kitchen while you're fixing supper, think nothing of it; he just wants to make sure that you have your shoes

on and, secondly, to see that you're not fixing rice. Incidentally the word "rice" should be avoided for quite some time, and at no time during his first year back home should you suggest eating in a Chinese restaurant. Hide the soy sauce and insist that he sits on a chair while eating rather than squatting on the floor.

5. HOLD HIS HAND WHEN CROSSING THE STREET. This may seem absurd at first but after watching him cross the street alone one time, your nerves will never be the same again. He will expect all drivers to avoid him and will make no attempt to dodge them. The sight of a motor scooter or motor bike will infuriate him.

6. Do not serve iced tea at any time.

7. When he pays the bill in a bar or restaurant, he will act nervous and check everyone in the room before he hands the waiter a five-dollar bill. The only thing you can do to combat this peculiar behavior is assure him that there are no C.I.D. agents present. He may ask the waiter what the rate is. If he does, tell him "One-thirty for one" and forget the incident.

8. He will stare at women and probably mumble something about "round eyes." There is nothing personal in this behavior. He still loves you. If he tends to drool, wipe his mouth for him and be understanding—it's been a long time.

9. He may spend much time in the bathroom flushing the toilet. Think nothing of it; he just wants to watch it work.

10. Don't let him order any drinks for you—unless you happen to like kool-aid, watered-down Crème de Menthe, or a very small glass of Coke.

11. If you want to have some fun with him, say "I love you too much," "Be nice, GI," or "you number one." Don't overdo it—he may go berserk!

12. A loud clap of thunder may have one of two effects on him. He may dive under the bed and yell "VC" or, if he recognizes the sound, he will grumble, "those &!?! monsoons are back again."

13. Above all—remember that he has been in man's closest answer to "Hell-on Earth" for ___ months. Pamper him and help him forget those months as only you know how.

Upon receipt of this letter, send no more mail to APO San Francisco 96243 because that man of yours has left Hell and is paradise-bound!!

February 9, 1967 / [No dateline]

Dear Alicia,

I've tried to tell you about as much of Vietnam as I have seen and about as much of the war there as I have seen and heard and felt. I want to tell you very clearly and without leaving any loopholes for misquotation or misinterpretation, that I have been given every facility for seeing every aspect of the country and the war.

The United States Armed Forces and the American civilian organizations as well as the government and army of South Vietnam have taken me where I wanted to go, have let me see everything I wished to see and have placed no restrictions or censorship on what I wanted to write. And this has not been special to me. Any reporter, from any country, can have the same facility of movement so long as he represents a newspaper or papers. If any reporter says that he has been restricted, I am inclined to believe that he didn't want to go. Those who stay safely and comfortably in their apartments in Saigon, reporting only the official reports and briefings available at 5 o'clock every day, do so because that is what they want to do. On the other hand, there are a goodly number of newsmen who cover the fighting areas personally and bravely and these should not be forgotten. The armed forces do us a further honor. They do not protect us in life and limb beyond the care they have for their own men. Any newsman is free to move about, to talk to anyone he wishes, and to report as he see fit.

There are some things I have not told you, but the censorship has been my own. I have gone in with certain operations which I have not reported for the reason that the moves have not been completed and that to tell plans, tactics and objectives at the present time might endanger first the men and second the operation, and that I am not about to do. But I repeat—the censorship has been my own. If there is criticism of the news about this area, it must be aimed at (1) those correspondents who do not wish to report it at first hand and (2) the editors and publishers, who by cutting and changing the material that comes to them, warp the news to their liking or limit it to the spectacular, the bloody and the shocking. All war is those things by its nature, but there are other sides to it—the helping, the rebuilding, the saving. It is true as it has always been true that civilians are injured and killed. In other wars there has not been as much care taken to avoid this as I have seen here.

Steinbeck getting firing instruction on the M-60 machine gun with a bipod front mount, top, and on the M-16 fully automatic rifle, bottom.

Steinbeck with U.S. Navy captain B. B. Witham aboard a PBR (Patrol Boat, River) in the Mekong Delta.

MARTHA HEASLEY COX CENTER, ELAINE STEINBECK COLLECTION. 0-888

PBR #37 on the Bassac River with Steinbeck aboard. At right with Harold A. Chase of New Bedford, Massa-chusetts (left), and Patrol Officer William A. Lee of Lebanon, Indiana (middle).

MARTHA HEASLEY COX CENTER, ELAINE STEINBECK COLLEC-TION. 0-264; 0-275

Steinbeck standing next to his assigned guide, Marine major Sam M. Gipson Jr. (middle), and an unidentified soldier in the South Vietnam Highlands.

MARTHA HEASLEY COX CENTER, SAM GIPSON JR. BEQUEST. 1-393

Steinbeck walking on patrol soon after arriving in South Vietnam in 1966.

MARTHA HEASLEY COX CENTER, ELAINE STEINBECK COLLECTION. 0-261

Steinbeck standing next to a UH-1 Huey helicopter. The man next to him is probably Captain Shaughnessey, D Troop, First Squadron, 10th Cavalry, because his ships were marked with green shamrocks.

MARTHA HEASLEY COX CENTER, SAM GIPSON JR. BEQUEST. 1-394

Steinbeck among soldiers behind sandbag fortifications, wearing a flak jacket and steel pot helmet.

MARTHA HEASLEY COX CENTER, ELAINE STEINBECK COLLECTION. 0-885

" . . . At the booby trap school near Da Nang is every kind of booby trap that has been found. They're pretty beastly."

  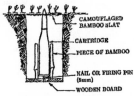

		CAMOUFLAGED BAMBOO SLAT
		CARTRIDGE
		PIECE OF BAMBOO
		NAIL OR FIRING PIN (5mm)
		WOODEN BOARD

In this booby trap, GI has fallen into pit where concealed Viet Cong is waiting to plunge a spear into him.

If a man steps into this pit, his leg hits' steel-spiked boards. These then pivot, wounding leg above the area protected by soldier's boot.

Only tip of cartridge projects above ground; it fires if it is kicked or stepped o

Drawings from booklet supplied U.S. troops.

HEADQUARTERS
UNITED STATES MILITARY ASSISTANCE COMMAND, VIETNAM
Office of the Commander
APO San Francisco 96222

30 JAN 1967

MACOI

Dear Mr. Steinbeck:

It was most thoughtful of you to write to me just before you left for Bangkok. It was our pleasure to help you get a close look at this complex and diversified undertaking, and I assure you that you will be welcome any time you wish to return.

It is my hope that you will have a chance to visit with my wife while you are in Manila. She would enjoy that.

Again, thanks for the kind words about the command and our performance here and for the articles you have written on these subjects. I have seen several of them and hope they get the widest possible display in the United States. The public needs the view through your eyes.

Sincerely,

W. C. WESTMORELAND
General, United States Army
Commanding

Mr. John Steinbeck
c/o Public Affairs Officer
Hq MACTHAI
U.S. Forces, San Francisco 96346

Top, *booby trap warning note, from a Defense Department pamphlet soldiers received upon arriving in Vietnam. Steinbeck sent the pamphlet to* Newsday, *which reprinted the drawings alongside three of his columns on January 7, 1967 (see p. 26). Bottom, letter from General Westmoreland, commander of U.S. military operations in Vietnam, to Steinbeck on MACV stationery.*

LIBRARY OF CONGRESS, HARRY GUGGENHEIM STEINBECK PAPERS

HEADQUARTERS
UNITED STATES MILITARY ASSISTANCE COMMAND, VIETNAM
APO San Francisco 96243

MACOI-C

28 April 1966

SUBJECT: Command Information Topic Number 3-66, Excerpts From Sun TZU's The Art of War.

TO: SEE DISTRIBUTION

1. Reference MACV Directive 360-1, 7 December 1965.

2. The attached topic consists of extracts from the military classic, The Art of War, by Sun TZU for the information of all military personnel.

3. Because this treatise embodies much of the military philosophy of the Viet Cong and North Vietnamese, COMUSMACV desires that it be brought to the particular attention of all commanders, down to and including platoon leaders and subsector advisors.

FOR THE COMMANDER:

1 Incl
as

HOWARD D. SCHULZE
Major, AGC
Asst AG

DISTRIBUTION:
A - HQ MACV
    100 - Cdr, 7th Air Force IO
    1,750 - CG, USARV IO
    500 - III MAF, ISO
    100 - COMNAVFORV - PIO
    50 - Capital Mil Region - IO
    75 - Dep Senior Advisor, I Corps IO
    75 - Dep Senior Advisor, II Corps IO
    75 - Dep Senior Advisor, III Corps IO
    75 - Senior Advisor, IV Corps IO
    75 - MACV-IO

11 Jan '67

To- John Steinbeck -
This is the extract.
Personal regards. WC Westmoreland

Cover page of MACV memo on The Art of War *that Westmoreland hand-signed to Steinbeck.*

And there is much coverage of these civilian casualties but little attention is paid to hospitals where they are treated, to the doctors who work to save and repair both the accidents of war and the civilian Vietnamese wounded by the terror tactics of the V.C., who claim to be trying to free them. I, myself, cannot see how any kind of liberation can come from a time bomb planted in a food market, or simple people coldly shot down by snipers. Yes, war is a sad and a savage thing and many people get hurt. But I have yet to hear of Americans or their allies slaughtering prisoners when they have to retreat, as was done by the V.C. in the Delta recently.

You remember, Alicia, when I came out here, I told you that I wanted first to see the war in Vietnam, and afterwards to visit the countries on the periphery, Laos, Cambodia and Thailand, where it is reported there is an attempt to spread the plague, and then to make a wider circle to those countries where the Communist method has failed, Malaysia, Indonesia, Korea, the Philippines, and last to see the places where it has not yet struck, New Zealand, Australia. All of these countries are deeply involved in the great plan which has been frustrated and staggered, and largely because our soldiers and those of our allies have been in Korea and in South Vietnam. Had we not been, I would not even now be able to visit the countries of Southeast Asia. Their borders would be closed, their plans secret, their produce subject not to economic law but to ideological whim and as a prop for a personality cult. And if soldiers and our government draw diatribes and foaming insults from certain sources it is not because we have failed but because we are succeeding. The screams are of frustration. And they thought they had it made.

Yesterday, in the mail, I received a translation of *Komsomolskaya Pravda*'s latest attack on my letters to you. No, I shall not answer it. The article is almost hysterical and sounds very like the denunciations during the time of the, sigh! sob! personality cult.

However, I would like to warn Youth Truth not to burn all the bridges and to save some adjectives for the future. Yesterday an editorial in the "Peoples" Daily, and quoted by the New China News Agency, referred to your nation, my dear Youth Truth, as "filthy, revisionist swine." The editorial could almost have been written in your office about me. I know you do not value my opinion or you would not devote so much space to refuting it. However, I am moved to offer, if not advice, at least a memory.

When Stalin, who misjudged and misinterpreted the German intention, made an alliance with Hitler and then found himself and his
country invaded, he suffered the further inconvenience of having murdered the best of his general staff for one reason or another. Remember
that then the Russian people put up a heroic resistance but it was badly
inhibited by errors and misjudgments of the past. It then became necessary for your government to ask our help in replacing equipment lost
in the opening days of the campaign or never manufactured at all. You
needed time to regroup and to re-equip, for your people to organize
defense and a new and dynamic military leadership to develop. And
we sent that help. Remember the solid line of trucks that moved up the
Baku road to replace your transport? Remember the swarms of C-47's
we sent you—some of which you are still using? Remember the con-
voys that ran though the submarine wolf packs to carry supplies to you
through Murmansk? You do remember that, don't you?

Well we didn't do it out of stupid philanthropy. Your enemy was our
enemy. In supporting you we supported ourselves.

What I am getting at is this—in the light not only of your being
"atrocious, bloody, filthy, revisionist swine," but also remembering
that you have a border with China 3,000 miles long, in addition bring
in China's demand for the eastern republics, roughly one-third of the
Soviet Union, sum it up with your built-in memory of invasion and
occupation from the east, and I might suggest that you keep a small
corridor open in you minds. For in China's paroxysm of fermenting
trial and error, made frightening by atomic and nuclear playthings, you
might find that far from being murderers and so forth, that we are as
before, defending your rear against a dangerous and an increasingly
fascist experiment.

Do you see no parallel between the Red guards and the Hitler Youth?
So leave a door ajar, *Pravda*—let some bridges be unburned. If you will
do that, you won't have to rewrite history after the fact, nor will you
have to insult the memory of my friend, Alicia Patterson.

February 11, 1967 / [No dateline]

Dear Alicia,

Don Besom of JUSPAD [the Joint U.S. Public Affairs Department]
invited Elaine and me to look at Long An Province, southeast of Saigon

in the Delta country, where the process of pacification is moving slowly forward. And since this action is a blueprint of what must be done in all of the Communist dominated parts of South Vietnam, I want to tell you about it in some detail.

But first, and by no means parenthetically, let me apologize for something I don't remember saying. Some magazine quoted me as saying that my lady wife was not about to fly in choppers. If I did say it, I'm sorry. She loves choppers and has covered a sizable chunk of the territory in them. What she does not do is to try to get into combat areas where her being there would deflect manpower for her protection, and this I approve of. Some young women have recently gone into forward areas for thrills and for publicity and have been damned nuisances to men who had other work to do. One young lady correspondent has disappeared for the second time. The rather cynical betting is that she will show up with a story and an increased price. But it is possible that she may this time be gone. It can happen. ([*Newsday* editor's note:] The correspondent, French newswoman Michele Ray, turned up unharmed last weekend after 21 days in Viet Cong captivity.)

We went from Tan Son Nhut by the Huey chopper I have learned to love. It carries six passengers besides two door gunners and pilot and co-pilot. From the airfield we rose quickly to 2,600 feet, which is out of range of small-arms fire. At that range Charley under a bush does not ordinarily open fire because the door gunners would instantly open on his muzzle flash with their M-60 machine guns and with their tracers they can rake a wide area and make a sniper's lot not a happy one.

Below us the Delta was spread like a patchwork quilt of oddly squared rice paddies. Rivers curled like snakes on the level plain and ditches cut straight as a string across the blanket of wet little fields. The rice harvest is nearly over now and the tree-surrounded squares of houses and villages stand out dark green against the browning paddies.

Our destination was Tan An, the largest town in the area with a bridge over the wide river. There are 35,000 people in Tan An but at 5 in the morning, when the boats of all sizes swarm in with market produce, the population rises to 45,000. It is a lovely town reasonably secured as is evident from the coveys and clusters of new small houses built by refugees who flee from the domination of the National Liberation Army or V.C.

Tan An is the end of the secure road from Saigon. Ahead are blasted bridges and the old road cut to pieces with ditches and littered with land mines. By these methods the V.C. have for some years blocked the flow of rice to the capital. Now Americans at battalion strength together with pacification teams of Vietnamese troops, village leaders, school teachers, knife on ahead, secure another town and rebuild the road.

Col. Sam Wilson, a very personable Virginian of long experience, commands this operation. We have heard a lot about Sam Wilson, who is more or less inventing his operation as he goes along. Don Besom, bless him, gave us his room, twin beds, and reading lights and inside plumbing.

We had lunch and then the colonel took us on a chopper tour of Long An Province, which lies along an extending dogleg of Cambodia. The towns and villages forward of Tan An were very different. The bridges were invariably down, the roads broken and a kind of dilapidation, like a skin disease, spread over the land. The fields looked untended and many of the houses were unoccupied. The river, teaming with traffic in the secured areas, was empty. At night of course Charley moves in the darkness and even in the daytime he brings a brooding darkness with him.

We cruised over the whole province, saw the new-built triangular outposts guarded by ARVN troops and subject to constant harassing fire. These outposts, their corners in redoubt form and surrounded always with deep moats and perimeters of barbed wire, are the first feelers toward security, a lonesome and dangerous business for their defenders.

That night, after dinner, the Tan An Music Lovers gathered. Five officers had bought quite good guitars for $7 apiece. Sam Wilson, who is an accomplished player, was giving this earnest group beginning lessons. The results were horrid but spirited.

We got out at 5 in the morning to see the market come into being. Hundreds of boats crowded the river banks and they were heavy-laden with fruits and vegetables, with fish, with small pigs in baskets and with thousands of white ducks. The Delta is duck country. From the air you see white clouds covering the wet country, ducks to make Long Island seem duckless. The street as the dawn came was completely covered with produce in little squares with only narrow paths between the individual stalls and each stall had its square sunshade of woven palm leaf.

A lovely Vietnamese girl, Miss Dang My Ha, explained to us the many fruits and roots and spices this rich land produces. A busy vital place Tan An, glowing with children. Maybe it seemed even richer and more lovely because of what I was to see later in the day. I'll write you about that.

February 11, 1967 / [No dateline]

Dear Alicia,

I wrote you about the teeming almost secure town of Tan An. Well this morning, I flew with Col. Sam Wilson a few miles deeper into the Delta to the hamlet of Rach Kien. This place was taken less than a week ago by the second battalion, 14th Infantry, First Brigade, 25th U.S. Division, Lt. Col. Charles A. Gillis commanding. With the battalion came U. S. Aid representative Jerry Mabe and MACV adviser Maj. Thomas Thompson. Also with them came the village chief, Truong Van Tran, and the hamlet schoolteacher.

It is hard to describe a place the Viet Cong have held for a considerable time. There are the obvious things—the schoolhouse blasted and torn apart and its brick walls cut through for gun ports. Then there is the old hospital, a sturdy structure with tiled floors and long open chambers which were once wards but now are deep in the manure of pigs and ducks. One other public building must have been defense and sleeping place for the occupiers—it is tunneled with deep shelters and its center is a bomb-proof place made by putting a thick mud roof over heavy logs.

The hamlet looks as though it had been through a long sickness; grass has overgrown the once neat paths, roofs are broken and falling in. The canals and waterways are foul with accumulated filth, the streets littered with stones. The will to be clean, to be neat, had long since gone, taken away by the V.C., who had offered to rise up and help the people against their oppressors. During the occupation many people drifted away to cluster near the secure areas, but some stayed because they had always lived there and many had never traveled more than five kilometers in their lives.

The hamlet chief and the schoolteacher had been early murdered, which is the V.C. method of eliminating traditional order and traditional culture; for which they substitute lectures, exhortations and threats, and gradually the light goes out of people and their eyes dim and they become listless and careless but at the same time they and the land grow unproductive. Flying over the V.C.-held parts of the Delta you can see thousands of acres of rich rice land, diked and edged and loved for a millennium and now lying fallow, the ditch banks broken down and no careful patient hand to guide the rice to its harvest and to trim the wild grass from the graves of the ancestors. The V.C. bring a blight on the people.

The hamlet chief who heads the restoring of civil government told me of one of the last acts of the Viet Cong before they were driven out. They demanded as tax 60 per cent of the diminishing harvest of rice. Two brothers, local farmers, refused the demand saying that if they gave that much rice they could not feed their families. The V.C. dragged the brothers to the marketplace where I have been sitting, convened all of the villagers they could find and held a court. They condemned the brothers to death, instantly shot them and then forced every inhabitant to pass the corpses and to strike them with sticks as they went by. It is a hard thing to understand. The hamlet chief thought that by this symbolic act of striking the dead, the V.C. hoped to involve the people in the judgment.

The chief repeated what he had been told by people who had been in the marketplace at the time. The thing backlashed. The people passing seemed to strike but really caressed the bodies with their sticks and the brothers became saints in their minds and their names were put in a song.

A week ago the battalion took the hamlet of Rach Kien after a sharp fight and drove the V.C. into the countryside where they still are— hiding and sniping. But the battalion secured its defenses, put up wire to inhibit harassment and intrusion and then pitched in to help put the town back on its feet. GIs were cleaning and repairing the school house. Two soldiers were repairing the broken school desks and spraying them with blue paint.

The hamlet chief was busy setting up his civil government and allotting training and defense roles to the popular forces that will one day be the protectors of the hamlet. And the people were beginning to come back. Already they had begun to cut back the raging grass, to clean out the waterways. Women came back to their homes carrying garlands of ducks.

From the ends of the hamlet streets, which disappear into tall undergrowth, sporadic sniper fire still spat into the town so that one avoided exposed places.

Meanwhile the battalion is clearing the road and repairing it, bridging the waterways with iron crossings, and a heavily guarded convoy starts back toward the secured area to connect Rach Kien with a world it has not known for a long time. It will not be easy. Every night the road will be mined, every day riflemen will fire on everyone they hope to frighten. But the security will spread out just as the blight did. The job is long and hard and seemingly endless but it must be done. For it's ourselves we are fighting for—ourselves we are defending lest we become so effete, so careless, so confused and so self-bedizened that we at home go the same way Rach Kien went.

There are rules of observation one soon learns in this twilight zone of hairy security. Entering a street, a village or a compound, you look first to the children. If they run to you, bright-eyed and curious, it is all right and you are safe. But if the children edge away from you and avoid contact with you even by looking at you—you'd better hit the dirt fast because Charley is there in the grass, waiting to put his rifle sights on you.

Rach Kien is a hamlet coming back to life after a long nightmare. And when you hear of the brutality of our soldiery remember the GIs, stripped to the waist, sweeping the filth from the schoolroom and painting the desks.

We had dawdled too long. We went quickly by chopper back to Tan An. Elaine was waiting impatiently. Col. Wilson rushed us to the armed Huey sitting on the pad with its rotors turning impatiently. We were about five minutes late. We clambered in, hooked the belts and Elaine was trying to get a scarf over her head when our chopper dived off the pad like a quail the day the season opens. The pilot hugged the ground, brushed his gear over a line of trees and then suddenly jumped for altitude like a skyrocket.

My dear wife shouted in the ear of the door gunner sitting beside her, "What's the hurry? We're only five minutes late." The gunner swiveled down the mouthpiece of his intercom. "Hell, lady," he complained. "They was shooting at us."

"Where?" she asked.

"Right back there on the pad, lady."

So you see, Alicia, even secure areas tend to grow a little hair.

February 11, 1967 / [No dateline]

Dear Alicia,

It is easy to remember how every war develops its wry and bitter personal humor. You will remember the "Dear John" letter of World War II as a stringent example. This action in Vietnam by its nature and place makes soldiers and American civilians kind of cut off. The newspapers they receive or the clippings sent to them in letters tell a story amounting to treason in attitude, a population reeling under the heavy burden of prosperity, a loud and headline-getting group of so-called Peaceniks or sometimes Berserklyites who not only do not support the war and our soldiers but actually do cheer on the enemy. The struggle for votes and jockeying for election position at home begin to flutter the politician in the uncertain minds of the electorate. During the next months he may and probably will say everything in all directions. Is it any wonder that a smart and amazingly dedicated army falls back on satire?

The following letter, like so many others, just appears. I don't know who wrote it but I admire him. This kind of thing passes from hand to hand. It is funny because it carries the sting of truth or suspicion of truth to many people here saturated with news stories of how it is at home, or of social, financial and ethical extravagance. The whole thing seems to me to have been brilliantly compressed in this letter.

Dear Joe:

Nothing doing back here. I sure do envy you out there in Vietnam right in the thick of things. Bet you never have a dull moment.

I was over to see your wife last night and I read all of your letters. You do write a bit mushy but I don't blame you. Frances is a swell girl with good looks and personality. The guys still whistle at her when she walks down the street.

Your brother-in-law, Smedley, dropped in. He was wearing the brown suit you bought just before you left. Frances gave it to him as she thought it would be out of style when you got back. Several other guys came in and we killed two cases of beer. We wanted to chip in for it, but Frances wouldn't let us. She said you sent her $10 extra for her to spend as she wished. One of the guys is buying your Wilson golf clubs that you bought last year and never got a chance to use. He paid $25 for them and will pick them up tomorrow. That is more than she got for your movie camera, hunting rifle, and projector.

Frances was the life of the party. I thought she would be a little shaken up after the accident last week on the way home from an anti-Vietnam demonstration she attended. She was involved in a head-on collision with your new Chevy and smashed your car to bits. That must have been something. If she hadn't been drunk and passed out like she did, she could have been killed. The other driver is still in the hospital and threatens to sue; too bad Fran forgot to pay the car insurance. But the funny thing is that she isn't a bit worried about it. We all admire her courage and nonchalance and especially her willingness to mortgage the house just to pay the bill. Good thing you left her power of attorney when you left.

Well, to get back to the party. You should have seen her do an imitation of Gypsy Rose Lee. She has the figure and was still going strong when we said good night to her and Claude. Guess you know Claude is rooming at the house. It is closer to his work and he saves a lot on gas and lunches and can stay in bed a lot longer in the morning.

Nothing much new with me except my wife got another raise. She's at $100 a week now, so we do O.K. It's getting late so I will stop. I can see through the window across to your front porch. Frances and Claude are having a little nite cap listening to the radio that was playing "Wish You Were Here." He is wearing your smoking jacket, you know, the yellow one you like so well.

Well buddy, I sure wish I could be over there with you and the action. Lucky guy!! Give those Viet Cong hell.

Your Old Pal,
Seymour

P.S. Pay no attention to the rumor that Frances is pregnant!

[No date] / [No dateline]

Dear Lou Schwartz:

Although I am numbering this enclosure [#30], it is more for background material. You can see how a whole language is building in South Vietnam under the impact of the war and the American presence. Now I do not know whether or not there would be any interest whatever among the subscribers. It will, of course, be of great interest to scholars of language growth. Also, browsing through the words and phrases, one gets a pretty good picture of attitudes.

Anyway—do what you want with this material—edit it, annotate it or eliminate it. But don't throw it away. It is the only copy I have.

SOME SLANG OF VIET NAM
SEPTEMBER 1966

ANH CA or ANH HAI—"Big Brother." Nickname for Prime Minister Nguyen Cao Ky used among his staff.

AN CHE—"Eat sweet soup, or syrup." To have a clandestine affair with a girl.

AN MANH—"Eat alone." To enjoy a good thing for oneself and by oneself.

BA MUOI LAM—Number 35. This has the meaning of "male goat" in a gambling game; from this comes the meaning of "woman chaser" or "hot pants," since a male goat is considered to be over-sexed. (De—"goat"—is used in same vein.) Also used at times as nickname for certain notorious playboys.

BA QUE—"Three sticks." A cheater.

BA VAN CHIN NGHIN—Number 39,000. A life-span or an old, old man. "Man can live only 100 years" (or 39,000 days). Also: Nil, insignificant.

BA XI DE—Vietnamese rice brandy.

BAI BAN—Shooting gallery. A place to take a girl for illicit pleasure. "He is looking for a bai ban." (An older term still in use).

BAN LUA GION—"To sell rice seeds." A con artist, someone you have to be leery of "or he will get you to sell the rice seed you need for your next planting."

BANH—"Smartly dressed." Respectful or admiring term for someone you consider to be really smart, extra bright.

BAY MUOI—Number 70. Denotes an old roué, alluding to a man's age and "foolishness."

BAY QUA DEN—"Black Crow Gang." A derogatory name for the government's Revolutionary Development Cadre. The V.C. propagandists are trying to get villagers to use this. (A crow is considered to be a noisy idiot bird).

BE TAY—"Arm twist," judo term. Force a person to do something, twist his arm.

BI BO—"Bo" from "Khung Bo" (terrorize). To get terrorized.

BI CAO—"Get shaved." To be scolded by one's boss or superior.

BI XAI—"Get scrubbed." To be scolded roughly, badly. Sometimes used to denote derogatory remarks about one's betters.

BIEN HOA—Crazy, a nut, nonsense, unbelievable. "He must be from Bien Hoa." Based upon the location of the psychiatric hospital, or insane asylum, at Bien Hoa.

BON DIT VIT—Pejorative name given to the Dai Viet Party by its political enemies, from similar sound of "Dit Vit" and "Dai Viet." Means "Duck's Rear-end Gang."

BON DUN—"Intestinal Worm Gang." Derogatory name given to the Duy Dan political party by its enemies.

BON QUYCH—"The Bumpkin (or Hillbilly) Gang." Name given to the VNQDD Party by political enemies.

BON SO BA—"Number Three Gang." Nickname for the Central Intelligence Organization, since it is located at No. 3 Bach Dang Quay.

BON VO TANH—"The Vo Tanh Gang." Saigon slang for the National Police, derived from the location of National Police headquarters on Vo Tanh Street.

BUI NHU—Nickname for Secretary of State Bui Diem among some GVN [government of Vietnam] officials and Dai Viets. Initially a joke by General Chieu, Secretary-General of the NLC, to tease about Bui Diem's position being similar to that of Nhu during the Ngo Dinh Diem Administration. A kindlier nickname, coined by Phan Huy Quat, is "Mcgeorge Diem" (after McGeorge Bundy).

CAO BOI—"Cowboy," a wild youngster. Early nickname given to Prime Minister Nguyen Cao Ky, as a fighter pilot turned political leader, which is gradually being superseded as he acts as a responsible national figure.

CAO DIA—Pejorative nickname given by political enemies to the Cao Dai [religion]. It means "High (Cao) land (Dia)."

CAO GIA (Also CHON GIA)—"The Old Fox." Nickname for Chief of State Nguyen van Thieu. In varying other contexts, this same nickname has been used for three different U.S. officials in Vietnam, one having been applied by the Communists.

CAU CO MOI—Nickname given by some political enemies to Thich Tam Chau. "Cau Co Moi" is a decoy goose which farmers use to attract other geese. In the same vein, "Cau co moi hoang quynh" has been used for Father Quynh.

CHAY—"Run." Know how to operate, in the U.S. sense of "I can get it for you wholesale."

CHI—Number one, the best. A more popular term is "So Dach" for "Number One" or "Super."

CHI HOA—Go to jail, in jail. After Chi Hoa Prison.

CHINH TRI XOI THIT—"Political-rice-meat." A political hack who will do anything for pay, i.e.: works only for rice and meat.

CHIU CHOI—"Accepts play." Ready to play along, a smart fellow. The negative is "Khong Chiu Choi"—refuse to play along.

CHO DI MO TOM—"Let go" (Cho di), "feel for" (mo), "lobster" (tom). To assassinate prisoners. From an ancient practice of killing prisoners, putting them in a bag, and throwing it into the river.

CHOI XO—"Play bad." To play tricks.

CHUI—"Slip." Surreptitious gift, a bribe.

CHUON—"Dragonfly." To slip away on tip-toes, take French leave (leave a restaurant without paying).

CO BA QUE—"Three stick flag." Communists' propaganda term for Vietnamese National flag. (See "Ba Que" above).

CO MEO—"Have pussycat." To have a girlfriend.

COM—A cop, a policeman. "Com chung" is a plainclothes detective, "long (i.e., long clothes) police." "Com coc" is a uniformed policeman, "short (from short coat) police."

CON SON—The prison island (formerly Poulo Condore) is often used in a political context. Some Vietnamese politicians have printed the legend on their calling cards: "Tot Nghiep Con Son" ("graduate of Con Son"), to show that they have suffered for their political beliefs. "Bi Day Con Son" denotes "exiled." "Bi Tu Con Son" is "jailed."

CU LAN—A vulgar person, impolite, or lack of fluent tongue.

CUONG PHO (Sometimes BAT PHO)—"Hover streets." To gad about downtown.

DA LAM—"Stone much." Stingy, avaricious.

DANH LEN—"Strike unknowing." Ambush.

DAO—Girlfriend, in some circles. More often, "actress." Common slang for "girlfriend" is "Em Ut" (little sister).

DAO MO—"Dig a mine." To try to seduce a rich girl.

DEP—"lay aside" or "put away" (such as a servant putting away dishes on the shelf). Pack it up, shove it away, it's no good.

DEU—Rascal. (Also DEIM).

DOC (also NOI COC)—To boast, boasting, not speaking the truth.

DON—A low blow, under the belt. A boxing term from the North. (See MIENG below).

DOP—"To snap (at bait)," a fishing word. To take graft or get easy money through shady methods. (An old slang word for "voracious eating.")

DOP HIT—"Snap and inhale." To eat and smoke, particularly opium. (Also same meaning as DOP, see above.)

DOT (Also VOT and DONG)—To "bug out," escape, flee rapidly, cut out.

DUT GAN—"Shake nerve." Sensational, nerve-shattering.

EP—"Press." To force someone to do something, coerce.

GENERAL TAO THAO—Upset stomach, bellyache. Among friends, a semi-joking excuse for leaving a social gathering or non-participation in a political event. From General Tsao Tsao, the chief schemer in "The Three Kingdoms" of Chinese lore, who uses this alibi for political ends.

GHIM—"Pin," for fastening banknotes together. 1,000 piastres.

HAI NAM MUOI—"Two Times Fifty." (See BA VAN CHEN NGHIN above.)

HAO NGOT—"Fond of sweetness." Fond of girls.

HAT CARRE—"H-Squared." Political nickname, somewhat pejorative, for the Hoa Hao [a Vietnamese Buddhist sect].

HET XAI—"Useless." No good any more, used up.

HOT BACK (and HOT CUA)—"Success gathering or harvest." Money, wealth.

HUI—"Leper." Pejorative for "policeman," from need to keep a distance from him.

KENG—A friendly term for an American. From the syllable "can" (keng) in "American."

KHO—"Dazed." Naïve, easily taken in.

KHO CHOI—A tough nut, difficult to get around, hard to fool.

KHO THUONG—"Hard (to) love." An unpleasant person.

LA DE (also LA VE)—Beer, from French "la biere."

LAM LE—From French "L'air." To put on airs, puffed up from own sense of importance.

LAU—"Clever." Sly, foxy.

LUU LINH—A confirmed drunkard. From a historic Chinese character.

LUU MANH—"Dishonest adventurer." Bad guy, dishonest person, scoundrel, the Ugly Vietnamese.

MAT DAY—"Thick Face." A person too stupid to be insulted. A thick hide. You often hear this in heavy urban traffic, as a driver gets emotional.

MEO—From the syllable "mer" in "American." Pejorative term for an American.

MEO NHIEU DON—Opulence. Often used to describe the status of the newly rich. (Meo: American, Nhieu: Many, Don: dollars).

MIENG—Dirty trick, low blow. From boxing term in the South. (See DON above).

MOT CAY—"A tree." An expert in something, an authority.

MUI DO—"Red nose." A foreigner.

MY THO—City in the Delta. Used also to mean "America" or "American." A use of "My" for "American."

NA—Hand grenade. Northern name for the knobbed fruit known in the South and Center as "Man Cau."

NGON—"Delicious." Someone you can respect or love.

NGOT MEO—"Sweet cat." Saigon student slang for a young American, such as an IVS (International Voluntary Service) type.

NHA QUE—From "Ngoui Que Mua" or "bumpkin." Pejorative name from French colonial times for any Vietnamese. Similar to thoughtless American use of the name "gook" elsewhere. French use of this name was deeply resented by the Vietnamese.

NHAY DU—Someone who gets ahead by pull, family, or graft. It is now being broadened to include illegal deals and going AWOL (absent without leave). Actually, it is the term for "airborne" ("Nhay" meaning "jump" and "Du" meaning "umbrella" or "parachute"). Illegal items are called "Nhay Du Salems," after Salem (Say-lem) cigarettes, an early black-market item.

NINH THAN—Flatterer, in the sense of "boot-licking," pejorative.

OK SALEM—A wry bit of Vietnamese-American slang recently coined in Da Nang and rapidly spreading throughout the country. It means agreed, or agreement to a deal. Also used by children begging for a handout. (Pronounced: Okay Say-lem).

ONG CO BAC (and Ong Di Duc)—Derogatory nicknames given to a political leader, for his reputed corruption.

ONG HOC BUA—"Mr. Hard (Hoc) Hammer (Bua)." Nickname for Chief of State Nguyen van Thieu.

ONG LABBE—"Mr. Labbe." Labbe is the name of a Saigon firm manufacturing bicycle tires (1940–1960). Nickname given to Father Lam, presumably from physical appearance (à la Michelin tire man in advertising).

ONG MOT DOI HAI DAO—"Mr. One Life Two Religions." Pejorative nickname given to Thich Phap Tri by his political opponents. Based on the fact that the Venerable Phap Tri was first (Mot) a Hoa Hao and then (Hai) a Buddhist.

ONG RAU KEM—"Mr. Tin Moustache." Popular nickname given General Nguyen Chanh Thi, former I Corps Commander.

ONG THICH AN NHAU—"Mr. Venerable Eating (An) and Drinking (Nhau)." An Nhau is a popular slang expression for eating, drinking, and playing around with girls. Nickname for Thich Thein Minh coined by his political enemies.

ONG THICH DA DAO—"Mr. Venerable Protest" (Da Dao "down with"). Nickname given by opponents and some friends to Thich Tri Quang.

PHO—(French: Feu). Fire, kill.

PHU QUOC—An island off the south coast of Vietnam, in the Gulf of Siam. Recently, it has been used to mean "jail" or "go to jail," due to gossip that Buddhist political prisoners from the 1966 Struggle Movement are being shipped to stockades on Phu Quoc Island. In mid-1966, this name started to supplant the old nickname of "Chi Hoa" for "prison."

QUA XA—"Too far." Extraordinary, super beyond expectation. A superlative superlative.

QUAN SI (or QUAN SU)—"Eminence Grise, Councilor." Nickname for Bui Diem and others.

QUAN SU QUAT MO—"Advisor Areca Fan." A technical advisor, mostly confined to those accompanying high government officials on trips and doing all the real work. Also, used pejoratively, to denote an evil advisor (since "quat mo," a fan made from the areca palm, is used to fan a fire or hide a face).

SAN BAY—Landing strip. New term for a place to bring a girl. "Does he have a San Bay?"

SUC MAY—A challenge of "you aren't strong enough (to do it)." Originally a taunt to would-be playboys by girls in Saigon bawdy houses, the term is now getting widespread usage. It is becoming common at top levels of GVN, in the RVNAF [Republic of Vietnamese army], and even among high school students in the provinces. Also used as a challenge for a drinking bout or similar feat. Also, starting to be used to dub those who fail to meet the challenge, such as a politician or civil servant who lacks capability to do his job.

TAY NINH—A city whose name is used also to denote "France," "Europe," "French," or "European." From "Tay" meaning "West."

THANG—"Fellow, guy." Commonly used in political and governmental circles to refer to a leader. "Thang so-and-so" means "That guy so-and-so." This rather irreverent title is in sharp contrast to North Vietnam's title of "Tong Thong" (Mr. President) for Ho Chi Minh (and South Vietnam's title for Ngo Dinh Diem in his first days as President).

THAY TIA—"Father." Bad news, the worst. "You get a bad blow on the head and you see your dead father."

THICH DOLLAR—Derogatory nickname for Thich Tam Chau used by some political enemies. The implication is that he was bought by the Americans with U.S. dollars. "Thich" means both "venerable" and "like," offering considerable play on words.

THICH MAT VU—"Venerable Secret Service (Mat Vu)." Nickname used by some political enemies for Thich Ho Giac, because of his reputed secret service duties for the Buddhists.

THICH THIT CHO (or THICH THIT HEO)—Literally "the Venerable Dog Meat (or Pig Meat)." Derogatory nickname given Thich Tam Chau by enemies during the Buddhist crises in the spring of 1966.

TIN VIT—"News canard." Rumor, false news. (Vit: "duck," French: canard).

TRAM MIENG—"Seal mouth." To stop someone from speaking, by
bribe or threat.

TROI OI—"Heavens! Oh God!" A common expression, often heard
in the heavy traffic snarls on Saigon streets. The American ear
picks it up as "Choy Oy!"

TRUM CHAN—Political fence-sitting. Literally, "to cover (with) a
blanket" or "go under a blanket" (to wait out the results of a
political conflict).

February 14, 1967 / Saigon

Dear Alicia,

I guess everyone who has been here has reported that the present
city of Saigon is a mess and getting messier every day. The traffic of
motorcars, military vehicles, motorcycles, Vespas, three wheel taxis
both motorized and pedaled and, in this bucket of worms, sometimes a
wagon drawn by oxen—it amounts to a nightmare.

Saigon is jumping in size and disintegrating at the same time. And
the constantly growing population of military refugees and the usual
camp-followers of a war spawn every kind of trick, hustle, con and
crime the world has ever known. Meanwhile the police do little to in-
spire confidence and, if the news reports are correct, are often more to
be feared than the criminals. If there were not an 11 o'clock curfew, one
would have to be invented because Saigon late at night is a secret and
stealthy jungle.

Among the most adept practitioners of theft and mayhem are the
"Saigon Cowboys." These are kids usually between 10 and 14, many of
them orphans of the war or the spewed-up unneeded and unwanted.
They are called cowboys because many of them in admiration of American western pictures, once wore blue jeans, until that garment came to
be the uniform of the young criminal.

These children live on the town, sleep, when they sleep, in door-
ways, in parks and in the crooked alleys of the city. For self preservation
they organize in large or small gangs. They are very like the wolf children who roamed the cities of Russia just after the revolution. They are
shifty, clever and incredibly adroit. They can drift in like smoke, strike
suddenly and disappear. At midday a boy on a bicycle pedals near to the

sidewalk, suddenly snatches a wrist watch from the arm of a stroller and is gone around a corner. They are purse snatchers, pickpockets and drunk rollers and they are rarely caught for they have the craft and energy of rats.

What little responsibility they have is reserved for their own gangs and here their loyalty is almost fanatic. In some ways they are like the kid gangs of New York except they do not fight each other. They conserve their efforts for the war against the civil and military population. They have nothing to lose and nothing except survival to gain.

And in many ways they are not the worst but the best of the species, the cleverest, the most versatile and intelligent. In one sense they are not criminals at all but successful survivors through sheer ability in an impossible situation that has been forced upon them. They could be very valuable people if their talents could be channeled.

I guess everyone has at one time or another on impulse to write a letter to authority. It is called getting in the act. If I should ever fall into this pattern I would address any letter to the head of state of the Republic of South Vietnam and it would go something like this:

Dear Marshal Ky, or your excellency or whatever:

Your young nation is at war with the Viet Cong and with the forces of Hanoi. In this war, we are your allies and in some cases your advisers in military matters. Having been in the field both with your troops and ours, I know that one of your main difficulties is the development of a good and reliable service of intelligence. Most of the time you do not know where the V.C. are, in what numbers or what they are planning. Very often you do not know where they are until they strike. I know that some villagers bring information, some defectors help with information, but all such people are deadly afraid of retaliation on the part of the V.C. toward themselves or their families.

May I suggest, sir, that you have available the best intelligence service conceivable. I refer to the kids of the city, the so-called Saigon Cowboys. These boys are more expert at concealment than the V.C. themselves. If they are thieves and lawbreakers, it is because nobody needs nor wants them for anything else. And yet through their very ability they are able to survive in a hostile climate.

These kids could disappear into the countryside, could live in the paddies, could infiltrate the enemy country as no one else could. They are tough and clever as weasels. They can hide, move in the night, appear, and disappear. I submit that these kids, this reservoir of talent, are no different than anyone else. They would rather be honored than punished. They would rather be needed than unwanted. I know, sir, that the nation is troubled about where the leadership of the future is to be found. Perhaps some of it is here in the streets. We have found in America that our leaders come from everywhere, from slums as well as from the universities. In fact, the very hardships in early life develop in some individuals the strength and resistance a nation needs.

What I am about to suggest would not be hard to try out. If it failed, it could be abandoned, but I believe it would have every chance of succeeding. I suggest that some of these street boys be recruited into an elite intelligence corps. The units should be small—three to five in each cell. They should be given training by the Special Forces and by Intelligence, training in what to look for, and how to communicate. They should know the danger they run but they should also be made well aware that their country needs them. Their reward for successful service should be honor and recognition and I don't know any human who can resist these rewards.

It is well known, sir, that the V.C. use children for many kinds of service. Why should your government deny itself these special gifts? You could start it with a small test cadre and if this were successful, use your first group to recruit and to train new groups.

The Republic of South Vietnam would have nothing to lose by such a test and it might find that it had much to gain. The older people are tired, confused and made cynical by many years of changing fortune. Many of them have lost their sap and have retired into a kind of hopeless wait-and-see attitude.

You are going to need your children for the future of the nation, need their energy and their enthusiasm. The old and cynical have little to offer.

I hope, Marshal Ky, that you will give my suggestion your consideration.

Yours Respectfully,

Now that is the letter I would write, Alicia, if I wrote open letters. But of course I don't. You know that.

Yours,

John

P.S. The darnedest things do happen. Since I wrote the above, I have heard that my plan is already being put into quiet practice. So it isn't my plan at all. I guess this proves that if an idea is good and practical, it occurs to many at the same time.

February 18, 1967 / Saigon

Dear Alicia,

You know how it is when large and maybe earth-shaking things are happening, and meanwhile the most important things of all are not reported, even not mentioned. I want to take a breather from the war and tell you about two really basic problems here in Vietnam. And they aren't new problems. They have been here all along and they still aren't solved.

The first is drinking water—not only for us and for our troops but for the great mass of people living here. This is probably the wettest country I have ever seen. More rainfall, more rivers and canals and ditches. The largest part of the producing land is under water a good part of the time and there is practically no drinking water. The ground water is sour tasting and unpalatable with soluble clays and decayed vegetation. Even when it is not poisonous with microorganisms, it is dreadful to the taste so that even boiled and sterilized, it is not usable. Filtered and treated water goes out of the center of Saigon every day in tank trucks to be sold to the people of the villages. The going price as the trucks leave the city is two piastres for two buckets, but as the truck gets farther and farther from the city, more and more taxes are placed on it by the local bosses until at 20 kilometers out, it sells for as much as five piastres for two buckets and that is more than poor people can afford to pay.

It sounds crazy but good well water is available, only it is very deep. Your well must go through the surface crust of clay and you can't get clean drinkable water in many places less than 200 to 300 feet deep, and that in areas where the surface water is everywhere. There's nothing new about this. It has always been so. The answer is either extremely sophisticated filtration systems to clean up the surface water, distillation plants for great size and output or government operated deep wells which so far are not even in process.

Our soldiers and those of our allies drink purified water, but it is so unpleasant to the taste that there is no joy in it. That is the reason so much iced tea is served, and so much beer is consumed. It is almost impossible to get a good tasting drink of water. Of course bottled waters are sent in from mountain springs but this is expensive and hard in these times to transport. It may seem a small matter and one easily overcome, but I assure you that you soon get to dreaming of good cool, clear tasty water and in plenty. In the hotels and billets, drinkable water, even water to wash your teeth in is brought to your room in big square gin bottles, one bottle a day. And GIs who are wet all day from splashing through paddies, have still to carry canteens of drinkable water. Canteens are in the survival kits of all fliers. It's kind of crazy. A few people have arranged catchments of corrugated iron to gather rainwater and to store it in large containers, but with the heat and the galloping growth of micro life of all kinds even this becomes foul very quickly. In a word, drinking water is one of Vietnam's greatest problems, and it is not near the solution.

The second and perhaps even greater problem is that of sewage disposal and I mean the sewage of human feces. In nearly every place I know, you can dig a hole and build a two-holer or if you are really fancy, you install a cesspool, which takes care of the matter by drainage and bacterial action.

But neither of these methods are possible in Vietnam and certainly the sewer is not the answer. If you dig a hole you get ground water and there is no drainage to make the cesspool practical. The result is that human waste is distributed as it occurs, that the small waterways and canals and rivers are polluted by it. If the rivers swept out to sea, there would be no problem, but most of the lowland country is within tidal range so that the filth is moved back and forth by the shifting tides to be deposited finally on mud flats or in the rice paddies themselves. In this situation the spread of disease is inevitable, and even where night soil is not used as fertilizer on growing vegetables, the water used for irrigation is contaminated. Furthermore, with the war causing more and more refugees to cluster to the cities and larger towns, the problem of pollution increases and will continue to increase. And sometimes when the tide is out, even in the middle of the city, the smell is dreadful. One of the often heard complaints against the government is—"We needed a garbage truck and they built a statue instead."

Now out of Taiwan has come an invention, simple, effective and not very expensive, which may in some future time help to solve the problem of human waste. It consists of two drums and a small combination sealing lid and small copper tubing. These metal drums are placed beneath the conventional two-holer but only one is used at a time. When one drum is partly filled, the head is sealed and a natural fermentation begins. The gas so formed burns with an odorless white flame and is very hot. It can be used for cooking, for heating or boiling water, or with a gas mantle to light a house. The human waste of a family of four produces enough gas to solve the cooking and lighting needs of a house. But there is a further advantage. When the fermentation is completed in the one drum, the residue has become a sterile and usable fertilizer, not only rich but safe to use on the gardens. By rotating the drums, a hut far from town is assured of sanitation, light, heat and fertilizer. It is a very cheap and practical thing. I have seen it work and later on this trip I will find out more about it because it could be a valuable thing for camps, for trailers and even, in reduced size, for boats. For we too have our pollution problems, haven't we? I don't suppose this system could be set up for communities though. The natural gas lobby would see that legislation against it was forthcoming.

This is a kind of scrimy letter, Alicia, but after all it is a scrimy war—but it does end on an upbeat, doesn't it?

February 18, 1967 / [No dateline]

Dear Alicia,

Students all over the world have become barometers of unrest, particularly here and I have wanted to see and to talk with student leaders to try to understand their thinking and its relation to the war and to the future.

I met the first group at Hue, far north of Saigon, the beautiful old capital with its moated, walled and citadeled Imperial Palace, which is said to be a copy on a slightly smaller scale of the Forbidden City of the Emperors at Peking. Hue is also the ancient city of culture, the seat of the oldest university, the accepted capital of learning, of culture and of the arts. It was also the center of the student riots against the present government not so long ago. Like most of this country Hue is part Catholic and part Buddhist, and these two larger groups are split in many directions. Sometimes several parties operate together and sometimes they split to fight against each other. It is very complicated. Nearly everything you learn is canceled by something else.

But do you know, Alicia, I have been kept from feeling superior by being asked to describe politics in our own nation, on a national, state or local scale. How would you go about explaining the intricacies of New York City—how the liberal Democrats are in effect the reactionaries, and how the reactionary Republicans have elected the liberal senators and mayor. As the King of Siam says in Oscar Hammerstein's words—"Is a puzzlement."

My first meeting with students was at Hue and it began ridiculously. I had been in outpost country and my fatigues were filthy with mud and sweat. My field boots must have weighed 10 pounds each with the accumulation of dense clay mud made even more sticky with strands of elephant grass. I had that rancid smell of foul water, decaying vegetation mixed with my own contribution from a bathless seven days. Do you remember Al Capps' Big Barnsmell, the outside man at the Skunk Works [a character in the comic strip *Li'l Abner*]? That's what I was like.

Furthermore it was Sunday when I arrived in Hue. The PX was closed and there was no way to buy clean clothes and too late to go to bed and have what I wore cleaned up. It had obviously become a time for borrowing. I began looking at people I met to see whether their clothes would fit me. I am wide in the shoulders and that limits me in scrounging. I had about given up when a chaplain came through who was as wide as I in the shoulders and a little wider in other places. He carried a submachine gun and a belt of ammunition over his shoulder and had obviously come from a mission of mercy in merciless country. I fastened on the good padre like a leech. He was Lt. Col. Lloyd, a Presbyterian, I believe, and he did have a spare uniform I could borrow for the evening. Bless him.

It was getting late so I bathed in a bucket, combed my hair, what there is of it and put on the chaplain's fresh clean uniform. I couldn't take off the insignia, the cross and the silver leaf of rank. They were of cloth and sewed on, so I promptly forgot them, being happy in my

cleanliness, had a quick drink and met my little circle of student leaders who were said to represent all parties and all sects. They were of all
kinds, some short and bushy and fierce, some smooth and careful and
some pale, wan and quietly worldly. I was glad to see that there were
two very pretty girls, one of the faculty of pedagogy of the University of
Hue, and the other a teacher in the Dong Khanh High School.

In any such confrontation you must understand, Alicia, there is
bound to be a period of formality very like the stiff, twittertail meeting of strange dogs. It is usually thus, but the tension can be eased
fairly quickly if one is careful and openly relaxed. But this evening I
got nowhere. The questions and answers froze in the air. The silences
grew longer and longer. I worked hard to uncork the meeting and was
thrown for a loss until I distinctly heard one of the girls address me as
"Father." I had completely forgotten the insignia on my uniform. I burst
into laughter of relief.

"You are misinformed," I said. "This is a masquerade. I am in fact
a wolf in lamb's clothing." I didn't tell them Col. Lloyd was the most
heavily armed lamb I had ever seen. But the tension did break and the
conversation began.

I discovered that as with most students, the complaints are against
the government, that they advocate a change of government to cure
whatever ill is bothering them. But I found another thing which was
true of all the other students and university intellectuals I met later in
other places. In this matter I think I can go out on a limb of generality.
In Vietnam as in other parts of Asia, the scholar occupies a social position greatly respected and completely set apart. The scholar belongs to
what amounts to a caste out of which he cannot nor does he want to
break free.

I asked these students, as I did many others later, what they wanted
for their country for the future, and they answered correctly. They
wanted freedom and peace and justice. They wanted honest government, and above all intellectual liberty. I could find no fault with their
aims, but when I asked how they would begin to go about getting these
things, there was only silence. These were difficult questions they said,
particularly with the government what it is.

"Very well, if the government is at fault, how can you change it—
short of revolution?"

"That also is difficult if not impossible."

"What is your leadership doing toward reform?"

In their own terms they told me that it was impossible to fight City Hall.

Then I asked about land reform.

That was necessary.

Had they a plan for bringing it about?

That is up to the government.

Then it must finally be up to the farmers, the paddy peasants who raise the food.

That is correct.

What do the farmers think?

A silence.

Do you know any farmers, I mean, personally?

That is difficult and dangerous because the V.C. are there and their propaganda is strong.

I was getting tired now, I guess, I said, "In other words, none of you know any farmers, that is roughly 90 per cent of your people."

Well, the V.C. and their propaganda.

But that is their propaganda. They are there.

"It is dangerous."

Hell, it's dangerous to be born. Everything is dangerous. Where will the leadership come from in this new nation?

It has always come from the educated.

And yet you tell me that the educated have no access to the bulk of the people?

That will, of course, be corrected when the government educates more people.

I know this sounds frustrated, Alicia, and it is. As far as I can learn, the intellectual in this country from a high and unassailable position maintains the right to criticize but does not take the responsibility to reform. It is always the government that is wrong and the opposition that is at fault.

I hope you don't think this makes me feel superior as an American. I've listened to so many political speeches, so many student complaints at home which are exactly the same things.

But one day, leadership is going to come to life in those same rice paddies and then the bewildered intellectual is going to find himself out on his behind, and he is going to wonder how it happened and what unfairness caused this to happen.

Maybe it will change from within. But I can't see that this process has much of a start yet. And it is perhaps one of the major problems faced by this truly new-born nation.

February 20, 1967 / Saigon

Dear Alicia,

One of the most interesting and perhaps one of the most important men I have met here is the Venerable Thich Tam Giac, pronounced Jack as near as my ear can make out. He is the leader of the moderate Buddhists. He is also head chaplain of the army of South Vietnam; he is also building a vast new temple in Saigon.

Giac is what is called a "clean man" here, and that is a rare animal indeed. It means he has made no deals, political or financial, that he has shown no ambition for increased power or influence, that he is not taking pay or bribes from the bosses, graft from the crooked nor is he putting the bite on the poor. In this confused but self interested polity, these traits make him as unique as Yellowstone National Park and as lonely towering as the Washington Monument.

Many Catholics are contributing both work and money toward the new temple which will be not only a place of worship but also a library, a meeting place and a retreat from a naughty world. Many of the younger army officers place great faith and hope in the Venerable as a force and as an example to the developing new nation—faith in his "cleanness."

There are many surprises about the Venerable Giac. Buddhism is a religion of peace and withdrawal from earthly conflicts and yet the Venerable, who lived for many years in Japan, is a judo expert and teacher. So far, he has trained between 6,000 and 8,000 judo men and women to the degree of black belt. Many hundreds of young people starting at 8 years old attend his judo school every evening. If Giac wanted power, he has at hand a trained and disciplined army that could take a city without the use of weapons and could police it too.

Through a Vietnamese friend, the Venerable Thich Tam Giac invited my wife and me to dinner and to visit his school, a walled structure containing a number of large roofed practice places, each larger than a basketball court, and each carpeted in woven straw to provide a padded flooring on the judo place.

He is a young-looking man to be called Venerable, his head shaved, his face composed and calm, the cheek bones prominent and the neck muscles rising to the head like the roots of a tree. His hands are soft and gentle as a woman's and his gestures have a slow rhythmic quality like those of a dancer. He wore a robe and sandals and spoke to us in English, making us welcome to his school.

We went first to the floor or court, or whatever it is called, of the youngest—boys and girls 8, 9 and 10, about 300 of them in long lines. They sat motionless, their legs crossed one above the other, the soles upward. Their palms were pressed together in the gesture of prayer and of peace and their eyes were tightly closed. The Venerable said, "Thus they prepare in peace and quiet the self-discipline that is required." Not a muscle moved in the long lines of children. They were relaxed but completely motionless.

"How long is this exercise?" I asked.

"About 10 minutes. They do it again at the end of the lesson. Self-discipline of the mind is required before the body can be disciplined."

"How do they come to you?"

"They come—and sometimes their parents bring them."

"Is there a fee for the lessons?"

"Yes, there is a small fee, unless they have nothing. Then there is no fee."

Suddenly there was a shout from the standing teachers and the children bowed to the floor, placing their foreheads on the mat and their palms flat down beside their heads. At another cry they took their places, some kneeling, in the center of the court and the others along the two sides. At a signal they flung themselves forward—dived in the air over the kneeling figures and struck the mat with a sound of a rolling drum. They are learning to fall, taking up the shock with a rolling distribution of weight. They leap and flit like swallows in the twilight, waves of little boys and girls leaping in the air and falling and rolling up to their feet. And any one of the falls would have killed me, would have broken every bone in my body.

"Now we must go to dinner," said the Venerable. "Afterwards you can see the advanced students if you wish."

The dinner guests were young army men in civilian clothes, and properly here since the Venerable is their chief chaplain. And dinner is entirely vegetarian but such vegetables as I have never tasted—nine separate courses, all different, combinations strange to our taste and delicious, black mushrooms and asparagus, celeries, carrots and strange varieties of cabbage. Soups with flavors new to me, a subtle and delicious succession of dishes all different and all pleasant. The dessert was fruit of many kinds, some that I knew and many more that I had never seen.

I fumble pretty much with chopsticks but we tried and the Venerable smiled sympathetically at us. "You should see me try to use a fork, much worse than you are doing."

"I am interested, Venerable, that you a man of peace should be teaching the art of private war. Can you explain this to me?"

"Yes," he said. "In Japan, where I lived for many years, I studied judo as a physical discipline to parallel mental discipline. Well trained judo men are not quarrelsome. They have no need to fight because they are not fighting within themselves. Angry people are usually those who are unsure of themselves, who must prove their worth and importance to others because they do not truly believe in it themselves. But a sure man does not need to prove anything."

"Yes, I can understand that. But why did you start the school here? Doesn't it alarm some of your contemporaries?"

"Perhaps," he said. "But their alarm would be their problem, not mine. When I came home to Vietnam, I found my people many of whom have never known peace in their whole lives, who have had nothing but defeat and frustration and confusion. This destroys a man's confidence, makes him unsure, and even treacherous. If it goes on too long that certainty, you in the West would call it pride, can be crippled beyond healing. But the young people and the children who have not been crippled, those are the ones I want to help."

"I have heard that you have trained several thousand up to black belt."

"That is true."

"You have then a disciplined force to be reckoned with. Have you any thought of using it?"

He smiled, "I have heard the question before. No, when a man is sure of himself, he is his own leader. He has no reason to follow anything but his own feeling and if that feeling is good—that is sufficient.

I would like ideally to create a nation of secure men, men and women who knowing they can defend themselves, do not have to."

"But suppose your secure men are attacked."

"A good judo man can defend himself without injuring his attacker," said the Venerable. "And this is usually sufficient. Now would you like to see the advanced students?"

We would and we did. The black belt engaged and instructing the blue belt and the blue belt the yellow belt, not single pairs but a hundred engaged on a single floor. The intricacy of motion, the applied leverage and the sprawling loser who on rising bowed to his teacher and went through the exercise again to see just how it was done and what had happened to him.

"It is growing late," said the Venerable. "These are working men and women. They can only come here at night."

There was a long shrill call. The engaged pairs fell into long straight lines. Then with their heads back they sang a chant, like something from the litany. Then they kneeled, crossed their legs, put their palms together in front of their faces and closed their eyes and were completely immobile, just as the children had been.

"I hope you will visit us again," said the Venerable.

"I wish I could enroll. I still have some angers," I said. His smile was very kind. He shook hands and gave us some kind of blessing and no one can have too many of those, don't you agree?

[No date] / [No dateline]

Dear Alicia,

Before I started this journey I had heard of Sun Tzu, the Chinese author of *The Art of War* twenty-five hundred years ago, but I had not read him. I also knew that Mao had taken most of his rules for guerrilla warfare from Sun Tzu, sometimes copying them word for word but of course without giving credit to the original author.

In Honolulu Marine General Krulak loaned me his copy of Samuel B. Griffiths' translation of the original work and I was able to read it quickly but was unable to make the loan permanent. To read Sun Tzu is to marvel that this ancient treatise has never been improved and is indeed applicable today and particularly in Vietnam.

Not long after I came to Saigon, General Westmoreland invited me to go on an inspection trip with him. In the course of conversation I mentioned Sun Tzu and was delighted to hear that the general not only knew his work but had caused *The Art of War* to be excerpted for the information of all officers "down to and including platoon leaders and subsector advisors." General Westmoreland believes, as do I, that the V.C. as well as all of the followers of Mao take these ancient precepts as their law and to know Sun Tzu is to know the mind and the plans of the enemy. I enclose the digest of these principles for your interest and edification.

After reading them I am sure you will be able to follow the war news more closely and with more understanding. I think it might be important for all Americans to read this treatise. It might clear up some of their misjudgments of this war and of the nature and the practices of the enemy. You see that there is little heed paid to ethics, to right or wrong—to anything in fact except winning. If we can just get this through our heads we will understand that the propaganda cries that issue from Hanoi and V.C. headquarters which so nourish and inflame our protesters are not related in any sense to moral outrage. They are simply another kind of warfare. On reading the following pages, we are not likely to fall into the trap that was set for the recent visitors to Hanoi.

I do hope you will find the enclosed pages informative as well as helpful. In haste now.

February 25, 1967 / Saigon

Dear Alicia,

It is time for us to continue our journey on to Thailand. We made the reservations to Bangkok and said goodbye to many friends. I know that I have not written you about everything I have seen. That would take a lifetime. But I have been six weeks here, about five of them in the field, and perhaps my years tell on me a little. I have often wished that if a war is necessary, it might be fought by men of my age rather than by boys with their whole lives ahead of them. The difficulty is that we wouldn't do it very well. Our bones would creak and our eyes might not have the clear sharpness required. Let's face it, Alicia, I get tireder quicker than the kids do and I don't recover as fast.

It was my last night and I had reserved it for a final mission. Do you remember or did I even mention Puff, the Magic Dragon? From the ground I had seen it in action in the night but I had never flown in it. It was not given its name by us but by the V.C. who have experienced it. Puff is a kind of crazy conception. It is a C-47—that old Douglas two-motor ship that has been the workhorse of the world since early on in World War II.

The one I was to fly in was celebrating its 24th birthday and that's an old airplane. I don't know who designed Puff but whoever did had imagination. It is armed with three six-barreled Gatling guns. Their noses stick out of two side windows and the open door. And these three guns can spray out 2,800 rounds a minute—that's right, 2,800. In one quarter-turn, these guns fine-tooth an area bigger than a football field and so completely that not even a tuft of crabgrass would remain alive. The guns are fixed. The pilot fires them by rolling up on his side. There are cross hairs on his side glass. When the cross hairs are on the target, he presses a button and a waterfall of fire pours on the target, a Niagara of steel.

These ships, some of them, are in the air in every area at night and all night. If a call for help comes, they can be there in a very short time. They carry quantities of the parachute flares we see in the sky every night, flares so bright that they put an area of midday on a part of the night-bound earth. And these flares are not mechanically released. They are manhandled out the open door by the flare crew. I knew the technique but I have never flown a night mission with Puff. I had reserved it for my last night in South Vietnam. We were to fly at dark and hoped to be back by midnight.

My lady-wife Elaine, who has taken everything in her proud stride to my admiration, did not want to sit alone in the Caravelle Hotel waiting for me, so Johnny Floyd, Regular Army, third hitch, recently wounded but recuperating, asked her to have dinner with him in a small restaurant near the hotel to wait out my return.

I went by chopper to the field where the Puffs live, met the pilot and his crew and had supper with them. Our mission was not general call. A crossroad area had been observed to be used after dark recently by Charley, who was rushing supplies from one place to another for reasons best known to Charley. We were to be directed by one of the little F.A.C. planes I spoke of in an earlier letter.

Because it was hot and no wind in prospect, I wore only light slacks and a cotton shirt. We flew at dusk and very soon I found myself freezing. Puff is not a quiet ship, her door is open, her gun ports open, her engines loud and everything on her rattles. I did not wear a headset because I wanted to move about, so one of the flare crew, a big man, had to offer me an extra flight suit and he said it in pantomime. I accepted with chattering teeth and struggled into it and zipped it up. Then they fitted me with a parachute harness and showed me where my pack was in case of need. But even I knew that flying at low altitude, if the need should arise, there wouldn't be much time to get out even if I were young and clever.

Forward of the guns and aft by the open door were the racks where the flares stood, three feet high, four inches in diameter. I think they weigh about 40 pounds. Wrestling 200 or 300 of them out the door would be a good night's work. The ship was dark, except for its recognition lights and a dim red light over the navigator's table.

They gave me ear plugs. I had heard that the sound of these guns is unique, so I put the rubber stoppers in my ears but they were irritating so I pulled them out again and only hoped to get my mouth open when we fired.

There was a line of afterglow in the western sky, only it was not west the way Puff flies. Sometimes it was overhead, sometimes straight down. Without an instrument you couldn't tell up from down but my feet were held to the steel floor by the centrifuge of the turning, twisting ship. Then the order came and a flare was thrown out and another and another. They whirled down and the brilliant lights came on. We upsided and looked down on the ghost-lighted earth. Far below us almost skimming the earth, I could see the shape of the tiny skimming FAC plane inspecting the target and reporting to our pilot. We dropped three more flares, whirled and dropped three more. The road and the crossroads were very clearly defined on the ground and then there was a curious unearthly undulating mass like an amoeba under a microscope, a pseudo-pod changing its shape and size as it moved. Now Puff went up on its side. I did know enough to get my mouth open. The sound of those guns is like nothing I have heard. It is like a coffee grinder as big as Mt. Everest compounded with a dentist's drill. A growl, but one that rocks your body and flaps your eardrums like wind-whipped flags. And out through the door I could see a stream, a wide river of fire that seemed to curve and wave toward the earth.

We flared and fired again and once again. Out on the edges of darkness there were the little winking lights that were ground fire aimed at us.

During the last five weeks, I guess I have been in areas and under conditions of danger. I've had a good normal fear that makes one keep his head down and take cover when it offers, the tenseness and crystal awareness danger brings. I guess it is fear all right but it brings compensations. But now, on the last night, with the mission completed and only the winking ground fire and that receding behind us, I was afraid. More than that—I was scared. I could see the stray and accidental shot hit a flare and the whole ship go up in a huge Roman candle of incandescent searing light. I thought how silly it would be on my last night. I think it was the first time I had thought of myself, me, as being in danger. And then curious memories came to me like movie shorts. I had a drink with Ernie Pyle in San Francisco. Ernie ordinarily dressed like a tossed salad but now he was wearing a new Eisenhower jacket. I said, "Just because you're going to the Pacific do you have to be a fashion plate?"

Ernie said, "It's new. I shouldn't have bought it. I'm not going to need it." And his first time on the line he got a bullet between the eyes.

And Capa leaving Paris for the war in east Asia. We made a date for dinner in Paris a week away. And Capa said, "I hate to go on this one. If I didn't need the money, I wouldn't go. I've had it. I tell you this is the last time." And it was.

And only last week lying in the bunker with a boy who said, "Five more days—no, four days and 13 hours, and I'll be going home. I thought the time would never come." And it didn't. He was killed on the next patrol.

I was cold all over and trembling maybe somewhat from the grinding of the guns. And already we were landing and the mission was done and we were back early.

I got to the hotel at a little before 10 and of course Elaine was not back from dinner. So I went around the corner to the restaurant. She and Johnny Floyd were sitting quietly and when they saw me come in they both jumped up. "How was it?" Elaine asked.

We have our privacies but not in big things.

I said, "I was scared."

"So was I. I had three martinis—and they didn't help."

And Johnny Floyd said, "I kept telling her you were all right. But I guess I oversold it. Because I was scared too."

Isn't that funny and strange the way the mind works? But that's the way it works.

And soon we will be in Bangkok and it will be very different.

March 4, 1967 / Bangkok, Thailand

Dear Alicia,

I must tell you that it is a delayed-fuse emotional shock to fly from Saigon to Bangkok, from South Vietnam to Thailand. For a time we were simply confused and perhaps a little suspicious. The Thai are a smiling, friendly people, outgoing and easy. What's so different about that? Well, Alicia, we have come from a people whose faces, whose posture, and perhaps whose souls have been wracked and battered with 20 years of war, not proud nor generous nor gallant war, but sneaking murder-terror, torture secret and nasty, designed to destroy the spirit so that it can be controlled and dominated.

The Thai people greet one another and us with the Wai, pronounced "wy." They place their palms together and raise the fingers to the eyes. In the West it would be a gesture of subservience or of prayer, but here the greeting simply means, "I respect you, not your position, but as a human." And the reply is the same gesture and it means, "And I respect you." It seems a lovely thing to us because we have come from a bitter place where the key word is not respect but suspect. Suspicion of everyone everywhere. That boy may have a grenade, those covered baskets on a shoulder yoke may contain plastic bombs. Of course it is not always true but true often enough to make everyone afraid of everyone, distrustful of everyone. And this is carefully designed to destroy the dignity and the respect which would permit a man to think, to question and to defend himself. Here in Bangkok, the necks are straight and respect and liking are close together.

The Thai are fortunate people in their country and in their history. Alone among the East Asian nations they have never been conquered nor colonized. They have been invaded, yes, but have driven the invader out before the corrosion of domination or the gangrene of colonialism decayed their souls. These people with the Wai can say, "I respect you," because they respect themselves. And without self-respect there can be no other kind.

It is almost too much for us here in Bangkok. We have a beautiful suite in the Oriental Hotel on the wide and fine river. We have, in fact, the rooms Somerset Maugham used to inhabit. And I guess we all got our first feeling about Bangkok from Maugham. From him I learned the word "Godown" [a warehouse for merchandise] but only now have I seen them and know what they are.

The rooms are spacious and comfortable. And at the Caravelle Hotel in Saigon we lived in a single room crowded by two single beds. If the telephone rang we had to leap over a bed to get to it. The furniture was 1947 Tijuana motel, the lights so dim that a perpetual night blindness set in. The water was not potable but water was occasionally brought in in square gin bottles. The air-conditioner either roared and froze the air, or, more often, went off, leaving the air a damp horror like warm chicken soup with bits and pieces floating in it. And for this gruesome pleasure dome we paid $28 a day plus a bribe to get in at all. For six weeks we maintained an armed truce with the Caravelle and we left it with the regret of a man saying farewell to Sing Sing.

And then to come into this wonderful place. A wide garden under our windows with gibbons doing acrobatics to make Ed Sullivan jealous and then the wide and luminous river—a broad highway for boats of every description, speed and purpose. Our rooms are far from cheap but we are getting what we pay for and that makes one hell of a lot of difference.

The first few nights we were uneasy here. Something was wrong. And then we knew—no gunfire, no hollow roar of howitzers, no flares hanging in the sky, no rattle of automatic rifles, no crump of mortars. It was all right when we identified the reason for our uneasiness. Bangkok is one of the rest and recuperation centers where our soldiers can come for a few days after a long and painful tour of duty. I've talked to some of them and they say they have trouble also getting used to peace, to kindness and to safety.

Everyone has written about Bangkok, about the Emerald Buddha and the Wats, the teeming city, and the even more teeming river and connecting canals. I am not about to write you a travelogue, Alicia. On the other hand I am reveling in comfort, in clean sheets, in hot water, in good and willing service, in cool drinks beside the wide river, where something is always going on. We are loving it, lapping it up without a twinge of conscience, Presbyterian or otherwise. I have always maintained that a man who protests that he does not like comfort, even luxury, is either a fool or a liar. I agree that contrast is needed to keep the ecstasy from becoming commonplace. But we are going to the northeast of Thailand, where the Communist terrorists are slipping in, to try to do to this happy land what they have done to Vietnam. That is rugged country up there, we are told, so right now we are wallowing in creature comforts, in music and laughter, in the beauty of women, the excitement of silk and gold and craftsmanship in wood and metal, in the sun sinking across the river and putting a red-gold glory in our rooms. We love it.

February 23, 1967 / Bangkok, Thailand

Dear Alicia,

This letter is not one of speculation. Rather it is the kind of question or questions one asks oneself. And sometimes the questions merge one into the other until they seem to be related.

The first part is this. You know of course that relations between Thailand and Cambodia have been broken off for some time. It was a gradually widening split. Cambodia wanted to be neutral but with an eye to China, and Thailand wanted to be real neutral, particularly from Mao Tse-Tung. Cambodia and Thailand might have stayed edgy (but no more than that) indefinitely, but suddenly a Cambodian train was blown up with loss of life and the Khmers pointed the finger of blame at Thailand. The Thais denied it, but the situation had got so bad that Cambodia broke off all relations with Thailand, South Vietnam and some others, which was not exactly bad news to Peking.

Now comes the news that in some part of Vietnam, where the fighting is, documents have been captured which show that the train in question was blown up by Chinese terrorists, sent down from Peking for just that purpose and to the end of breaking relations between the two countries. And in this the move was very successful. End of first subject.

Second subject.

Not very long ago Hanoi charged that the U.S. had bombed civilian areas in the city of Hanoi. The U.S. Air Force denied this, and said it had bombed only military targets but admitted that if civilians were living near those targets, they might have been hit. To prevent this the Air Force had dropped leaflets before bombing, said leaflets warning civilians to get out of the target area.

Hanoi countered by charging that we had bombed the homes and apartments of people. The outcry in the protesters' groups was very loud. It was the finest propaganda pitch Hanoi had put on maybe ever. And then to cap it, Harrison Salisbury of the *New York Times* and later William C. Baggs of the *Miami Daily News* were invited to Hanoi to view the damage to residential districts, to photograph the wreckage, and they were furnished with lists and numbers of the killed and wounded. Their words and pictures made liars of our Air Force and our government. A squeal of joy went around the world. The American image plummeted, shot down in a large part by Americans. Actually it was the most perfectly planned and coordinated propaganda set piece on record—almost too perfect.

But who am I to sit way out here and question the reports of two reputable American newsmen? I met Mr. Salisbury some years ago in Moscow and I know his devotion to certain principles, which if not practical, are surely not immoral. Mr. Baggs I do not know.

Then why should I raise an eyebrow? Well, for two reasons. First I know an awful lot of our fliers, Army, Navy, Marines—the lot. Some of them are pretty raunchy. All of them are braver than I am and in my experience, none of them are liars.

I was uneasy when I read of the Salisbury reports and the noise they were making in the world. But out here, papers get to us late. It was only a few days ago that the newspapers came through with pictures of the destroyed residential areas. It was pretty complete wreckage all right and very sad. I wondered why I had a curious uneasy feeling about the pictures of splintered and broken houses. Even in the coarse grain of newspaper reproduction something seemed wrong. I've seen a lot of bomb damage in World War II and recently in South Vietnam. Still I'm no authority. Did Mr. Salisbury or Mr. Baggs actually see the bombs fall and identify the aircraft flying them?

There is something very wrong with the pictures. I suggest that our explosives experts study the pictures closely. There's something missing in the pictures that a bomber pilot would know. This is only an open question because I would like to know the reason the pictures do not look like bomb damage to me. They look like dynamite. Look closely at the pictures and see what I mean. A powder man would.

And it would be a small price to pay for propaganda to change and harden world opinion.

Third Subject.

A dynamited train in Cambodia, and residential destruction in Hanoi. If I had access to the ear of official Russia, I would suggest that their ships proceed toward Hanoi with great caution. Remember the Cambodian train. A mine in the channel and a Russian ship blown up would cause great tension between our nations at a time when there is a chance of light. Remember who would hate a Russian-American accord of any kind and who would do anything to prevent it. Cambodia! Cambodia. And please watch out for mines. If they happen, they won't be ours. Neither of us should fall into that old trap.

March 14, 1967 / Bangkok, Thailand

Dear Alicia,

You remember how, when you are going away for the summer, and the last evening you open the refrigerator and take out all the leftovers, bits of pate, a small square of corned beef, tomatoes that have seen better days and a single wedge of lemon meringue pie. So you have a clean-out-the-refrigerator dinner and anything left over, you throw away.

Well, in the last nearly three months, I have stored small leftovers, observations, ideas, pictures, hopes, speculations and jokes to tell you, I have a notebook full of these. They are not important nor illuminating nor even very instructive. But hating waste, I propose to write you a clean-out-the-notebook letter and what is left after that I'll throw away. Okay?

Here is a note that says, "Remember Corporal Chatterley's round-up of the war situation."

I remember it well, it was in an area near An Khe in a barracks, if you want to call it that, decorated with mosquito nets, ammunition boxes, rifles and the debris and gnawed bones left by the let loose dogs of war. Cpl. Chatterley, called "Lover," naturally, a snub-nosed philosopher with a misbegotten look and a taste for rye whiskey "in" Coca-

Cola, was holding forth on the military situation not only in his own sector but about the world. He sat on a jerry can of drinking water and gestured with the Coca-Cola bottle in which he had fitted a warhead of Canadian Club.

"We got ourselves in a bind," Lover said and pointed his weapon at his tonsils. "Here we are a paid professional army of killers, armed to the teeth, whatever that means, brutes, without feelings of conscience. Killing women and children is our pleasure, although I must say it ain't economically sound what with the increasing cost of military hardware, but let's say us paid professional killers have got to have our fun."

A small voice from the dark depths of a netted bunk and never identified said, "Yeah! Let's say that."

"But it ain't right and we all know it," cried Lover, shaking his bottle under his thumb and then spurting the charge into his mouth like wine from a Spanish wineskin.

I said, "Different people have got different gouts. At least we aren't mean."

"But we are being punished," Lover said. "Would you like to hear me analyze the whole situation from beginning to end?" There was no response. "Good!" said Lover. He stood up and walked to (forgive the expression) a two by four stud to which was fastened a contour map of something between twin Fujiyamas and Jayne Mansfield. Lover pointed his bottle at the left one. "Now here we are here! And right up here beside the nose is the V.C. and up about the hairline, it might be, are the battle ready divisions of North Vietnam, poised for combat, right?"

"Right!" said the voice from the net.

"But we can beat them," cried Lover. "We have beat them over and over."

"Then why don't we?"

"Why? I'll tell you why just as soon as—anybody got a bottle opener? Now, while I'm busy, don't anybody break in and roil up my train of thought, because in the lonely boondocks with no company but my darling M-16, name of Doris, I have figured the whole thing out."

"A regular Walda Lippmann," observed the hidden man.

"No sir," cried Lover. "Don't you think that I would presume to climb to . . . to . . ."

"Olympian heights?" I suggested.

"Or Lippmannian. No sir. I admire Walter, if I may call him that, and I do not have his advantage of not being here. I am blinded by proximity."

Vernon P. Calhoun, who from his accent was obviously a foreigner, or a recent immigrant, broke in irritably. "Get on wi' the war, mon! Gie us your interpretation, and perhaps your prog . . . prog . . . Ah! the hell wi' it."

Lover said, "Show me a good listener and I'll show you a man I love. Now you shut up back there and you, sir (to me), with all respect to your gray hairs, stand back! Interruptions, even helpful ones, will only confuse me further. Now, where was I, yes. We can and we have licked the V.C. or as they call it on the Berkeley campus, the Peoples Liberation Army. We can and have licked Uncle Ho's boys ditto called the Peoples Republic of North Vietnam."

"What's holding us back Lover, besides the sporting laws the Pentagon is putting on us? Open season, closed season, only take so many in one week, don't go near the game refuges and if you see any MIG-21s sitting on the ground, for God's sake don't shoot them. They might get extinct like whooping cranes."

"There's that," said Lover. "But that's not really our problem because I feel that deep down the Pentagon is on our side."

"No sir. We've got a real hard core problem. In fact we're surrounded. We got Fulbright on our right flank and *The New York Times* on our left flank (and if you think that's a slip of the tongue, you're nuts). And to top it off, or maybe bottom it off, we've got poets and folk singers snapping at our heels. It makes a paid professional killer feel kind of frustrated."

From the net—"You said you were going to prog . . . whatever you said. Hell! We know our enemies. Who are our friends?"

"We got no friends," said Lover, "unless you'd want to admit you kind of admired those Korean soldiers or maybe the better bunch of ARVN or the tough Filipino outfit, or the Thais that are coming in or maybe that ringtail bunch of Aussies with balls [*Newsday* changed this to "muscles"] big as grapefruit. Outside of them we got no friends. On our flanks and rear we are surrounded by paid professional non-killers and that's the most dangerous kind."

I said, "Do you think we could join up with Hanoi and turn on the whole bunch of them? I bet we could beat even the acid-heads, if they'd just amend the game laws."

Lover nursed on his bottle and then suddenly unplugged the vacuum and the air rushed in and foam rushed out. "Only one thing to do," he said judiciously. "We want peace, don't we? Sure we do. Well, we try Hanoi and we get turned down. So what's our next move?"

"What? Do I hear you ask? Well we try to make a separate peace with the *New York Times*."

"They're pretty bitter."

"Well then we try to negotiate with Fulbright and Sen. Morse."

"With elections coming up? Are you crazy?"

"Well do you suppose we could get Joan Baez to the peace table?"

The voice behind the net said, "I don't think she'd do it. She hates war so much that if there was peace she'd be out of a job. You can't ask a girl to take her eminence right out of her own mouth."

Lover made a new move, which shows his versatility. He poured Coke in the rye bottle (or maybe it was Pepsi-Cola). "I guess that does it. I thought I had a good idea there. Looks like we're forced to go right on killing and injuring women and children and old people. But I don't want to hear of anyone of you slaves of capitalistic imperialism mistreating a dog. There's such a thing as being un-American. Lord! Lord!" said Lover, "for a moment there, I thought I had it made. Divide and conquer. That's what I thought."

"Live and learn," I said. "Die and forget it all."

So you can see, Alicia, that the soul searching is not limited to the battlements of Academe or the pads of the "turned on."

March 20, 1967 / Bangkok

Dear Alicia,

I'm not going to give you a geography lesson because I'm kind of hazy myself and as for place names, that's one of the troubles with moving about. In Saigon I had got to a point of excellence so that I always mispronounced the same word in the same way. Now we have moved to Thailand and it's all to do over again. Instead of places like Tan An and An Khe and Da Nang and Pleiku, you're going to hear about Sakhon, Hakhon and Nai Amphae and Amphae Wanon Niwat.

What most people know about Thailand is that in Bangkok they make beautiful silk, have a thousand temples, and a young king who plays the saxophone and has a lovely queen. Apart from that our information comes largely from the Rodgers and Hammerstein musical *The King and I*. To us this fabulous but savage kingdom was ruled by Yul Brynner and civilized by Gertrude Lawrence. Those were facts to me and I'm sure to most Americans. Imagine my surprise in coming here to learn that not even the movie version of *The King and I* has ever been permitted to be shown here. The Thais, right or wrong but surely stubborn, have taken the dangerous position that Yul Brynner was never King of Siam, and that Gertrude Lawrence did not civilize them. They hold rather passionately that they might have civilized her if that were possible. They find other inaccuracies in the Rodgers and Hammerstein account.

It is just stubborn these Thai people are. That's one of the main reasons they were never conquered and never colonized. They have a naïve but brass-bound conviction that they want to rule themselves in their own way, accept those foreign ways and methods they need and want, and reject those they don't. They must have refused to allow Rodgers and Hammerstein to play here for historical reasons surely. The Thais have sunk even lower than that. They don't let sex magazines in or nudies. What kind of country is it that won't license a bunny club no matter how much cotton there is in the brassieres? But they have done even worse. Lately I have been traveling in the upland country with Police Maj. Gen. Amroong Skultratana, a very big wheel indeed in the national police structure. One day at lunch the general said, "Do you know a magazine called *Playboy*?"

"Indeed I do. It is the bible of young Americans before they learn to read."

"But you are a part of that magazine, aren't you?"

"Only indirectly," I said. "When my boys were in prep school, they used to bring it home and also I see it in airplanes."

"Very strange," said the general. "You see this magazine *Playboy* applied for a license of import to Thailand. Such licenses are in my department and after looking through this magazine, I decided that it was not the kind of bible we older people could recommend for our children."

"You see," he went on, "in Thailand, we adults take the responsibility for making decisions for our children. Perhaps it is wrong, but we have always done it. My colleagues agreed with me and I rejected a license for the importation. You understand—anyone may bring a copy in, but it is not permitted to be imported for general sale."

"In the United States, there would be a protest march by teenagers," I said.

"So I have heard," said the general. "This morning I had a letter re-applying for the license and giving you as an example of the kind of writers they printed."

"Nice of them," I said.

"Do you write for *Playboy?*"

"I don't write for anyone, sir, but if *Playboy* says it has printed some of my work, I presume it has."

The general smiled and when a Thai smiles it spreads all over. "Then you would suggest that we reconsider the license?"

"That's very flattering, sir, considering everything. At present I have nothing in which *Playboy* would be interested—but you could reserve your decision until I do . . ."

"It would put you in a good bargaining position," he finished the sentence for me.

"I never bargain," I said more haughtily than I felt—because I can't for the life of me remember selling material to *Playboy* to put me in the proud position of fronting for it. But naturally I'm open to offers. Then suddenly a dreadful thought came to me. "General, are you saying that United States servicemen can't get *Playboy* in this kingdom? Why, we can't fight a war without mammary incentive."

"Don't excite yourself," he said. "They can buy it in the post ex-changes. It's only general sale I am resisting. And perhaps that, too, is a losing battle." He sighed. "I wonder what has happened. You know, in my young days we liked women, even admired some of them. And of course, there was love."

"Maybe the eye changes," I suggested diplomatically.

"Surely it does, but not that much. It seems to me that the modern young western man hunts a woman like big game, to show off her pelt to friends, and the woman defends herself with the tools and tactics of the fox, the leopard and the cobra. It's a savage sport."

"That's what you feel about the West, sir. How about Thailand?"

"Perhaps we will lose," he said. "But we do what we can. I have re-jected the license."

Now, isn't that an outrage, Alicia?

March 4, 1967 / Bangkok

Dear Alicia,

This flitting about may make me appear to you like a disturbed bat in a daytime attic but actually it does follow some kind of pattern. I have come from Vietnam, where the Communists have had a long time to dig into the skin and to become actively parasitic on the body of the polity, difficult to expel until some vermifuge of reason and kindness is introduced consistently.

Apart from the spawning ground in China, the cancer has metasta-sized into the surrounding geographic tissue, gruesomely in Vietnam and parts of Laos, and it is just beginning to move into the northeast of Thailand. In other places the disease was ignored too long. Thailand, fortunately, is alert and taking measures early on in the sickness. That is why I wanted to go to the northeast to see what means were being tried to excise this carcinomic nastiness.

Now I have been and I have seen. I think they have caught it in time. I devoutly hope so. But it is not easy. Last week in a remote village of a northern province of Thailand, a schoolteacher was taken by a band of infiltrating terrorists. He was killed and his head cut off and put upright in the middle of a table. Then the other schoolteachers of the district were forced with weapons to sit and regard this horror. Always the same pattern, destroy the teachers and the local leaders and terrify the rest. There have been 600 reported acts of terrorism in the north-east in the last few months.

In Bangkok, rich and smiling, it is hard to believe these reports, but going over the country makes it very real. On the map, Thailand looks like a headless animal with a long tail. I haven't been down the tail yet, which is the Malay Peninsula, but I have been about in the body of the sitting-up animal and it isn't what it looks like on the map. From Bang-kok on its lovely Chao Phya River, a little north of the Gulf of Siam, there is a great, level, rich alluvial plain, an enormous checkerboard for rice and fruitful in all tropical and semitropical growing things beyond belief. It is a tended, cared-for country and the land in small farms is privately owned beyond anything known in Asia.

Flying north, one sees this fortunate land extending to the horizon until at last a range of mountains cuts across and bounds this bountiful plain and on the other side of the mountains there is higher country, upland, still fruitful but drier in this dry season and dustier and studded with maverick trees. But this land, too, is terraced in paddies to catch the wet time rain and push up the rice.

The upland rises to another range of mountains and beyond that and as far up as the stately Mekong River, which bounds the north and east of Thailand, it is a strange lost and forgotten country. At least it was until recently, when the Communist terrorists, trained in Hanoi or Peking, found it a possible place into which to move their cells, to set their claws and push outward as they have done in Vietnam and parts of Laos.

The northeastern provinces are a part of Thailand which until a short time ago was not so much neglected as forgotten by the central government. And it is easy to see why. The land is thin, a red ferrous soil that rolls up in muddy dust in the dry season and washes away in the rains. Some forests of huge hardwood there are, but mostly the land is covered with a scabby scrub, low and difficult but almost without value except for burning. What surface water there is is sour and undrinkable and a well to reach sweet water may require a hole as deep as 60 or 100 feet.

Until recently there were no roads. The villages were isolated, self-sufficient if you want little. It is a sparsely inhabited place, but the people are clever and intelligent and tied with light strong webs to customs that spin out of a remote past. The small amount of cotton they raise they spin and dye and weave into beautiful and very durable cloth. Their houses are of wood raised high on posts for air and to provide under the family a shelter for the chickens, the snub-nosed, pot-bellied pigs and the water buffalo, the work animal of the area, which is eaten when he is no longer able to pull and plow and turn and tread. The village gardens yield tobacco, melons, peanuts and soybeans with some root vegetables. These are watered, in the dry season, from earth-built reservoirs and from wells which only reach the bitter tasting surface water.

The villagers grub out a life. In the past they have had little knowledge, contact or interest of, with or in the central government and the central government has had little contact with or interest in the villages. They have nothing of value to export to interest the capital and the taxes were so low, and hardly collectable, that the village was only vaguely conscious of the capital. And that's the way the northeast is, Alicia, with variations. But one thing interests me. In this vast brush and tree-covered area, I saw no wild animals, no rabbits or hares and consequently no predators or birds of prey, in fact few birds of any kind. And when I asked, "Where are the birds and the beasts?" the reply was, "They've eaten them all." More on this strange and now-important area soon.

March 11, 1967 / Northeast Thailand

Dear Alicia,

I wonder whether I made it clear in my last letter that this northeast is really frontier country, rough, scrub-wooded and settled by scattered villagers living a remote and marginal life—no roads, no power and very little communication. That's how it has been for hundreds of years and perhaps that's how it would have continued had not the Peking–Ho Chi Minh axis decided that this area was ripe for infiltration and excellent for the tactics of terror and the hit and hide methods of guerrilla war.

It was not that the indigenous people in their villages had grievances against the rather benign constitutional kingdom of Thailand. They had barely heard of it. The northeast shoulder of Thailand, defined by the great Mekong River, hunches against the mountains of Laos at its narrowest. From here it is less than 75 miles to North Vietnam and it is down through these mountains the Ho Chi Minh trail snakes its tortuous way, the supply route to the Viet Cong guerrillas. A short turn right and across the largely unguarded Mekong River and those same supplies and terrorists were in the wild country of Thailand. That is not what they could do. It's what they did do.

To complicate this situation, the genial governance of Hanoi with the blessings and explosives of Cousin Mao had caused between 70,000 and 80,000 North Vietnamese to stampede with terror across the narrow Laotian waist, across the Mekong River and into northeast Thailand in the area around Nakhon Panom. You can look for that on the map but I know you won't. That's a lot of refugees for a pretty poor part of the country. The Thai government began sending them back to their homes in North Vietnam but soon Hanoi refused any more of its own people and slammed its border closed, leaving 35,000 refugees in Thailand.

There were two reasons for Hanoi's decision. First, they didn't want the refugees back, and second, a large concentration of Vietnamese made a perfect cover for the infiltration of terrorists, and how can you tell who is a terrorist and who isn't unless you catch him or her in the act? If the movement had been in the other direction, the Communist command would have cheerfully slaughtered the refugees or put them in forced labor camps, which is a little slower way of doing the same thing. But the Thai government was hog-tied by its traditional distaste for slavery and murder. It still has not solved the problem. The refugees still cluster near Nakhon Panom, very many of them good and honest people and a sizable number just the opposite, judging by their work. But to remove the poison sac would make it necessary to kill the whole snake. Over and over in this part of the world where a struggle for survival is going on, we find ourselves and our allies hampered and stymied by our own rules of justice and decency, which rules are considered by the other side as symptoms of weakness, indecision and decay. And isn't it interesting, Alicia, the screams of outrage against us when we do something by accident which the Communists do regularly coldly and by plan.

Anyway, that's the background on the northeast, a rough, undeveloped, under-populated country which suddenly becomes terribly important by being used as a staging and training area for the never-changing process of terror and takeover we have seen before, always the same and always directed from the same source.

The Thai government freely admits that it has not paid enough attention to the provinces of the northeast. The infiltration by terrorists is still in its early stage, but the pressure is increasing as the Communists grow aware that they cannot win in South Vietnam, that they have lost in Malaysia, Indonesia and Africa.

The Thai government, having before it the unvarying blueprint of Communist activities in other countries, is going about the job in a reasoned and methodical way. In this they are helped by the great Communist failing. Once having set down a principle and a technique, the plan goes forward with little or no gift for change to meet changing conditions. Again and again when their practiced plans have run into obstacles, the field cadres have either tried to bull it through to the point of suicide or have panicked and disintegrated.

The point of attack is usually an area where communication is difficult or impossible, or vulnerable to a quick cutting of all means of communication so that the infiltrated community loses all contact with the outside world. The party is then able to tell its hostages anything it wishes without fear of rebuttal. The second punch is to murder all local leaders, schoolteachers, priests and police. In a rough and sparsely settled district this is easily accomplished by sudden sneak attacks at night.

The Thai government, with U.S. advice and technical assistance, begins by pushing roads into the wilderness at the greatest possible speed and to place bodies of national police in strategic areas so that they can quickly answer calls for help. These police forces are large enough to defend themselves and to extend their patrols deeper and deeper into infected areas. In the villages, local defense units recruited in the villages are trained and given two-way radio communication with the national police units.

The points of penetration are invariably those where the people are poor and standards of health and living are low. The parallel counteraction to the forced propaganda meetings is carried out by teams which carry out such projects as medical aid and inoculations, digging of wells or water purification, improvement of agricultural methods and introduction of new food crops. [They work on the] improvement of local livestock and [the] introduction of new kinds, teaching of new handicrafts and development of new products so that the villages may have something to sell or trade and encouragement of movement over the newly opened roads from village to village, which is another kind of communication. Dispensaries are set up at intervals and midwives trained, and the local scourges such as malaria and meningitis are treated or prevented. Serious agricultural sicknesses are attacked. For instance, the gall midge, which attacks the rice crops, can be brought under control by aerial spraying.

All of these approaches are designed to work together, coordinated by the governors of the local provinces, who are given new authority to act quickly as need arises. Needless to say, this is a slow, ponderous, plodding procedure, but where it proceeds the Communists are forced to give ground and the villagers themselves find resources in themselves for defense and development.

It was this combined operation we went to the northeast to see. Our schedule was planned and shepherded by Peter Davies, assistant director for rural affairs of the U.S. Operations Mission to Thailand. He is all of that but he is also Nada Barry's brother and that's pretty important to people like us who live in Sag Harbor, L.I.

March 11, 1967 / Northeast Thailand

Dear Alicia,

In my last I started to tell you about Northeast Thailand, that strange country separated from Laos by the Mekong River, and a line of peaked and domed mountains which look like those old Chinese ink paintings. I always thought those were fantasies or dream mountains, but here they are very real and very rugged.

We flew to the northeast and then drove in jeeps over the new roads which are being pushed into this harsh country which has been chosen by the Communists for "liberation." Water is the problem here as it is in so much of the world. During the rainy season the rains come in sheets. The river rises out of its bed and floods huge areas, destroys villages and ravages the land. Then follow five dry months. We are in them now. The red ferrous earth turns powder dry and huge cracks open up and, except on the river's edge and near the small areas of standing water, no green thing grows. All living things shrivel and die if they cannot retire deep into the earth. As we drove in jeeps over the newly bulldozed roads we put up a cloud of red dust as fine as pumice, but so very light that it hung in the air a long time. It covered us with a red film, and breathing it caused painful irritation in our throats and chests.

You must have been in places where you felt and knew something was wrong but could not isolate the cause of your unease. I finally found the cause of this feeling—no wild animals, small or large, no birds or very, very few. No soaring members of the hawk family searching for rodents. Here is a dry country surely, with a rough brush cover almost devoid of living creatures. In Death Valley there is some life, but here, very little. No insects, consequently no birds. I can't remember anything quite like this. When I spoke of it to our jeep driver, a southerner from a rich area, he replied, "No birds, no animals because the people have eaten everything—everything." This is the kind of traveler's statement which in all history from Herodotus, through Marco Polo to certain present-day reporters, has been put in evidence and then has hardened to conviction almost completely fact-resistant. So simple—no life because people have eaten it all.

Prince Bhanu [Bhandhu] of the Thai royal family has studied the northeast for years and has written a number of papers about this little-known part of his country. It is his contention that it is the extremes of wet and dry which make it impossible for animal life to develop. Those species that thrive near or in the water are desiccated and roasted out of existence in the dry season, while those which in desert countries have developed physical techniques for conserving and storing water, these are drowned and washed away in the flood season. In our deserts the cacti which are storage reservoirs for moisture are available, but in Northeast Thailand cactus would be washed away.

As for the statement, "The people have eaten all living things," Prince Bhanu told me some findings of his own. The village people of the northeast, he said, whose staple diet is the rice quick planted and harvested in the wet season, have a protein deficiency and a protein hunger. They raise chickens and some pigs, but so far not enough for their needs. As a result they eat insects, locusts, lizards, and any other reptiles they can come by, and they need their protein food. But the people of the south, who have access to the unlimited animal riches of both sea and land, find the scavenging food search of some parts of the north amusing and primitive if not disgusting. For myself, Alicia, I have never understood people who while guzzling oysters, snails and shrimps are horrified to learn that maguey worms and beetles are eaten in Mexico, grubs by American Indians and locusts nearly everywhere.

It is not difficult to see why the northeast is not more densely populated. Life is hard here. Wherever there is access to water, however little, a complex of villages is found, the houses perched high on stilts. Here they raise the quick rice, cultivate the fruits and coconuts they can hand water from the bitter earth cisterns. They pick wild cotton and weave an excellent and beautiful cloth, and they survive. But by far the greatest number of northeasterners cling to the edges of the river, the life bringer, even though they know it may flood them out and wash away their houses, their livestock and themselves in any year.

And this is the area the Communists, trained in Hanoi and in China, have chosen to enter and to liberate from the Thai government, which is trying to bring in the capitalistic poisons of food, transportation, education, communication and security from terror. We stopped in many villages and in most of them the people came running with greetings, with green coconuts to drink from, with ceremony and speeches of welcome. The children crowded close chattering with excitement, for many of these people, until recently, had never seen a stranger, even a southern Thai stranger, let alone foreigners like ourselves.

In most of the villages we were accepted with pleasure and curiosity, and then one day we passed through three villages where the Communists had been at work. No one has to tell you. You know. The children run and hide. Only a few young men stand about sullenly, staring at the ground. They will not reply to a greeting. The women and old people peer from the semidarkness of the stilted houses. And the young men continue to stare at the ground and refuse to meet your eyes and then you know that in the brush nearby there are men with guns watching every move, and others dressed as villagers recording every expression. And when we move on, if any villager has given us aid or comfort even to the extent of ordinary courtesy or response to a greeting, that villager will be punished viciously or killed. Does this seem melodramatic? It isn't. It happens every day. The agents of liberation do not change and their currency never varies—promises of a better life in the future, but for the present, absolute obedience with the alternatives of torture and death not only of the rebel but for his children and his relatives. These are the hostages, the children, the wife and the parents.

I wonder how brave we would be, Alicia, if everyone we love and revered were held as surety for our conformance and by an enemy to whom pity is a weakness and forgiveness a completely foreign conception. How brave would we be? The thought makes us hesitant about giving advice before we can offer protection.

March 18, 1967 / Bangkok

Dear Alicia,

I've probably tried to tell you more about the wild northeastern provinces of Thailand than you want to know. But to me it is important because here is the battle front of methods and ideas, the true confrontation of our allies and ourselves with the Communist pressure for power. And it is in places like these that we will win or lose and the future of the world will be decided—not in Washington, or Moscow or Peking, but in the rice paddy, the hill village, the fishing boat, and the conservers of the crafts of weaving and pottery, and the thousand products of the bamboo. This is the heart.

Item: In the town of Nakon Panom, there is a hotel and pleasure garden named The Civilized, and so it is. At the entrance to the garden, where in the evening civilization is kept alive, there is a large sign that reads, "Girls without V.D. cards not permitted." And inside the garden tacked to a tree the sad printed statement, "V.D. cards #139, #85, #62 and #18 are not valid." How civilized can you get?

Through no fault of our own but probably better so, since Elaine has no V.D. card, we were booked not at The Civilized but at the Grand Hotel, a marble structure with bathrooms each of which contained a shower, a basin and a toilet. This is pretty grand all right even if the toilet seat is broken, but in the two days and nights of our occupancy no water graced any of these luxuries. We carried buckets for the absolute necessities. Now, we have stayed in many places where there are no facilities and with perfect happiness. Why is it that when surrounded with trappings that do not work, we become furious? Elaine renamed the Grand Hotel "The Uncivilized," and so we will always think of it.

Item: Lt. Dick Platt commands a small detachment of Seabees in the village of Ban Nong Chon near the river, an area that was flooded and chewed up during the terrific floods of the last rainy season when the river leaped its banks and went berserk. The Seabees' project is to teach the digging of deep wells to reach potable water, to teach the building of permanent bridges constructed of heavy timber, to bring some kind of medical help to a people who have none.

Platt has young blue eyes and a nose which will not tan. It burns, peels and burns again. Having the same trouble, I sympathize with him. Not many men in the unit were at the base. They never are. In small squads or groups they are out living in the villages. A project is decided on by the village. The Seabees design it, whether a bridge, a well, a schoolhouse or latrines.

"The people do the work," Dick Platt said, "They cut the trees, saw out the lumber and do all of the digging and hauling. We teach them to make the forms for concrete well casing but they mix the cement and pour it and do the digging. All we contribute is methods and a few things they can't get—like nails. That building over there is the new school and meeting place. It has gone up in a week. It will be finished in another week. They won't take a day off. It's theirs and they want it finished. That's the thing. When they find out it's theirs and they build it themselves, you can't stop them."

I asked, "Well, will they be able to carry on when you pull out?"

"Sure," he said. "We've got graduate well diggers and bridge builders working upcountry right now."

"How about the Seabees out in the villages? They must get pretty bored."

"Well they don't," he said. "They only come in when they run out of food. They've got too much to do to be bored."

"How about you?" I asked

"Me? I love it. I think maybe when my service is over, I might come back here and go it alone."

I looked around at the wasted country and the poor gallant attempts to survive and continue. "Why do you like it?" I asked suddenly.

Platt's eyes began to shine. "I've thought about that. No rulebook. We're writing it as we go. We're making it up. When something is needed we do it. Same with the men out in the villages. It's wonderful."

And it is wonderful. It's what every man of energy wants—to be needed and to fill the need by his work and his mind and his imagination and in the end to have something that wasn't there before. It is the dream of creative man—to be creative whether it is interlocking those logs in the bridge there so that pressure only makes them more firm or whether it is art or music. It is the thing a man does at his best and it is the thing that makes him happiest. And Dick Platt put his finger on it—"No rulebook." Only us—here.

Item: Mike Fields, a Peace Corps teacher, wandered in to say hello, and to pass the time of day.

"Were you here during the flood?"

"Yes. I couldn't leave. I got a boat. People were stranded, some of them in trees. I couldn't leave."

"What did you eat?"

"I had eight chickens and a monkey. I was trying to raise chickens. We ate a chicken every other day. Someone ate the monkey."

"How are you getting along?"

"Well," said Mike, "You know how it is. When I first came, it was tough. But when the flood came and I stayed, you know—my stock went way up."

March 18, 1967 / Bangkok

Dear Alicia,

The year is running and it is time for us to move on. We will go to Vientiane in Laos and see what is there. Laos has been under great pressure from Hanoi and China, but we will see what is there when we get there. I would like to go on a rice drop up there if I can. But one thing at a time. Only there are too many things. Can't see them all and can't write as much as I see.

Odd things happen, Alicia. Do you remember an idea I had for using Alnico magnets to drag the ditches in search for weapons hidden there by the Viet Cong? Well I looked all over Saigon for magnets and so did many of my friends—no magnets. I thought I would have to get home before I could find some.

And then a letter was forwarded to me here in Bangkok from Saigon. It was from Edmunds Scientific Co. of Philadelphia. They had been trying to telephone me in Saigon but the circuits were filled through the end of February. It seems that they had sold me the magnet I have at Sag Harbor that I use for picking up things lost overboard. They said they wanted to send some powerful magnets to try out in the ditches but couldn't find where to send them. You can be sure I got in touch with them right away so in the near future Col. Hyatt may get his magnets to try out. That and some other things. But I'll tell you about that when it happens. And I hope something comes of it.

Here's something that came to me in the night when I was trying to go to sleep. I find that this war, and it is a war, is with me pretty much all the time. And as with Dick Platt of the Seabees, there is no rulebook. The thing has to be made up as we go along. We can't look up precedents, procedures of the past. They don't apply. A planning board in Washington, taking a decision, often finds that it arrives too late or that it is irrelevant.

One of the matters of greatest concern in this whole action has been communication, not with our people but with people held or terrified by the enemy. When we were inspecting boats and sampans down in the Delta we found that quite a few people had small transistor radios. Whether they listened to V.C. broadcasts or ours, or both, I don't know, but I'm pretty sure they would not turn on ours in V.C. country. A radio, even a little one, has a penetrating voice that comes through walls and windows. Then I remembered when my kids were growing up they used to buy little radios usually shaped like torpedoes. They had two wires—one you clamped on a water pipe or a nail in damp soil for a ground and the other you threw over a bush. You listened to this thing with an earplug and it drew so little power that you could get a strong signal from quite a distance. I don't know how they were powered. After months when they finally ran down, you simply threw them away. I seem to remember that even at retail these things cost less than $2, which probably means they cost about 50 cents to make.

Well it seems to me here is a fine means of communication. A man who wouldn't dare turn on a speaker would listen with the earplug. Also the whole thing is small and concealable. Distances are short here and in the lowlands there is nothing to get in the way. We could buy and drop 10,000 of these things for the cost of one 2000 pound bomb and 1,000,000 of them for the cost of a bomber.

What would be the advantage? We could talk to our friends and to our enemies. We could refute the V.C. stations or take over their wavelengths. The only thing that would strain would be our programming. We would have to be more interesting as well as more truthful than our opponents. We could also issue requests, warn of impending action, describe people to be watched for, give news of families where separated.

What do you think of this? These tiny things could be spread by the thousand by little paper parachutes which could be printed with instructions. And if anyone says they wouldn't be used, and concealed and the messages repeated—that person is crazy.

Maybe some people like Edmunds Scientific Co. will come up with a design and price low enough so that we could really talk with people and privately. And don't think the V.C. wouldn't listen. They would. And that could be valuable also.

Anyway, we're off to Laos now. Everything different.

March 25, 1967 / Vientiane, Laos

Dear Alicia,

A traveler is reported to have said, "There is no such place as Laos, and I can prove it because I have been there." Having been here, this seems to me to be a very fair statement. Laos is all boundaries with a long thin country in between. Name any country in southeast Asia and Laos is pretty sure to be bounded by it—Burma, China, North Vietnam, South Vietnam, Cambodia and Thailand.

If this is what is meant by a buffer state, Laos is about as buffeted as anyplace I have ever seen. It is the unwilling but helpless proprietor of the Ho Chi Minh Trail in the north and the Schanauk [*sic*, presumably Sihanouk] Trail in the south. Armies of North Vietnamese troops and Viet Cong guerrillas move about Laos almost at will, organizing, arming, commanding and robbing a punch-drunk bunch of bandits called the Pathet Lao. This is called, naturally enough a People's Liberation Front, although who they are liberating and from what, is not very clear. The only tangible evidence of this freedom movement is burned villages and the removal of the rice crop and anything else they can drag away.

Laos is a neutral nation, and I'm not about to explain that to you, Alicia, any more than I could explain the Lao government. It is a kingdom, of course, with a prime minister, who is also minister of defense, education, home affairs, foreign affairs, nearly everything except finance. That portfolio is held by a bright and earnest young man who seems to be in a state of shock. You see, there is a constituent assembly but it won't vote taxes, not even on liquor, or French perfume, not even on opium, which is lawful to raise, to use and to sell.

Can you see the difficulty? Thailand and Cambodia and Burma and South Vietnam all have laws against opium. The only outlets are China and North Vietnam and both of these countries, the first with weapons and the second with soldiers, are engaged in freeing the Lao people from Laos. But it isn't only Lao people who are involved. In the south in the mountains are many tribesmen of the same Polynesian ethnic background as the Montagnards of the central highlands of Vietnam, a clever and energetic people, and perhaps despised for that very reason.

Then in the central and northern mountains are numerous groups of Meo (pronounced Mayo) people, who in some ancient time drifted down from China, as did nearly every other people in Southeast Asia at one time or another. Without boasting I can tell you that I learned to recognize four different kinds of Meo. The white Meo wear black pajamas with a tight crotch. The black Meo wear black pajamas with a low loose crotch. The striped Meos wear stripes and the blue Meos—well, they wear blue. That's not much knowledge but it is enough to keep confusion alive.

Laos was, of course, set up as a buffer state by the Geneva Convention, and that brings me right back where I started and maybe I shouldn't have—started, I mean. A buffer is a thing which takes up the friction between two heavy bodies and in the process gets worn out. Laos takes friction from six or more and it is getting pretty frayed.

We flew into Vientiane, the capital, from Bangkok. It lies just across the great Mekong River from the northeast corner of Thailand and in the distance it looked like a dust storm which, in this dry season, it is. The Mekong flooded earlier this year and when it retired deep within sandy boundaries, the dust got up. Vientiane is a medium-sized orientalized French provincial town largely made up of embassies and unfinished monuments. Because Laos is neutral by act of the Geneva Convention, it has more embassies than London or Paris or Washington. I guess every nation in the world has an embassy here, all except Taiwan.

Now and then, Alicia, I have a sense of delight in the formal nonsense with which serious nations indulge themselves. You know how it is when next door neighbors get mad at each other. When they have to communicate, they get the family across the street to take the message. In international politics, the family across the street is a "neutral" nation. It's silly but that's the way it is. But truly neutral nations are rare. Nearly every country is mad at some other country. A truly neutral nation has to be so scared of everyone that it doesn't dare have either enemies or friends. Laos is the perfect neutral because in addition to having neither friends nor enemies, it was designated neutral in Geneva. This means all the other countries can have representatives in Vientiane and these statesmen can get together in this dusty or drowned capital to talk things over. They can also spy on each other and evaluate, and report.

China is here and North Vietnam and Cambodia, but in addition Vientiane has an embassy unique in the world, I think. The Pathet Lao, the Communists who with the Chinese and North Vietnamese weapons and troops are at war with the nation of Laos, also have an embassy in Vientiane. It is a low, thick building surrounded by walls and barbed wire and guarded by small unsmiling dark men in shabby uniforms and armed with Chinese rifles and fixed bayonets. At first this seems ridiculous but it really makes sense. Where you really need diplomats is not with your friends but with your enemies. When I looked over the barbed wire at the Pathet Lao embassy the guards scowled at me and waved their bayonets. They were not friendly at all.

I was delighted with this diplomatic nosegay in this dusty Eden. The ambassador of Her Britannic Majesty is Fred Warner, plus titles. He sent a note to my hotel to remind me that over 20 years ago, he commanded a small cluster of motor torpedo boats of the British Navy, and that I had sailed with him in the Tyrrhenian Sea on a mission which over the years I have come to believe was a lie and a fabrication. The triumphant finale of this improbable sortie was the bloodless capture of the Island of Capri. HRM's ambassador invited me to dinner to cut up old touches and to reassure each other the lies we have been telling all these years had some basis in truth. And since our stories matched, it apparently really did happen, much to my wife's disgust. Nothing spoils a good story like corroboration.

I have more to tell you about the diplomatic façade of Vientiane, about the Chinese Embassy and that of North Vietnam, but it's too long for this letter. And that's all for now.

April 1, 1967 / Vientiane, Laos

Dear Alicia,

As you may know, the subject of visas has always been near and disgusting to my heart. Before starting this present piece of quixotic tourism we had to get a lot of visas and while *Newsday* and my dear wife did most of the work, I was around enough to reconfirm that the smaller and poorer and more miserable and no account a country is, the harder and more expensive it is to get permission to visit there. Only the tiniest and brokest and hence the proudest nations require my grandmother's maiden name on the visa application.

Whenever a nation is real mad at us, it pulls up stakes, puts its affairs in the hands of some other nation and closes up shop. I guess we do the same thing, but that doesn't make it any smarter. Hoping that countries won't act like spoiled children doesn't seem to help them to grow up.

Cambodia is one of the countries I want to see, and that because I have seen pictures of Angkor Wat. But in New York, I found that Prince Sihanouk, who is the regent of Cambodia, is mad at us so his affairs are in the hands of Indonesia. When application was made, the inspector looked at my profession, said, "Cambodia does not want writers," and closed me off.

In Saigon, Cambodia is mad at South Vietnam so the Australians handle their affairs. The Australians were very helpful. I couldn't pass as a tourist, they said, and writers were not wanted but they suggested that I wire personally to Prince Sihanouk asking his permission to enter his country. This I did in a cable dripping with respect and humility. But, alas, Prince Sihanouk had gone to Grasse (no joke) in the south of France for his liver. Cambodia having been until recent changes a colony of France, it is natural that the prince's liver has a French tendency. Also, the prince may possibly feel that he has backed the wrong horse and that it might be just as well to stay away from the track until the race is over. Anyway he left what is called a shadow cabinet in charge of the business. I don't quite know what a shadow cabinet is but I can guess.

To continue—I had this cabled reply to my visa request: "Samdech Norodom Sihanouk etant absent du Camoge Regrette Vivement ne pouvoir reserver suite favorable a votre demande visa stopend, Directeur Cabinet Chef Etat." In other words the shadow chief of state said "no." I could wait for a change in Prince's liver and/or policy and try again.

Well here in Vientiane in Laos there is a real blowed-in-the-glass Cambodian Embassy, the first one I had come across. But more than that there is a Chinese Embassy and a North Vietnamese Embassy, and I have long wanted to go to both countries, and particularly North Vietnam to verify the facts and figures of Harrison Salisbury. My try for China goes further back.

A number of years ago Dag Hammarskjold [Swedish diplomat and second Secretary General of the United Nations], who was my friend, dined with me. I told him I wanted very much to visit China, but that invitations were rarely issued to Americans. He suggested that I write a personal letter to Chou En-lai [Premier of China], said he was a tough but fair man and might well invite me. I did write such a letter but since my passport is not valid for travel in or to China, North Vietnam, North Korea, Albania and Cuba—before I sent the letter I queried the

State Department asking if they would give permission to go to China if I could get an invitation. The reply was about 13 pages long and its burden was that State could not permit me to go because they could not protect me in China.

You know, Alicia, how too much nonsense brings a kind of wave of weariness? All I could reply was a short note which said, "Hell, you can't protect me in Central Park. I asked for permission, not protection." State did not continue the correspondence. And there the matter lay until just before I came out to East Asia. In Washington I spoke with what we call a high official. I told him the story of my China try and its end. He laughed and said, "Well, you're going where there are embassies, why don't you apply for a visa?"

"But how about my passport?"

"You get the visa and you'll have the passport," he said.

"How about changing it now?"

"No hurry. But give it a try."

So I did. The Chinese embassy was blinding white in the sun and its shadowed door and windows correspondingly black. There is a high wire fence with a heavy duty gate and beside it a little gate house which was empty. But beside the locked gate there was a bell button which I pushed and when nothing happened I pushed again. The front door of the embassy opened a little and a young man in black trousers and an open white shirt came to the gate and looked at me without speaking. I said, "I would like to see the Chinese Ambassador."

The young man looked more puzzled than angry. "He is not here."

"When will he return?"

"I don't know. He is in Peking."

"I see," I said. "But you must have someone in charge. Is there a charge d'affaires?"

"Yes."

"May I see him?"

"He is busy. What do you want?"

"I want to apply for permission to visit China."

"Why?"

"Because I want to see it," I said. "I work for a newspaper. I want to report what I see." I thought a shadow of weariness crossed the young man's face. "You wait," he said, and left me in the blazing sun in front of the locked gate. But it wasn't long before an older man came from the embassy. He unlocked the gate and led me, not to the embassy but to the gatehouse where there were chairs and magazines printed in China in French and English and a pile of color pictures of Chairman Mao.

My new friend sat me down. "Now," he said.

I explained again. He listened and thought of other things. His eyes were soft and uncritical. "May I see your passport?" he asked.

I gave it to him and he looked at the proper pages, where issued and when, where born. Then he glanced through the pages and pages of visas, stopped at the South Vietnam page for a moment. "You are a journalist?"

"Yes, but I have written other things, novels, plays, short stories."

"Would they be known in China?"

"I don't know. I haven't been there."

"Can you tell me some titles of your books?"

I did and he wrote them carefully. "I will cable," he said when I had run out of titles. "But, look. You can't go to my country. It says so here."

"If you will get me a permit, that will be changed."

"I will cable," he said. "Where can you be reached?"

"The American Embassy will find me."

And that was that. He let me have one of the color prints of Chairman Mao and he went away thinking his other thoughts. I wish I knew what they were.

The North Vietnamese embassy was snappy and businesslike. "We are allowing a quota of reporters in—so many a month. The quota is full for this month. I will put you on the list."

"For how long is it full?"

"I can't tell you."

"Who picks the names?"

"I don't understand."

"I mean if Burchett is doing your screening—forget it. I just thought you might like some reporting."

"The quota is full. I will put your name on the list."

"Do that," I said, "for the record. And never say I didn't try."

So you see, Alicia, when I came to the only Cambodian embassy of my career, I was weighted down, kind of drawed out and tongue dusty.

Young man behind a counter: "Visas—fill out three copies for each person—three photographs." He handed me a sheaf of six sheets.

"I've already done this twice," I said.

"Just fill it in in full. Three pictures for each applicant."

"I've got a great idea of something Sihanouk can do with Angkor Wat."

"Pardon?"

"Forget it," I said. "Wouldn't work," and I handed him the six blanks and went out through the dusty heat looking for a beer. Maybe I should stay away from diplomacy. It bugs me.

April 8, 1967 / Vientiane, Laos

Dear Alicia,

I guess I learn slowly but I do learn. In Thailand, after I got the runaround from officials who should have known better, I asked to see the foreign minister, Thant Khoman, a charming and intelligent man. I asked him to tell me the ground rules, what I should see and what not, and of what I saw what I could write without being a nuisance or a danger. He told me I could see anything I wanted to see and write anything I wished so long as it was true and I did not endanger lives. But in both cases, he said, I would have to use my own judgment. After that meeting no one tried to razzle-dazzle me anymore.

On arriving in Laos, I thought to do the same thing—to go to the top first. The prime minister, Prince Souvanna Phouma, is also foreign minister. He was deeply immersed in prime ministering and set a meeting forward, so for eight days I moved about the long thin country of Laos. Since roads are practically nonexistent, this can only be by foot on narrow mountain trails or by aircraft of one kind or another. Laos has mountains, the strangest I have ever seen.

In some places thin shafts of limestone stand high, thin and sharp as knife blades. And then there are the ones that look like animals, like cats and furry snakes, and like hornless cattle. Much of the mountain country of the north and middle is heavy with brush, which on approach turns out to be trees. Foot trails wind in the canyons by the water courses connecting little villages—houses set high on posts, woven bamboo siding and palm thatched roofs.

And where the hills are gentle enough so that a man does not fall off, the little fields of slash-and-burn agriculture can be seen from the air. The trees are cut and the brush slashed down and burned. Then the mountain farmer plants his rice sometimes tethering himself to a stump lest he fall off his farm. The cut trees lying in careful patterns hold back eroding soil in the hard rainy season and draw and hold moisture in the dry. But in about five years when the trees have rotted so that the water escapes, at just about this time, the thin soil is cropped out and the farmer must find another place to slash out a field and burn in a little richness. His old field goes back to jungle and perhaps in 20 years, he, or his sons may slash it out again. It is a haphazard wasteful way of staying alive, but it is the only way the mountain people live.

From Pak Pong, I flew to Sam Thong, the kingdom of Pop Ewell, in about 30 minutes. I asked how far it is, and was told eight days on foot, with belongings, meaning women and children, four days by the river but then there are the rapids and the Pathet Lao, and 30 minutes by Porter airplane. It doesn't seem fair.

Pop Ewell, the middle-aged, Midwestern American farmer, sometimes known as Mr. Laos, had just returned from a trip to the States and was being welcomed with an enthusiasm that might well make the Lao king a little restless. Pop Ewell founded Sam Thong. He walked all over these, I almost said, God's mountains. He brought in the hospital, the school, worked away at the small dusty airfield. But mostly he built this structure with the bodies and brains of the Meo tribesmen. Once over lightly is not good enough for Pop Ewell. He deserves and will undoubtedly have a book written about him. I think Pop is an example of how the ancient gods were born and preserved in the minds and the carven images of people all over the world.

Remember, Alicia, how the story invariably goes—in olden times the people did not live well as they do now and they practiced abominations. Then a stranger appeared and he taught us to use the plow and how to sow and how to harvest. He brought us writing so we could keep records. And he gave us healing medicines to make us healthy, and he gave us pride so we would not be afraid and when we had learned these things he went away. He was translated. That is his figure there, carved in limestone. Well, I don't think Pop is likely to be taken up in a sweet chariot even if he had the time or the inclination, but that ancient story is Pop Ewell's story. Whether you believe it or not, Alicia, there are still giants on the earth.

For eight days I moved about—to places with names you don't lightly forget. Luang Probang to Ban Nam But to Sam Thong to Tranninh on the edge of the Plain of Jars, which is a rebel stronghold. I went with some Baptist missionaries to take some medicines to a tiny Christian village, way to heaven and gone in a pine forest on a mountain top. And then we moved far south near the Cambodian border, to Savannakhet and Pakse and up to the fertile Bolovens Plateau where a cluster of 44 villages of hill people are learning to plant new crops and to improve their chickens and pigs, and to move water about, to raise it and hold it back in storage. It is like the world we knew in prehistoric times. Fred Hubig, David Teller, and Ben Revilla showed us around Houei Kong, where they are creating a new world by suggestions and example. Ben Revilla made us a treat which should clang the name of Houei Kong throughout the world. It was cheddar cheese ice cream and it was delicious.

Late in the afternoon my old bad habit reasserted itself. I draw fire. Two battalions of V.C. crossed from Cambodia, overran Attopeu and started up the cliff-like edges of the plateau. I guess word of the chickens and pigs and lush vegetables of the 44 villages of the Bolovens cluster had got about and that was enough to fire up the liberators. They were not about to permit the villagers to languish in that kind of tyranny.

The firing was getting closer to Houei Kong when a chopper dropped in to pick us up and evacuate us to Pakse. But the news came out anyway. It seems that the 44 villages had successfully resisted liberation thus proving to the world that they are lackeys of Western Imperialist Capitalism. You know, benighted as they are, those people seem to like it. They drove the Freedom Heroes back down the slope. That's all for now.

April 15, 1967 / Jakarta, Indonesia

Dear Alicia,

By now I know some things about Vietnam and the war there that I do not believe to be opinion but a pattern of fact if such a thing exists outside of special force forward areas of the New York Post and such like battle weary outposts. Sometimes I could wish that they would at least rewrite Hanoi's copy before they reprint it. But some of our editors even take the typographical errors as matters of faith. [This paragraph was deleted in the published version.]

Before the whole world sinks helplessly into a thick semantic smog, I would like to discuss the civil war in Vietnam with which we should stop interfering. The proponents of non-interference in Vietnam are by no means in favor of non-interference in other areas closer to their hearts. Thus it becomes apparent that it is not interference they oppose but place. This letter is not for those brave defenders of obvious and arrant nonsense. They would take it as an attack on the freedom of the press, which I expect it is.

Anyway, Alicia, I do know some things now outside the reach of editorial rearrangement and, as I am ridiculously human, to know a thing is to tell it. If governing groups want to consider what follows as unsolicited advice, they are free to do so, since they are not paying.

The first great truth is this: America and the allies can help South Vietnam to ward off defeat and subsequent subjection, but no amount of help military or economic can make it free. That must be done by the South Vietnamese themselves and all by themselves. The V.C., backed by the North, by China and by the USSR, could be uprooted, defeated and destroyed for all time if the problems which follow could be solved. They are not new problems. They have been festering and swelling in Vietnam for many hundreds of years. In the north, Ho Chi Minh has damned [sic] up the uneasy flood in the usual Communist way, by taking the country away from the people and then dribbling a percentage of it back to them, charging as interest only their freedom to think, to plan, to move, to create as individuals. In this transaction, while something is gained, something very precious is also lost, namely the individual, the only truly creative unit the world has ever produced. But having eliminated, for the time being at least, the individual, the North has been able to eliminate some of the poisons which do and will threaten the people of the new little country of Vietnam. Without the pressure of war and possible defeat, it is probable that the problems would never have been faced except by periodic use of force or threat of force.

I have not dug these things from darkness, Alicia. They are there, open and ulcerous and if they are not solved in the near future, a great many people are presently dying to no purpose whatever.

I do not know Prime Minister Ky but he doubtless knows what has to be done. I wonder, however, if he knows how very soon it must be started. Since he is the national leader, and regardless of how he achieved that position, he must make the first moves toward the future. If, as he says, he does not wish to remain head of state, it will be easier for him. It is true that he did call a constitutional assembly, protected the election and saw to it that a constitution was written, not a constitution without holes in it but better than what went before. And Marshal Ky has promised that in the near future a general election will be called to create a civilian government to take over from the military dictatorship. If Ky is honest, he must be haunted by the lurking dangers of the future.

It is so much easier to tell people what they must do rather than to teach them to do it themselves. For this reason democracy cannot be created by decree. It is the end product of a long period of learning, usually by trial and error. Democracy cannot be given. It must be wanted, and after that it must be learned as a child learns to read. And in the process of learning there will be many mistakes. The danger now is that a mistake which normally might be corrected, at this time might throw the learners to the simple solution of Ho Chi Minh.

While there are many subtle and unseen dangers in the path of the little country the main hazards are open for all to see. First there is the history—many hundreds of years of domination by conquerors, warlords and landlords. Wherever the poor farmer has looked, maybe forever, he saw only a deputy of an absentee god to take from him everything he and his family could produce from the land. He was allowed to keep enough so that he did not die of starvation because only through him and his children could the land he didn't own be made to produce for the owner he never saw. To keep him at a distance and still producing, a class or caste had the job of farming the farmer. For purposes of regional safety against foreign intrusion, but mainly against dissatisfaction with the cockeyed system, another caste grew up—a soldier caste, men proud of their calling but servile to their proud commanders, who were in turn very humble toward the cocks of the roost.

It is obvious that education is a luxury and an interference to a farmer. It takes time and sometimes, when exhaustion recedes, dissatisfaction may arise. On the other hand accounts must be kept, poetry written, genealogies dusted off and improved, architecture piled up and religion designed in the image of the boss. There must be a heavenly retinue to parallel the army and an academy of saints. The only people on earth who didn't have heavenly equals were those same poor damned farmers. The lords, the bureaucrats, the soldiers and the scholars ganged up with their deified equals and all of them rode herd on the rice paddies. And as though that and dysentery and meningitis and malaria weren't enough to keep the farmers in line, somebody invented devils and evil spirits and that required a caste of soothsayers and demon tamers to sort out the traffic jam piled up around the half naked, ignorant, ant-hill of sub-humans without whom the whole pyramid would have collapsed.

Maybe it wasn't quite as simple as that but pretty nearly. In addition, every caste was paid off with the privilege of holding everyone below in contempt. And far from being a crime, it was an honorable requirement that theft could only be committed against your own caste or those above you. Anybody or anything else was fair game. And that's the way it was until the enlightened colonizers came in from Europe. Vietnam was privileged to get the civilized but realistic French, who added only one rule. They stole from everybody, but kept the system going.

Of course there were all kinds of little refinements. The graves of the ancestors were in the field the farmers didn't own, which kept him from running away. Simony, far from being held in disfavor, was an honorable duty. The first duty of a provincial governor was to get his nest feathered quick before something happened. Under him, the first duty of district chief was to help with the governor's nest so he could get to his own. This was the way life was—and to some extent this is the way it still is.

Land that can produce three crops a year brings in only one. Why should a farmer produce more since it is going to be taken away from him anyway? He has been rolling with the punch so long that his neck is a spring. When the Communists came in, they had very fertile minds to work on. They could promise anything since they had no intention of delivering anyway. It was only when in some districts they had settled in and taken over, that the farmer discovered it was just new words for the same old malarkey he had heard for a thousand years.

Well that's the background of this new little nation. The old habits die hard. Integrity is a strange word with a foreign flavor. There is no way to judge honesty because it has never been tried.

It is odd that in this unlikely soil something is germinating a change, an idea, perhaps even an ideal but not without teeth and claws. I am not making this up. This constitution must work. This general election must be held. The districts must be elective and must be a check on the national government. The land must be distributed—not promised but put under the calloused hands of the families. The education, so long withheld, must be given and given freely.

These are the problems that must be faced and put into execution—land, government and education. The castes, so long powerful, still exist but they are shadow things. The strength of the country lies in the farming people who, through the ages, have been ignored. Not only must the self-defense of the nation come from them but the local leadership of self-government. If the central government does not know these things, the V.C. do. Their first victims when they take over a village are the local leader and the schoolteacher.

The next few months will determine the future. The armed forces, Vietnamese and allies are winning but unless the peace forces of civil government move with equal speed and determination the military victory will mean nothing. We cannot do this for them. They must do it for themselves and by themselves. All we can do for them is to give them the time to make their nation.

April 22, 1967 / Bali

Dear Alicia,

This is a place of dream. I suppose everyone, weary with wind and weather, with the combined rat-maze the world makes for us with our own frenzied help, all of us, at one time or another, in horror or just plain weariness, have felt that we could make a better and more beautiful world without half trying. Well, Bali is that world. [James] Michener or Rodgers and Hammerstein called it Bali Ha'i.

Rousseau painted it from the memory of longing. I suppose very many thousands of people have seen Bali but I have never heard it described nor seen a picture which gave me any impression of what it is like. I think perhaps Bali is not transmittable. Your self must see and feel it, but it is not mysterious. It is wide open to the eye and the feeling—just not capable of being captured and capsuled and taken home to be put in the parlor under a glass bell.

Alicia, I might argue with myself that I find Bali exquisite because I have so recently seen the disease of flood and desert, the appalling distortion and ugliness of war, the crawling confusion of fear and cruelty and crippling poverty. But I am sure this is only a small part of my

THE DISPATCHES | 139

passionate wish to keep Bali in myself forever. And I am sure of this because for thousands of years no stranger has left Bali without longing and no Balinese has ever willingly gone away at all.

We have not been here long enough, no one is, but against this beauty the rest of the world is helpless. But it is personal, not private but personal.

For the few days of this other-worldness, the last several months have passed in review to be inspected, reseen and judged. You remember that I came to the world of East Asia because it seemed to me that something of the utmost importance to the world is happening here and the reports I could read of it were not all satisfying to me. I imagine my letters have been no more satisfactory to anyone else.

Perhaps my vision has not been in depth, my judgments and opinions, based on the quick look—superficial because of the short time and the insufficient knowledge or insight. But is this entirely true? The very strongest and most unshakable opinions about the war in Vietnam and our part in it seem to be held by people who have never been there. These people are absolutely sure of their positions, if the letters I get are any indication. And why should duration have anything to do with superficiality? Sometimes the fresh quick look with an unprepared and unindoctrinated eye and brain is more clear and penetrating than long experience which has dulled this facet, edited out this one, built this one out of personal need or gain or frustration. No, duration—length of experience with a place or a situation—suffers from our human tendency to bring our own world to dim or even to blot out what is there, and this too is opinion but for some reason, this kind of opinion is greatly respected.

Some years ago, when Ed Ricketts and I were collecting marine animals for fun and very little profit, we would come to a beach or tide pool near which people had lived all of their lives and they would never have seen many species that were constantly under their eyes. They had to be shown what was there before they could see it. This little example has often frightened me with the question, how many things are there under my eyes that I cannot see? I am sure there are very many.

For that matter, how many things are in the fields of vision of governments, of generals, heads of departments and heads of state which are invisible to them for one reason or another, sometimes for reasons imposed by the blinders of policy. At a party recently, the Swedish ambassador to an East Asian country said to me, "You have been to South Vietnam. We only go to North Vietnam."

"Why?" I asked.

"Because we do not approve of your policy."

"But what has approval to do with seeing? I would like to go to North Vietnam but its government will not permit me. Policies may be as blind as people. And isn't it strange how self-defeating it can be?"

An honest writer is at the mercy of what he sees and hears and feels. Only a propagandist is committed before the fact and can come to a conclusion without contact with reality. And yet there are many governments which will not permit a writer to enter unless he has proved in advance that he favors that system or policy or government as opposed to any others. A writer who can arrive at a conviction by remote control is either stupid or paid for and in either case a bad writer if not a dishonest one. The result then of excluding all writers who do not in advance agree with you is to guarantee inferior products.

If I had been permitted to move about freely in North Vietnam, seeing what I wished, talking without hindrance to anyone I saw, it is quite possible that my opinions might have undergone a change. In South Vietnam I saw only the cruel, ugly treachery of Viet Cong and North Vietnamese, and that is the only side I saw, the booby traps, the mutilated people, the policy of terror by torture, the gray creeping murder of the guerrilla. These things I know to be true. I have seen them, not once but many times. But let us suppose there is another side, a sweet side, a lovable, even a reasonable side to Ho Chi Minh. It is reasonable to suppose that this is so, but I am not permitted to see it if such exists. I am condemned to see only the bad. On the other hand, those journalists who are welcomed to the North are those who have never seen the bad side and are thus convinced that it does not exist. They have blinded themselves to a half of reality.

I do not believe that any system or policy is without fault. South Vietnam, the U.S. and the allies all have many faults, but among them is not this one. Any writer with any kind of conviction can come to South Vietnam, can see what he wishes and can report to his readers any opinion or observation that may come his way. The result may seem like anarchy, but I believe it to be more permanent and healthful in terms of history than the channeled publicity which in a short space of time turns out to be a lie. We may not be perfect but we do not have to rewrite our encyclopedias every 20 years to match changing leaders and varying policy.

Now and then in this East Asia so far from the vortex of emotional conviction without representation I see the American newspapers—the full-page advertisements paid for and signed by devoted, and I am sure, honestly perturbed people who are opposed to American participation in the war in Vietnam. Moving slowly about, talking with everyone, I have yet to see a corresponding conviction among the people directly involved. No South Vietnamese, American, Australian, Korean, New Zealander, Thai, Lao or Malayan has this opposition at all. In fact the opposition seems to increase in direct relation to the distance from the danger. The most hysterical objector to this war is the man or woman farthest from it. I suppose this is invariably true.

There are many American writers whom I admire and respect who find themselves in violent opposition to this war. And they are writers of enormous diversity and background. Indeed they have only one thing in common—they have not been there.

I can't believe that writers like Arthur Miller, Saul Bellow, John Updike, Tennessee Williams, Edward Albee and many others can wish to be uninvolved with one of the most important events of their lifetimes. In the body of their work they have looked at life before they have reported it or formed an opinion about it. Alicia, I wish I could appeal to those I have mentioned and to many more, to come to Vietnam—North or South, preferably both but to associate with this conflict.

They could do it. Nearly any newspaper would send them, particularly *Newsday,* and the forces at least in the South would surely accredit them. Also I am sure that their copy would not be interfered with except perhaps at home. I could hope that they might wade in the rice paddies, sit with the hurt and troubled old people, listen to the frightened or rambunctious children, walk through the hospitals and look into the great suffering eyes. (It seems to me that the smallest little person always has the biggest eyes.) I wish also that these writers would go out where the fighting is—sit behind sandbags with the kids they call murderers, fly with the airmen or if they feel particularly adventurous, go in with a First Cav strike, hit the ground and take cover, or if they wish really to know something about fear and gallantry, I could wish that they might go on a night patrol in the Delta, where every tuft of grass may hiccup a burst of fire and any small stab or pain is probably a needle-pointed punji stick smeared with human excrement and poisonous as a snake bite.

If they will do some of this I can promise them they will at least have to reorganize their thinking, and perhaps revise some of their preconceptions. There is the problem of course that a claymore mine plays no favorites and a grenade tears writer flesh like any other. Then there is a chance of being killed. A number of writers have been. But, hell, everything is dangerous. One might lose an eye on the corner of a protest placard, or be garroted by a guitar string.

But one thing I will promise any fellow writers. If they will come out and associate with the war they detest, they will not hate war the less, but at least they will know what they are talking about, and this is a valuable thing for a writer, as you well know, Alicia.

April 29, 1967 / Jakarta, Indonesia

Dear Alicia,

I recently was present at the last scene of a strange, through-the-looking-glass piece of world history. It took place in an enormous sports court and was witnessed by tiers of ambassadors, assemblymen and some journalists like me. The area of the Sports Palace on the outskirts of Jakarta was guarded by heavily armed troops and on the approaches there were armored cars and tanks deployed to discourage civil commotion.

For a week the National Assembly of the nation had debated whether or not to remove its permanent President Sukarno on the grounds that he had participated in a plot to turn his country over to the Communists. The meetings constituted a kind of court-martial. The assembly found against him and put in a temporary president, Gen. Suharto, until a new general election can be held.

In the Sports Palace, the band played, the decree was read, the oath of office administered to the new president and the band played again. This was the occasion of the retirement from public life, it is to be hoped, of one of the most improbable characters in history, Bung Karno—which means Brother Karno or Comrade or Bud. This chubby man who smiled with tinseled teeth could charm any audience at any time with oratory which was perfection if only you did not inspect what he said. He regularly raised his followers to cheering frenzy, or lulled their fears or conned them out of everything they possessed, and accepted their thanks for the privilege.

Bung Karno—The Bung. At the end of the last war, he made a nation out of the collection of great rich islands we used to call the Spice Islands. It is more than a great sickle-shaped archipelago. It amounts to a subcontinent. It has a population, as nearly as can be guessed, of perhaps 120,000,000 people. In area it is larger than all of Europe from Spain as far into Russia as the Ural Mountains. It is potentially rich beyond dreams of any kind of avarice.

Before the war the Dutch owned it, or acted as though they did, then the Japanese captured it and finally the Bung got it and made of it the nation called Indonesia. But where the Dutch and the Japanese only tousled the lovely place, the Bung raped it and was greatly admired for so doing.

What a character the Bung was, or is, I suppose. He is presumed to be somewhere under house arrest and many people here and on the other islands still adore him, still would cheer his meaningless oratory and burn an embassy or overturn automobiles and riot in the streets at his suggestion. If this were not so, the assembly would doubtless have ordered him to trial for treason and he would have been shot.

This chubby man reminds us of so many people we know of because he studied and stole from the great hustlers of all time. Like Caesar, he was a greatly publicized seducer of women. Like Huey Long, he was everything to everyone. He admired Hitler, took poses and sentences from Mussolini, whose "Vivere Pericaloso" ("Live dangerously") became his motto, which he said and, as with Mussolini, his nation lived.

The Bung was fabulous. He created a dream state, a combination of classic Rome and a World's Fair, a nation with a huge army with which he threatened the peace of the world and which he used chiefly for parades. I wish I had known him but not with more than a dollar in my pocket, because he had the ability to make men and nations believe anything he wished and furthermore, to pay for it.

Governments vied with one another for the privilege of giving him money to be used either for monuments to himself or to be used against them. He got money and equipment from everyone and he double-crossed everyone. He got American aid and burned our libraries, took Japanese reparations and built huge hotels, inaccessible places. You can see the working of his mind in the enormous unfinished buildings in Jakarta, skyscrapers that have not got past the stage of standing iron skeletons, half-finished palaces in weed-grown compounds. The great shaft of the national monument has a flame made of many hundreds of pounds of pure gold and its base still has the concrete forms in place. The Russians built him one of the great stadia of the world for the Asian Games, which never quite came off. The city is like the work of a rather talented child whose interest wavers before the piece is finished. He ordered trucks and heavy machinery by the hundred-thousands but no spare parts, so that in this city over 70,000 heavy trucks stand rusting away, and in this city, with an estimated 4,000,000 people, there are only 80 buses still in operation. He built, or rather conned, a navy that has no unsilted harbor and the great dredges happily given to him lie in the sea with the waves and the salt eating them away slowly.

There is little on this archipelago the Bung did not handle, change or redesign. He was Big Brother in an Orwell sense. Father and creator of his country, president for life. He held all portfolios of government, designed decorations and medals. The bank of ribbons he wore on his uniform was about the size of a chest X-ray plate. His dream of a nation caused Javanese, Sumatrans, people of Borneo, Bali, Celebese to believe they belonged to one nation, where before they had been slaves of invaders or subjects of predatory European colonists. This identity the Bung—Big Brother—gave them, but only gradually did they discover that since the Bung had invented them, the Bung owned them.

It is strange, or is it, that no dictator has ever been able to avoid the actions, the traps which inevitably destroy him. Big Brother fell into the trap.

A dictator must be very clever but not intelligent. Perhaps if he were intelligent, he would not want to be a dictator. That requires a single direction and an egotism of monstrous size and child-like simplicity.

Big Brother Bung freed the people from the domination of foreigners. Only gradually did they discover their new stylish velvet-covered chains. The prisons began to fill with people who asked questions and particularly who wrote questions, for to a Big Brother a question is treason. Newspapers became advertising tracts, their editors in prison. All foreign press was forbidden entrance. Books were carefully inspected for poison and the mail scrutinized, inspected and censored. Communications with the outside world ground slowly to a stop.

Then, as all dictators do, the Bung created an outside enemy to take his peoples' attention away from the fact that he was robbing them blind. First Malaysia was the enemy and must be conquered—Malaysia and the British. Malaysia must in fact be conquered and annexed to become a part of Big Brother's dream empire. His new army mobilized to protect the homeland and to invade the neighbors. Communications with the outside world were broken. There was a confrontation which stopped all trade.

From his actions it is possible to read the Bung's comic-strip visions of grandeur. In his Sopwith Camel, he daily flew out to engage the Red Baron. When the United Nations censured him for a particularly smelly action, he not only withdrew from the UN but formed his own Asian Union, which was to rule first the Far East and later the world.

In his jerry-built capital of Jakarta, bands of Bung zealots roamed the streets aching to prove their devotion to Big Brother, particularly if it involved destruction and looting. These were not mobs in the usual sense. They were organized and well directed. They only looked like uncontrolled rioters. When Bung Karno didn't like the English, his mob burned the British Embassy. His defiance of the U.S. brought an arsonist mob down on the American library and a violent attack on the embassy. One by one the Bung made calculated enemies of those nations which he had conned, milked and razzle-dazzled to the limit.

Did you ever hear of a dictator who didn't do it for the good of his people? In the last 100 years all dictators have proclaimed themselves socialists and more recently Communists. This indicates, of course, that the savior is taking the ill-gotten gains of the rich to return them to the deserving poor, particularly those poor who have been most useful. That these ill-gotten gains stop halfway and stick to the hands of the saint, this fact never gets inspected or if it does, the troublemaker who messes around where he is not wanted is quietly put away either behind bars or under ground. It is always so, it is the dismal repetition in different parts of the world that makes me wonder whether we are fit to be let out where we might get rained on.

There is no question that the Bung is a gifted man. If he were not he could not in such a short time have taken one of the richest areas in the world and through his own efforts built an astronomical bankruptcy perhaps unique in history. People still take bets as to the numbers of millions the Bung has in anonymous numbered accounts in Switzerland. And he might have none.

This is real crazy, Alicia, and it proves that only the ridiculous is believable. While Big Brother Bung Karno was working at his nation and dream worlding an international empire, what was happening to the people he so dearly loved? Well, it can only be told in comparative terms—a college professor's monthly pay is half as much as it costs him to take a bus to school. No government employee can possibly live on his pay. A man to raise a small family must have at least three jobs and put his children to work at something soon after they learn to walk. A hotel bellboy makes more money than a cabinet minister. University students sometimes found they couldn't get to school on foot and couldn't afford a bus. A bicycle is a major investment, hard to come by and even harder to keep.

While glory flamed about the brows of the Indonesians, they were broke, busted, smashed. The rice farmer could feed his family, but the average man had only the army for shelter. Then at least he was fed and clothed.

I am simplifying as much as I can, Alicia, but this insane story, to be understood at all, must be told in some kind of detail. If you are still interested and you should be, I'll have to tell you how it came out in another letter. And if you are confused—think how mixed up I am, who know much more about it.

I'll continue the story of Snoopy and the Baron in my next.

May 6, 1967 / Jakarta, Indonesia

Dear Alicia,

I guess you can call this letter Bung II or Bunged Again. I am sure that the moment I leave these fabled shores, I won't believe a word of what I am writing now. I don't know why I should expect you to believe things I have doubted, while watching them happen.

Let's see, where was I? Oh! Yes—the Bung was well into his marriage to his fourth wife and his fifth bloodless war. Apparently his department of accounting had long ago given up keeping books. His credit for loans from foreign business and government was just about exhausted. But the Bung still had the power of hypnosis. If he could get a man or a woman alone in a room the man would emerge smiling and with his pockets inside out and the woman—smiling. But the field of operations was growing smaller.

From the first the Bung had trumpeted his socialism and later, when he successfully put the bite on the Soviet Union and on Red China, he went even further and indicated to them that deep down inside he was really a Communist and that when the time was ripe he would openly proclaim his convictions and join Indonesia to the great peace lovers who have kept the world on edge for 50 years. The Communists of various Peoples Republics were delighted that Big Brother felt this way, and they were prevailed on to show their pleasure in a material way with loans, equipment, machinery and all of the trappings of international love.

It can only be a guess, but with the past record in hand, the guess is probably accurate that the Bung was up to his old tricks. He would take his new friends for everything he could get and then give them the heave ho. Now his Communist brothers offered to help in an organizational way to introduce orderly government in the far-flung islands and peoples of Indonesia to the desirable end that all Asia would defend itself against the Imperialist West, which is Soviet talk for invasion and conquest by infiltration and subversion.

Now the Bung must have been pretty far gone in pleased self-admiration. He was particularly pleased with the offer of his new friends of finding and eliminating the enemies of the people wherever they might be found. In Communist terms an enemy of the people is anyone who disagrees with the boss. Bung's jails were bulging with enemies of the people but he welcomed help in cleaning up those he had overlooked. So the brotherhood moved in using their traditional methods. And the Bung seems to have been so far gone in self-affection as to believe that when they had finished the job for him, he had only to kick them out and take over. He had done it very often before.

You know, Alicia, there are three basic rules of life which are invariably forgotten by would-be dictators. These are (1) You can't miss them all, (2) you can't take it all and (3) you can't put them all in the pokey.

At this time Red China and the Soviet Union had not started slapping each other around. They were as close as two acid-heads with one lump of sugar, and here was the Bung, wide open, a patsy and a pigeon. It is more than probable that they had the same plans for Big Brother as Big Brother had for them. So they all went happily to work setting up Indonesia for the kill.

But the rules still operate. There were some the Bung had not won, there was a moiety he hadn't stolen because he couldn't find it, and there were some he hadn't jailed because he didn't know who they were. And lastly there was the danger that always haunts a dictator. He must have an army to exist, and at the same time the army can wipe him out. This is why dictators invariably lavish honors, funds and privileges on their armies. There is nothing else they can do. You can't put an army in jail.

In the Bung's army, there were the usual main chancers, but there were also some men of intelligence and integrity, who just did not believe that the Communists were motivated by an undying love for the common people and unquenchable desire to help them to freedom. Some of Bung Karno's generals had heard of Finland, of Lithuania, of Estonia, of West Germany, Poland, Hungary, Rumania, Tibet, Korea and North Vietnam, just to mention a few. Some of these generals began to be a little itchy about the aid being given in the organization of their country.

In the light of subsequent events, it is reasonable to suppose that these generals, together with a number of civilians who had managed to remain un-Bunged and still alive, that these men began to look into what was happening to their country, and that they carried on their research without Big Brother's knowledge. It is also possible that they discovered things Big Brother did not know about his new friends and advisers.

It is the invariable practice of the Communists to work very slowly, to tighten the noose so gradually that the victim believes it is a new necktie. Then when all is ready, they strike, instantly and mercilessly. All opposition is slaughtered and the poor idealists who helped them in are shoveled out on the dung heap. The process never changes.

Since the Bung has not so far been brought to trial, what actually happened is only known from others who seem quite willing to testify. Apparently, the time came when the loyal friends called the Bung in and said, "Time's up! We're going to take over now. The time is set— hour, minute, second. It will happen simultaneously all over the country. We've done it before. It should not take more than two or three hours."

Now the Bung has claimed he did not know about it, but there are many others who say that he did know but that in his usual manner he covered himself so that he could come out as the victorious leader of whichever side won out.

In the history of Communism I can find no exact parallel for what happened. The generals and their civilian aides had made an exact study and had made exact plans. They too knew the moment set for the Communist coup. It had been set up days in advance. Troop movements were slow and units deployed so that they seemed almost casual.

Part of the plot was to be the kidnapping of key military men. Just before the H-hour, the army struck and caught the cadres before they could move. The fighting was merciless. There was no quarter given or asked. But the generals had been captured and a number of them were tortured to death. But the Communist coup was broken and the organization driven and harried. There was great bloodletting all over Indonesia, but when it was done, it at least for the present is done.

Meanwhile, what of Big Brother? He moved about smiling with his tinseled teeth, making his jokes, patting ladies' behinds. He was the permanent president, the father of his country, the founder, the Bung. His friends and associates were charged with treason and murder, convicted and shot. The Bung smiled on, denied everything. His newest little Japanese wife was about to have a baby.

Under increasing pressure, the National Assembly held a meeting. The motion was made to depose the Bung and to try him for crimes against the state, capital crimes. It was a tricky thing this assembly undertook. Many people all over the far-flung country still believed the dream world the Bung had preached. They did not know about his treachery, his bankrupting of the nation. It would not be a good thing to kill him. A little time and diseased kidneys will do that job. But where would he be likely to do the least harm—in exile, or at home? It was decided that it would be better if he stayed home where he could be watched. And it is to be hoped that he is well watched, for this man like all dictators would destroy his people to save his power.

And so, sitting in the sports palace, I heard the band play, and then the decree of the assembly was read removing the Bung from the presidency and binding him to refrain from political activity of any kind. And then Gen. Suharto took his oath as acting president.

The Bung is living in one of the delightful palaces he built for himself. The gardens are thronged with statues of naked girls. He is no longer president, no longer a general. The last line of the verdict left him only his scholastic title. He was called Engineer Sukarno. And the snaggle teeth of unfinished buildings in Jakarta are the monuments to his ability.

Don't you wish you could know what his thoughts are?

May 13, 1967 / Tokyo

Dear Alicia,

I remember promising you that I would be a China Watcher and give you a rundown on what is really happening in China. Well, we arrived in Hong Kong, surely an improbable place—the Neiman Marcus of the Far East. All of the beautiful and desirable movable goods of the world at bargain prices, a citadel of opulence in a sea of confusion and failure. I was prepared to become a China expert once removed at a moment's notice.

You remember Cynthia Walsten [sic], don't you? She promulgated the rule of "No good deed goes unpunished." What the Viet Cong or accident—fire, flood and bombs bursting in air—failed to do to me was accomplished by a kindly impulse. In our hotel I saw a small but earnest oriental porter trying to pull a hand truck loaded with three cases of beer up a staircase not quite making it. So I gave him a hand and together we worked the stuff up to the next level. My impulse was casually benign but the next morning I couldn't walk, and the hotel doctor said I had slipped a disk in my back and the only treatment was to lie flat thereon on a fracture board. My good deed had drawn maximum penalty.

Fortunately, I had looked over the desolate border into China, which is a little like looking into the Jersey marshes from the top of the Empire State Building. So you see I could not go to the China Watchers, but fortunately some of the best of them came to me. A number of the best of them gave me the benefit of their knowledge. I shall not mention names. A China Watcher worth his salt protects his sources and so shall I.

I was particularly impressed with China Watcher No. 2. There are five No. 1 watchers and they, to a certain extent, cancel each other out. But No. 2, not having to protect his position, was very helpful—also much less fearful of making a mistake. Since I don't even have a number in the watchers' hierarchy, and am not a bit afraid of making a mistake, I am able to tell how it is in China and what is likely to happen—all of my information coming from experts may be a little confusing to you at first, but you will get used to it as I go along.

The first question is, of course, what is the struggle all about? My own answer is that as with all struggles from the beginning of time, one side wants to get something and the other wants to keep it and so they fight. It is exactly like "King of the Mountain" played by children.

Chairman Mao Tse-tung is an old man now. Some demi-experts think he is dead, others that his mind is gone and the third set of experts cover their bets by holding that Mao's mind is good sometimes and slips out of focus sometimes. However, there are some points of agreement. Mao did accomplish a revolution of enormous extent. To do this, he laid down a set of rules, some of them after the fact. Some of his decisions brought about catastrophes but those have been erased from history. Like most successful old men, Mao cannot conceive that there are two or more right ways. And a successful leader cannot accept change. Are you with me so far Alicia? I hope I am.

To accomplish and lead a revolution is very different from devising a productive and an organized people. The first requires military control and the second a delegation of power to bureaucracy. Whether you call it one thing or another, local management is required to raise food, build houses, introduce education, mine materials and make them into usable products and police the whole project at the same time. But bureaucracy, no matter where it occurs, has a universal tendency to be bureaucracy whether it is in Red China, the Soviet Union or the State of California. It is an organism having its own directions and tendencies. And it is the opposite of active revolution, which is the destruction of present organization. For this reason, revolution accomplished becomes automatically counterrevolution. This is what Mao calls revisionism. If you do not keep to a line, even where it has proved wrong, you are a revisionist. When Mao saw that his own personal revolution was taking the inevitable path of trial and error, he could not tolerate it. He called on the toiling masses to rise up and fight again. But the toiling masses were doing pretty well, better in fact than they had ever had it.

Then Mao raised the danger of Russia, the traitor to the revolution—war in the offing, of Imperialist America aching to invade China, as though we didn't have enough trouble defending our nation against Lurleen Wallace [wife of Alabama Governor George Wallace] and the toiling masses of Alabama. So that didn't work either. There was only one huge reservoir of people ready and anxious to drop everything and go into perpetual revolution and that was the millions of school kids who seem to have the same aversion to work as ours have. They rushed out, marched, cheered, made decisions, charged everyone who disagreed with them with treason and in general had one hell of a fine time.

But in the process the factories dropped production, the crops weren't planted, the army took a dim view of being shouldered aside by punks. And then the inevitable happened—the kids began fighting among themselves. So Mao, or whoever speaks with his voice, ordered the Red Guards to go home, back to school, back to work. That hasn't worked out very well. They don't want to go. And they are constantly finding enemies of Mao to march against. You can't march around giving orders, living off the country, feeling important and then go back to long division and history, even the fascinating rewritten history of China.

I hope I am not oversimplifying, but this is what most of the China Watchers agree on. Whether Mao is active or not is fairly unimportant. One indication that he is not is the emergence of his wife, an aging actress who until now has been kept under a bucket. The feeling is that if Mao felt good, she would still be there.

For many years Chou En-lai has perfected the art of egg walking. He has weathered all storms, soothing this side, hiding this set of figures—a real fixer and very good at it. The proof of his efficiency is that he is still alive. But all of my China instructors agree on two things. The first is that there can never be peace between Madame Mao and Chou En-lai. One of them has to go down. The second agreement is that no matter what emerges from the free-for-all, it is going to be called Mao-ism, just as in Russia it is always Leninism no matter who is in charge. For that matter, our own foibles are always ascribed to democracy. If Mao should die right now, or if he is already dead, anything that happens in China is going to be called by his name. I have read a lot of Mao's thinking and it has that wonderful quality of being able to back up anything you want to do. So Maoism it is, no matter what side wins or who takes over.

What will happen is what happens everywhere. Eight hundred million–odd people will get tired of slogans and directives if they have not already. They will get back to their basic problem of getting enough to eat, of the problems of drought, epidemics, distribution and the personal relations of family, district, village, children and the vicious practices of the new man in town. They will want what everyone wants— comfort, security, health and enough leisure to get into a little local trouble. That is what will happen and I'm going way out on a limb—but it's an old limb polished over the centuries.

That's China, Alicia, but if I were a real expert I could have made it much more confusing and thus more erudite. But there remains the question of what we should do. And again I'm going to shine up that limb.

We should sit it out, the way we sit out our children's discovery of sex and profanity, but while waiting we should trade with China to the limit of our ability. We should sell them our things, haggle with them over prices not ideologies—the more trade the better, the more association, the better. A bulldozer is a better weapon than a bomb and a shipment of vaccine is a far more effective weapon than a shipload of napalm.

We should not give, but trade, and if in the process, we should lose a little face—we have plenty left. You know as well as I do, Alicia, that the only people who have to save face are those who aren't sure they have any. So let us lose some face in the interest of the future. China is going to be China for a long time—not Mao—but China. I think trade restrictions with any country in the world are stupid and self-destructive. Can you suggest anyone in our power structure who might listen to the unchanging music of history?

(Editor's Note [from the editor of *Newsday*]: This is the last in a series of reports by John Steinbeck from South Vietnam and other countries in East Asia. Steinbeck and his wife, Elaine, after viewing every phase of the war in Vietnam for five months are returning to their home in Sag Harbor, Long Island. Steinbeck, whose 20-year-old son John is serving with the U.S. forces in South Vietnam, lived with the troops under fire, flew with them in every type of combat aircraft and relaxed with them when the guns were quiet. The following column sums up his views on the future of the area.)

May 20, 1967 / Tokyo

Dear Alicia,

Our time is nearly up now. Our son, who is now Specialist 4, got five days Rest and Recuperation and joined us here and we all went to Kyoto in the prime of the cherry blossom season, probably one of the very most beautiful things I have ever seen—things to stare at for storing to remember later.

John was nervous at first, as we were, coming out of Vietnam. Traffic moves too fast. No care is taken about road mines. People move near to cover without caution and at night you can walk alone in safety. It's a frightening thing and takes some getting used to, but he didn't have time to go really soft. Last night he went back to his post—and because we know what it is, a big hunk of us went with him. He went loaded down with presents, mostly for Viet kids, the ones the protest-marchers claim he is murdering.

You know, Alicia, I do hope I have sense enough when I go home not to argue with those convinced people who don't know what they are talking about. I don't suppose I am that smart but I'm going to try to be.

But this pattern is nearly complete. Remember what the original plan was? To go to the center of the trouble and then to move outward on the periphery to see what the effect of Vietnam was on its neighbors. I've never done anything which stayed so close to plan. We've trooped all over South Vietnam, Thailand, Laos, Malaysia, Singapore, Indonesia, Hong Kong and Japan. Cambodia and Burma (U Thant's home country) wouldn't let us in nor would North Vietnam nor China, but wherever we could go, we went. And I have tried to write you what I could about it. There is, of course, much that can't be reduced to words—fear and pride and companionship and the trust in good men whose lives are in your hands and yours in theirs. I don't think such matters can be communicated. They are personal. And just as personal is my deep conviction that we are properly involved in East Asia and that we will be for all time, not in a military sense nor in any way a colonial or imperial sense, but simply because it is a huge and largely undeveloped part of the world and that we can and will creatively help [it] to develop without owning it. It will be that way in spite of all the shouting and the politicking about the world.

I had always thought of East Asia as old, old in the sense of being tired and worn out, and second of being unbearably overpopulated. Neither preconception is true. The people are young and fresh and inventive, the lands are huge with enormous unpopulated areas and the natural resources are comparatively untouched—the rivers, the hardwoods, the electric power, the food, the incredible richness waiting for peace and the creative hand to raise them. And I feel that we will be involved in this creating. Conquest is no longer possible or desirable but cooperation is not only necessary but inevitable. Our young of energy and imagination are going to be drawn westward as they always have and the new West is Asia. I know of no great movement of people or animals that has ever moved from west to east. Always we follow the sun and find our dreams not in its rising but in the direction of its setting. Probably all humans began in what we call the East. Now we have finally come full circle. The East is become the West. And if you don't believe this, talk with any young man or woman who has ever been in Asia and watch the eyes when he answers. France, England, Italy never caught our young men the way the so-called Orient does, for the Orient has become the Occident.

I have tried to write what I saw and felt and thought in this part of the world. My letters have by necessity been simply impressions, perhaps neither profound nor permanent but as true as I could make them and I'll back them against the granite convictions of those who have never been here.

I'm moving in on an ending now. I know what I want to say but not quite how to say it. I've been accused by the interested but uninvolved of being a warmonger, of favoring war and even of celebrating it. I hope you will believe that if I could shorten this war by one hour by going back to Vietnam, I would be on tonight's plane with a one-way ticket.

What I have been celebrating is not war but brave men. I have in a long life known good and brave men but none better, braver nor more committed than our servicemen in the far east. They are our dearest and our best and more than that—they are our hope.

AFTERWORD

As his biographer Jackson Benson noted in *John Steinbeck: Writer*, Steinbeck's opinion of the Vietnam War followed "a curve, from great doubt about our involvement, to very strong support of our policy, particularly in defense of the integrity of our troops in Vietnam, to doubt once again about the wisdom of our participation" (967). The Letters to Alicia mark the top of that curve. In them, he put aside any reservations he had and threw himself wholeheartedly into making the best case he could for the war. Although he insisted he was going to the combat zone to observe and draw his own conclusions, he declared his full support to reporters in Hawaii before he got there.

Steinbeck was strongly loyal to President Lyndon Johnson as a friend and as a fellow New Deal Democrat, but his support of the Vietnam War was based on broad intellectual agreement with LBJ, not just personal feelings. Like Johnson, Steinbeck believed in the domino theory, and viewed the Vietnam conflict as an East-West showdown of global proportions, in which Chinese-style Communism would sweep through the region unless it was countered aggressively by the West. He had been to the Soviet Union and its satellites in 1963 on behalf of the Kennedy administration and had personally witnessed what he saw as the life-killing oppression of leftist totalitarianism. He assumed that both China and the Soviet Union were determined to impose this hellish version of society on South Vietnam and beyond. In a column written from Bangkok, he referred to this aggression as "the great plan which has been frustrated and staggered, and largely because our soldiers and those of our allies have been in Korea and in South Vietnam. Had we not been, I would not even now be able to visit the countries of Southeast Asia" (71). It was America's task to halt this collectivist expansion and Vietnam was the place to draw the line.

The second premise Steinbeck shared with Johnson was that South Vietnam was a small and overwhelmed nation struggling toward democracy and in need of help to ward off an enemy of freedom every bit as ruthless and evil as the Nazis. This idealized view of the situation ignored the deep corruption of the Diem and Ky governments, the French colonial underpinnings of the struggle, and the Catholic-Buddhist cultural clashes in the region. It reduced the struggle to one of freedom versus totalitarianism. As Johnson phrased it in a speech, we were in Vietnam to "defend the freedom of a brave little nation." Notably, this language also ignored the fact that Vietnam was not small; the combined population of North and South Vietnam was almost 80 million.

The third premise Steinbeck and Johnson shared was that America could regenerate itself through rising to this great challenge. All three of Steinbeck's last published works, *The Winter of Our Discontent, Travels with Charley,* and *America and Americans,* were essentially treatises on the decline of America's moral values. In one essay in *America and Americans* he wrote, "John Kennedy said his famous lines, 'Ask not what your country can do for you—ask what you can do for your country.' And the listening nation nodded and smiled in agreement. But he said it not because this selfishness might become evident but because it already is evident, and increasingly so. And it is historically true that a nation whose people take out more than they put in will collapse and disappear" (397). Remembering what his generation had lived through in World War II, Steinbeck believed, or at least hoped, that our defense of South Vietnam would bring out the best in America as that war had and return us to the greatness of that time.

Given these views of Steinbeck's, it is easy to see why the war protesters were so odious to him. He simply could not ascribe any legitimacy to their point of view. It was the soldiers who were demonstrating how much they were prepared to do for their country. It was the soldiers who were putting in more than they were taking out. The protesters, on the other hand, were against the war, but not "for" anything. Not only that, he suspected their true motivation was cowardice. This dichotomy is one of the most consistent ongoing themes in the Letters to Alicia. In one of the harshest moments in the series, he wishes he could "run a protest parade down a V.C. trail" (26–27). The servicemen Steinbeck always depicted as brave and admirable. Benson even suggests that he equated them with the heroic Okies of *The Grapes of Wrath:* "They displayed for Steinbeck the same kind of nobility, born of adversity as his characters faced in dealing with the Dust Bowl, the banks, and the jeers of native Californians. Our soldiers were fighting for the survival of others and for human dignity"(969).

Dissent was not something Steinbeck's previous experience as a war correspondent had prepared him for, and as his wife Elaine noted, reliving that time was a significant part of his motivation for taking on the Vietnam assignment, a daunting one for a man in his mid-sixties. The whole country had been behind World War II, and Steinbeck approached Vietnam with the mindset of that era, using the same Ernie Pyle–style, human interest focus he had in his pieces for the *Herald Tribune* from Europe in 1943. He sought out and reported "small and shining things" as he termed it, stories that he felt would make the war "feelable and personal" (34), such as the K-9 corps, a Buddhist martial arts instructor, a bull session in a barracks, and local water and sewage issues. As he had in World War II, he tried to present the common man's view, though this was obviously difficult since he was escorted by high-ranking officers almost everywhere he went. In fact, *Newsday* owner Harry Guggenheim sent notes to several ambassadors and high-ranking military officers asking them to help Steinbeck in any way they could, implying that his views were sympathetic and would help secure American public support for the war.

Ever the folklore collector, Steinbeck passed along to readers such circulating GI lore as a satiric "official" note to loved ones on how to treat their newly returned soldiers and a comic letter from home about a soldier's wife's high times in his absence. Early on he used sarcastic humor, as in his column on bugs as military agents, but as he realized the grimness of the circumstances, he dropped that tone. One aspect of the conflict he often featured was military technology. He loved the helicopters, grenade launchers, and illumination flares on their technological merit and did some of his best writing describing these tools of the war. An essay that particularly upset doves back home was his paean to the firepower of "Puff, the Magic Dragon," the military transport plane modified to be a gunship. The fact that technology was so important and made such a difference in World War II may have encouraged his missing an essential difference between the wars—namely that Vietnam was an insurgency without set battles or amassed enemy troops. It did not occur to him how detrimental Puff would be in winning Vietnamese "hearts and minds," since its configuration would not allow pilots to distinguish between combatants and innocents.

In several pieces he offered concrete, specific ideas on how to improve mission performance. For instance, he suggested the use of five pound "alnico" magnets to search for weapons caches in the rivers and even asked Guggenheim to look into shipping some to him. In one essay from Laos, he suggested the military give the locals small radios that would only receive American radio channels. A less practical suggestion was his idea of transporting groups of the roving homeless street boys called "Saigon Cowboys" to the rural areas where they could serve as an intelligence gathering corps.

By the end of January 1967, after five weeks of almost nonstop observing and reporting from the field, his narrative voice had changed. Writing from a desk in Bangkok, he dropped his jaunty adventurer's style for a somber one tempered by the whirl of experiences that were fresh in his mind. He had lost some certainty about his opinions, but he had gained a more informed sense of the complexity of the situation. In early February he wrote, "There are no good wars, and I can find no soldier to disagree with me" (54). Doubt even crept into his previously ironclad belief in the overall integrity of the American effort. In the same piece he asked, "Who is guilty and who is innocent?" (54). That air of lost innocence became especially sharp after he visited Northern Thailand and Laos, where he saw the clandestine American operations that were going on and the devastating effect the U.S. bombing campaign was having on the landscape and the people. In these pieces, he often reminded his readers that "war is a sad and a savage thing" (71).

And a confusing thing. Steinbeck's character sketch of a colorful GI named Corporal Chatterley did not lionize its subject as one of his World War II pieces would have. Instead, Steinbeck used Chatterley to showcase the confusion and frustration of a soldier who is not allowed to operate in a military manner because of ambiguities and restrictions in the rules of engagement. And he began to express the possibility that America could actually lose the war. In a column from Jakarta he wrote that unless the Vietnamese got serious about the war "a great many people are presently dying to no purpose whatever" (135). He voiced what would later become the formal U.S. policy of "Vietnamization," writing that "no amount of military or economic help can make Vietnam free. That must be done by the South Vietnamese themselves" (135).

A palpable feeling of relief was evident in his sketch of "Pop" Ewell, an energetic and effective agricultural advisor in rural Laos. In Edgar Buell (Steinbeck evidently misheard his last name), he found an admirable American individual doing unequivocally good deeds in the back country of the war zone. Buell, and the Baptist missionaries who were working in the same area, were, in Steinbeck's words, "creating a new world by suggestions and example" (134). To be reminded that America's original mission was one of advising and building up, not destroying, helped him regain his moral footing, if only for one essay. The piece showed how much Steinbeck still yearned for a gallant, larger-than-life figure. He felt that his friend and president had let him, and the entire country, down. In a despondent letter to Guggenheim after Johnson's State of the Union speech in January 1967, Steinbeck wrote from Saigon, "He'd better come out of his slump or hurt feelings or whatever they are and come out fighting for us. The President does not have the right to sulk in his tent" (Guggenheim Papers). And in another letter to Guggenheim a week later he made it clear that he didn't trust General Westmoreland or his lieutenants and that he had no faith in the new Vietnamese leader, Nguyen Cao Ky. Aside from random heroes like Buell, he could no longer find anyone in a position of responsibility for the war who was proving true and not faltering.

It is important to remember that the major literary project Steinbeck had been engaged in just before his Vietnam tour was a translation and modern rendering of Thomas Malory's *Morte d'Arthur*. No matter how hardboiled he was externally or how much he claimed a naturalistic, non-teleological approach, Steinbeck believed in the mythic ideal of Arthur, the Round Table, and Camelot. Though he was not religious in the usual sense, he considered the Arthurian cycle more than a set of stories. To him, they were a mythic pattern that informed a worldview, and he worked from within that mythic framework all his writing life. A letter he wrote to Jacqueline Kennedy after her husband's assassination is his clearest statement of this. On February 25, 1964, three months after Kennedy's death, he wrote

Since I was nine years old, when my beautiful Aunt Molly gave me a copy of the *Morte d'Arthur* in Middle English, I have been working and studying this recurring cycle. The 15th century and our own have so much in common—loss of authority, loss of gods, loss of heroes, and loss of lovely pride. When such a hopeless muddled need occurs, it does seem to me that the hungry hearts of men distill their best and truest essence, and that essence becomes a man, and that man a hero so that all men can be reassured that such things are possible. The fact that all of these words—hero, myth, pride, even victory, have been muddled and sicklied by the confusion and pessimism of the times only describes the times. The words and the concepts are permanent, only they must be brought out and verified by the Hero. (*Life in Letters*, 792–93)

Warren French was the first Steinbeck scholar to discuss the Vietnam columns in terms of the Arthurian story cycle. In a 1975 essay titled "Steinbeck's Use of Malory," he called the Kennedy-Johnson years a "shattered dream of Camelot" and suggested that Steinbeck played the role of a defeated knight defending a defeated king when he "became too involved in the defense of Lyndon B. Johnson, dreamer of the 'Great Society'" (Hayashi, 11). And Tetsumaro Hayashi, in his 1986 monograph *Steinbeck and the Vietnam War*, also saw the connection and characterized the Asia trip as "a quest that epitomized his personal search for the grail . . . one that left him a deeply wounded knight bitterly denounced by both his friends and foes" (4).

In physical pain from a back injury and exhausted from frustration and disillusionment, Steinbeck closed the last Letter to Alicia by answering critics of the columns who had called him a warmonger. He wrote, "If I could shorten this war by one hour by going back to Vietnam, I would be on tonight's plane with a one-way ticket," and ended with the following salute to the soldiers: "I have not been celebrating war, but brave men. . . . They are our dearest and our best and more than that—they are our hope" (155). Thus, while the rest of his Arthurian construct had collapsed, the troops remained chivalrous American heroes in his mind. John IV's description of the days just before he left for the war in *The Other Side of Eden* shows the extent to which Steinbeck had mythologized the soldiers, including his own soon-to-be soldier son. After he formally presented John IV to President Johnson at the White House on the eve of the son's departure to Vietnam, Steinbeck and John IV had a session the latter called a "warrior's passage." His rendition of the evening is telling: "He bought me a lovely Colt derringer as a personal sidearm. For close-in fighting, don't you know. I mean two lousy shots for chrissake! We were obviously in some reverie of war fought in the mists of make-believe" (98).

But Vietnam had a distinct way of killing naive dreams of glory. John Hellman's book *American Myth and the Legacy of Vietnam* argues that it disrupted our entire national mythology. "Americans entered Vietnam with certain expectations that a story, a distinctly American story, would unfold. When the story turned into something unexpected, the true nature of the larger story of America itself became the subject of intense cultural debate" (x). Steinbeck's encounter with the Vietnam War, entwined as it was with personal friendships, liberal ideology, patriotism, fatherly pride, and romantic mythology, was a microcosm of that national experience. Like "his" president, the generals, and the politicians, Steinbeck went into a mythologized Vietnam. He went for two reasons—to voice support for our gallant defense of a weak and oppressed people, and to chronicle the moral redemption of the nation. While there, he saw the war's ambiguity, horror, stupidity, and destruction, and came home questioning its execution and legitimacy. Like the entire country, he was traumatized by all this, but unlike the rest of the country, he wasn't given the time to process the trauma, recover from it, or heal. His death on December 20, 1968, meant he did not see the end of the U.S. combat mission, the Paris Peace Accords, the fall of Saigon, the killing fields of Cambodia, or the dedication of the Vietnam Veterans' Memorial in Washington, D.C.

In late May 1967, Steinbeck debriefed Lyndon Johnson; after their meeting Johnson asked him to repeat his ideas to Vice President Hubert Humphrey, Secretary of State Dean Rusk, and Secretary of Defense Robert McNamara. This second briefing was recorded and is archived at the Department of Defense. He gave only tactical advice, suggesting things like reloading and abandoning old mortar shells with explosives set to detonate on use, dispensing medicines from air drops to show our good intentions, and using retrained captured Viet Cong soldiers in combat. He did not engage big questions like those Henry Cabot Lodge, the former ambassador to South Vietnam, posed after the war: "Was the United States mistaken in its determination to intervene? Was the United States engaged in an imperialist adventure far from our own shores? Or were we defending a small nation, pledged to a democratic government? Did the limitations placed on our use of military force keep us from a swift and decisive victory? Or were we engaged in a war that could not be won even with the most sophisticated and lethal of weapons? Were the Vietcong freedom fighters seeking to liberate their country, or were they simply blood-thirsty terrorists?" (Barden, 23).

Steinbeck did, however, raise those issues three months later in a letter to Elizabeth Otis. To me, this letter constitutes the true "lessons learned" briefing he might have given the men at the pinnacle of American power when he met with them. It is a remarkable document. I want to quote it at length in the hope that readers of this book will think of it, as I have come to, as a kind of coda to the Letters to Alicia.

August 31, 1967
Sag Harbor

Dear Elizabeth,

I know I have been greatly remiss about writing or even communicating, but this has been so in all directions. It starts with the stupid feeling that I have nothing I can or want to communicate—a dry as dust, worked out feeling. The only simile I can think of is those mountains of mine, tailings from which every vestige of value has been drawn. Some people, I know, work the tailings and get a small amount of very low grade ore. . . . The pain from spine and legs has been quite sharp but I halfway believe that the pain and the verbal impotence are a part of one thing in spite of what the X-rays say. Strange isn't it, that none of this happened until after I left Vietnam. I have seriously considered going back to get rid of my devils, but so far that would only be repetition.

I understand your feeling about this war. We seem to be sinking deeper and deeper into the mire. It is true that we are. I am pretty sure by now that the people running the war have neither conception nor control of it. And I think that I do have some conception but I can't write it. I know we cannot win this war, nor any war for that matter. And it seems to me the design is to sink deeper and deeper into it, more and more of us. When we have put down a firm foundation of our dead and when we have by a slow losing process been sucked into the texture of Southeast Asia, we will never be able nor will we want to get out. If we should win this war, in the old sense of defeating and deadening the so-called enemy, then we would become just another occupying army, and such an army loses contact with the place occupied. But we are not winning in that sense and we will not. In many directions we are being defeated by more successful techniques and attitudes than our own. We have no choice in the matter. . . .

Maybe I should go back. I seem to be becoming a vegetable here and now, thinking little thoughts or no thoughts at all, and I am sure boring the hell out of Elaine. She is conducting a business as usual campaign but with me it is not business as usual. The constant rain is getting tiring. One can find so many pains when the rain is falling. And I seem to have lost touch with things. . . . It is not that I am obsessed with myself. The opposite seems to be true. I cannot seem to draw my mind back to myself. Maybe that is what the pain is trying to do—but it is failing. But the curious retirement to the cave has given me no direction to follow. There is something sly about the whole thing, as though I were the butt of an ancient practical joke.

Anyway, I'll try to keep in touch from here on in—I hope. Love, John (*Life in Letters*, 847–49)

As his letter indicates, by the end of the summer of 1967 Steinbeck had finally grasped the great intractable predicament of the war, the thing that the best and brightest military strategists kept missing—that the American presence was, in the eyes of the Vietnamese people, an army of occupation. In his book *A Dove in Vietnam*, Mike McGrady, the *Newsday* reporter who covered the war after Steinbeck, quoted a poll showing that only 4 percent of the South Vietnamese wanted "victory over communism" while 81 percent wanted the foreigners to leave (198). Back in 1942, in *The Moon Is Down*, Steinbeck had understood this and stated it eloquently: "The men of the battalion came to detest the place they had conquered, and they were curt with the people and the people were curt with them, and gradually a little fear began to grow in the conquerors, a fear that it would never be over, that they could never relax or go home, a fear that one day they would crack and be hunted through the mountains like rabbits, for the conquered never relaxed their hatred." But in that book he had been writing about fascist occupiers, not his beloved American GIs. To realize that the great liberating army of World War II had gotten itself into this position was surely as painful to him as his back injury. His great memorable line in *The Moon Is Down* had been "The flies have conquered the flypaper," but this time it was us, the Americans, not the Nazis, who were turning out to be the flies.

His wife Elaine was emphatic about his "hawk to dove" conversion. In an interview after his death, she said, "John changed his mind totally about Vietnam while there, and he came home to write it and spent the rest of the time dying. That's not an apology for John. That's true." From his apprentice writings to his last novel, *The Winter of Our Discontent,* Steinbeck consistently placed moral dilemmas at the center of his plot structures. He saw such dilemmas as the wellspring of great storytelling. It is ironic that his last published work would display before the American and international public a wrenching moral dilemma that was both national and highly personal. And it was truly an "ancient practical joke" that, since he was not creating this dilemma as a fiction but living through it as a human being, he could not craft its proper ending.

His letter to Elizabeth Otis implies he knew what that ending should be but could not write it. Over forty years later we are left with a big "what if?" What if he had been able to write his views and they had been widely circulated? What if he had declared something on the order of Walter Cronkite's famous pronouncement on the *CBS Evening News:* "It is increasingly clear to this reporter that the only rational way out will be to negotiate, not as victors, but as an honorable people who lived up to their pledge to defend democracy, and did the best they could." Would Steinbeck's famous and trusted voice have changed the course of the war, of the Johnson presidency, of American history? In the last essay in *America and Americans,* in the chapter called "Americans and the Future," he wrote, "What happened to us came quickly and quietly, came from many directions and was the more dangerous because it wore the face of good." I wonder if he realized, as he lay in his New York hospital bed, how well that sentence described the war that was the old knight's final, if dubious, battle.

I want to close with a personal note: I was a twenty-three-year-old lieutenant when I arrived in South Vietnam in June of 1970. A full colonel, I remember his last name was Lewis, flew me out from Saigon to the fire support base at Tay Ninh where I was going to take command of a battery of the 2nd Battalion of the 32nd Field Artillery Regiment— "The Proud Americans." After he showed me around and introduced me to the other officers, we took a walk along the barbed wire at the end of a small airstrip on the west side of our compound, presumably so he could show me things I needed to know about the defense of the perimeter. As we walked he asked me what I thought about the war. I said a few things, as I recall, about Vietnamization being good and that we couldn't win if the people didn't want us to.

What he said in reply still rings in my ears after forty years. He said he was a history buff and had studied his way to the conclusion that the war wasn't about Communism. It was about overthrowing an occupying army, us. He said that long ago, we, the American colonists, had beaten the British in our own revolution not because we were better soldiers, but because we were in a winning situation. We knew the countryside, we could hide in the trees and bushes, we got aid and comfort from the sympathetic civilians around us, and we didn't stand and fight pitched battles unless we knew we could win them. "Sound familiar?" he said. I said it did. He said, "We're the redcoats in this one, lieutenant. Don't be John Wayne. Take care of your men and get everybody home. We won't be here much longer." I thanked him for the advice and he went back to Saigon leaving me to think about his analogy. I am still thinking about it.

That's how, one morning in Tay Ninh, I learned the lesson Steinbeck spent the last years of his life learning the hard way.

NOTES ON THE DISPATCHES

1   "To me, very exciting news": No dateline was published, but Steinbeck datelined it New York in the handwritten original. It ran in *Newsday* on December 3, 1966, inaugurating the series. Steinbeck apparently did not consider it an "official" column, since he did not number it as he did the rest. *Newsday*'s editors called it #29 in their in-house numbering, continuing the sequence of the first series of Letters to Alicia.

1   "You must have seen a crowd of": *Newsday* #30. No dateline was published, but Steinbeck again datelined it New York. It ran on December 10, 1966. The initial Yevtushenko exchanges had occurred in July; Yevtushenko came to the United States in late November and the two met and embraced warmly. The essay seems to be a direct response to that meeting and the subsequent re-emergence of the controversy.

3   "Every year about this time": *Newsday* #31. Its published date was December 17, 1966, but it was likely written before December 8, 1966, the Steinbecks' departure date. The importance of the People's Republic of China to the Vietnam conflict was on Steinbeck's mind as he began his journey. This and the following column were written in blue ballpoint pen unlike the black used in all the others, indicating possible earlier composition.

5   "The bugs are in again in Vietnam": This piece was not published in *Newsday* and was not given a *Newsday* number. When it ran in the *Philadelphia Bulletin* on Christmas Day, 1966, it had the dateline "En Route to Vietnam."

7   "We stopped here to be briefed": This piece was not published in *Newsday* and was not given a *Newsday* number. The date, December 9, 1966, matches the Steinbecks' travel itinerary. He mentions their arrival in Saigon "tomorrow."

8   "Remember how the lordly jet cuts": *Newsday* #34. Steinbeck's reference to being in Saigon for two days indicates that this was his first dispatch from the ground in Vietnam, though *Newsday* numbered it after the "Christmas truce" piece (see p. 12). Both were published on December 31, 1966. *Newsday* editors deleted a direct appeal to the American leadership to drop the Christmas truce and the restriction against incursions into Cambodia and Laos. They also dropped "and by this letter I am trying to get it," following the phrase "If I had the ear of authority." There were several other non-substantive editorial changes as well.

10 "I must say I'm glad to be getting": *Newsday* #32. Steinbeck mentions getting back to Saigon before the Christmas truce, so he had been to the field, although the focus of the dispatch is the city at the holiday season.

12 "The Christmas truce is over": Newsday #33. This piece ran in *Newsday* on December 31, but came in the same mailing as a letter to Guggenheim dated December 26, so that is its likely date of composition. Note the reference to the NVA and Viet Cong having no respect for the Western concept of honor in relation to breaking the Christmas truce.

13 "Strange happenings are": *Newsday* #35. *Newsday* used the dateline Saigon, but Steinbeck titled it "Dialectic Dementia" in the space where he usually wrote datelines. The "youth" (*komsomolskaya*) edition of *Pravda* must have been following Steinbeck's columns closely because the topic of this piece is their calling Steinbeck an accomplice to murder, based on a column he wrote only six days earlier.

14 "Just back from a field trip": This column was not published and not given a *Newsday* number, although a transcribed copy titled "Letter No. 8" is in the Guggenheim files at the Library of Congress. Despite the mention of an enclosed map, none was with the typed copy or with the originals in the Pierpont Morgan Library. The apparent locale was Saigon, since Steinbeck said he was just back from the field.

16 "If I had any ambition": This column was not published and not given a *Newsday* number, although a transcribed copy titled "Letter No. 9" is in the Guggenheim files. Its mention of flying to Pleiku places it as written on January 3 or 4, 1967.

19 "Where do we get our impressions": *Newsday* #36. The typed transcription in the Guggenheim files is dated December 29, 1966. Note the mention of Steinbeck's getting high-level briefings whenever he visited a unit, either an American or Vietnamese one.

22 "I would like more than anything": *Newsday* #37. *Newsday* gave the dateline as Pleiku, but Steinbeck originally wrote "Dateline—a tiny circle cleared with machetes, just big enough for a chopper to set down, in the mountains northwest of Pleiku." It ran in *Newsday* directly after the previous column, on the same day. In the published version, the *Newsday* editors added the term "Vietniks" used to describe the war protesters, apparently in trying to fix a clumsy sentence.

25 "Do you remember my telling": *Newsday* #38. Published in *Newsday* on the same day as the previous two columns, as the third piece in a sequence in the *Weekend* section. Steinbeck used the dateline "Pundit Manor," an ironic reference to the Caravelle Hotel in Saigon, although the piece was about Pleiku. This was changed to Saigon by *Newsday*. The drawings of the three types of booby traps were from a booklet supplied to the soldiers

when they arrived in Vietnam. Steinbeck sent it in the packet with these dispatches (see gallery).

27 "Here in Vietnam, people": *Newsday* #39. Interestingly, the writer of this tribute suggested "chivalry" as a possible motive for Steinbeck's trip to the war. Perhaps he knew about Steinbeck's interest in Arthurian legend.

30 "This war in Vietnam is very confusing": This column mentioned traveling with General Westmoreland. A cordial letter from Westmoreland in response to Steinbeck indicates that Steinbeck must have written the general after their time together (see gallery). Obviously, his positive impressions of the war were important to the American military leadership at the highest levels. Note that the column closes with Steinbeck's first hint of doubt about the prospect of a quick victory. This is one of the few dispatches to be reprinted after its initial appearance; it appeared in *America and Americans and Selected Nonfiction*, edited by Susan Shillinglaw and Jackson J. Benson (Penguin, 2002, 297–98), with the title "Vietnam War: No Front, No Rear."

32 "I want to speak of our troops": Not numbered by *Newsday*. Before the published opening phrase, Steinbeck's unedited version of this piece began: "Tomorrow I'm going south to the Delta country, to look at what has to be the next phase of this war, but now . . ." Since the columns have typically been referred to by their openings, this has led to confusion, including the assertion by one scholar that it is not in the Pierpont Morgan Library files. It is. The edited *Newsday* version had the headline "A Look at the New GI."

34 "I have to tell you about the massive": *Newsday* #42. *Newsday* used the headline "Canines vs. the Viet Cong" and ran two Associated Press photos of trainers with their scout dogs, one of which was wounded. The caption notes, "The dog survived." A reader, a recent K-9 corpsman in Vietnam, sent a letter to *Newsday* complaining of inaccuracies in this column, but it was not published. The corpsman wrote of his "concern about some misinformation" in the piece and mentioned three errors: (1) sentry dogs were not fitted with steel fangs when their real teeth wore out; (2) dogs were not destroyed if their handlers were killed; and (3), contrary to Steinbeck's listing of breeds, no poodles were ever employed in the K-9 Corps in Vietnam.

36 "By chopper to Delta region of Vietnam": *Newsday* #43. Published in *Newsday* in the *Weekend* section. *Newsday* used Steinbeck's full dateline, "Can Tho, 70 miles Southwest of Saigon," in the headline, and added "Steinbeck in Vietnam: Action in the Delta," which was superimposed over a photo of a River Patrol Boat (PBR) on the Mekong River. This column contains some of the best descriptive writing in the series and marks Steinbeck's first actual field encounter with Vietnamese people. It was also reprinted

in *America and Americans and Selected Nonfiction* (299–303), under the title "Action in the Delta."

40 "I wrote to you about the quiet patrol": *Newsday* #44. This piece was a continuation of the column above and ran in the same *Weekend* section of *Newsday*. There were two captioned photos, one of a Navy river patrol questioning two Vietnamese men on a sampan, credited to Woody Dickerman, a *Newsday* journalist and photographer; and one of Steinbeck looking through binoculars at a sampan on the river, credited to the U.S. Navy. The column was reprinted in *America and Americans and Selected Nonfiction* (304–6) under the title "Terrorism."

42 "Want to hear some pure James Bond": This column was not published and not given a *Newsday* number, although a transcribed copy titled "Letter No. 20" is in the Guggenheim files. The handwritten version was dated January 13, 1967.

44 "I came up here to visit the": *Newsday* #45. *Newsday* kept Steinbeck's full dateline. The official name of the mountain is Pussai, but Steinbeck, like the troops in the area, seemed to prefer the alternate spelling. This field trip gave him a chance to visit his son's Armed Forces TV detachment and spend time with him while also seeing a more northerly region of the country.

47 "In my last I told you about": *Newsday* #46. Again, *Newsday* kept Steinbeck's full dateline. *Newsday* gave this continuation of the dispatch from his son's unit the headline "One of the Strangest Nights I Ever Spent," and used the following as a pull quote: "Tonight was dark, a velvety crumbling dark, no firing, no earth-lighting flares swinging from their parachutes. No, it was dark and it was quiet." John IV wrote about the same night in his book *The Other Side of Eden*. Here's his version: "I saw my father behind some sandbags overlooking my position with his M-60 at the ready. There was nothing particularly awkward here. We both knew and liked guns, but there was something incredibly touching and hilarious about the operatic quality in which all our metaphors had crystallized. I mean, who, in God's name, was producing this movie?" (106).

49 "Soon after I arrived in South Vietnam": *Newsday* #47. *Newsday* gave this column the headline "Aerial Eyes on Charley." There was a noncredited photo of an O-1 Bird Dog F.A.C. airplane flying over rice paddies, shot from above. The caption read: "A single-engine plane carrying Forward Air Controllers over rice paddies in South Vietnam, on the watch for signs of Viet Cong." "Bat" Masterson, a frontier lawman and U.S. Marshal in the 1880s American West, was the basis for a popular 1960s TV show, so the name would have been widely known to Steinbeck's readers. Captain Masterson took off in an A1G Skyraider on October 13, 1968, from Nakhon Phanom

Airfield in Laos and was subsequently shot down. He was recorded as Missing in Action. The full report on him can be seen online (http://taskforce omegainc.org/M021.htm).

52 "As I told you in my last letter": *Newsday* #48. *Newsday* did not give this piece a dateline, but Steinbeck wrote "FAC Mission No. 2" in the area where he usually wrote datelines. It is a continuation of the last column and ran the next day. *Newsday* gave it two headlines, "Steinbeck in Vietnam" and "Air War Is Just as Ugly," and ran this phrase on the second page of the article: "Viet War Is Just as Ugly From Air, Says Steinbeck." Although Steinbeck said he sent a declassified photo with the essay, none was in the Guggenheim files at the Library of Congress or at the Pierpont Morgan Library.

54 "Ev Martin, who is Bureau Chief": *Newsday* #49. Someone at Edmund Scientific, the company in Tonawanda, New York, that sold the alnico magnets, read this column and followed up by writing to *Newsday* and sending a shipment of the magnets to Col. Hyatt's battalion of the 25th Infantry Division.

59 "Very often you read in the papers": This column was not published and not given a *Newsday* number, although a transcribed copy titled "Letter No. 34" is in the Guggenheim files. There are no copies of the actual leaflets Steinbeck sent in the Guggenheim Library of Congress files or at the Morgan Library. *Newsday* ran a story on February 4, 1967, on the leaflets with the headline "The Paper War," noting that they "were collected by *Newsday* columnist John Steinbeck." Since this story did not have the "Dear Alicia" opening or Steinbeck's byline, it has not been considered an "official" dispatch by some. *Newsday* ran graphics of the leaflets themselves as well as a photo of a helicopter dropping them over the countryside. The layout divided the leaflets by type—"Target: South Vietnamese Civilians," "Target: Communist Troops," and "Target: North Vietnam."

64 "Very often since I have been 'in country' ": *Newsday* #50. This is a continuation of the last column, and both ran together in the *Weekend* section. *Newsday* gave them a common headline on the second page: "On the Trail of the V. C." They also included two pull quotes: "This is prime sniper country and it doesn't pay to bunch up," and "I have seen the desperate terrain where the V. C. must live." An unattributed photo showed Steinbeck in a flak jacket and steel helmet standing next to his fellow Long Islander Captain Turchiano.

67 "As you are well aware, wars": This column was not published and not given a *Newsday* number, although a transcribed copy titled "Letter No. 25" is in the Guggenheim files, which would place it as written in early February. There was no dateline and the location Steinbeck used was "Saigon-on-

Styx." Xerox copies of the instructions on how to treat a returning GI were in the Library of Congress's Guggenheim Steinbeck collection.

70 "I've tried to tell you about as much of Vietnam": *Newsday* #51. *Newsday* did not give this dispatch a dateline, but it was written from Bangkok, Thailand. This was the first of the summing up columns written from the relative calm of the Steinbecks' suite in the Oriental Hotel, rooms that had once been Somerset Maugham's Bangkok residence.

72 "Don Besom of JUSPAD": *Newsday* #52. This and the next two pieces, though *Newsday* recorded them as posted from Saigon, were written from Bangkok. They were published together as a long spread for the *Weekend* section. Steinbeck couched them in the past tense, accentuating their reflective mood. On the second page of the feature, *Newsday* gave the headline "Letters to Alicia from Vietnam," and included the following as a pull quote: "The bridges were invariably down, the roads broken and a kind of dilapidation, like a skin disease, spread over the land. The fields looked untended . . ." This and the two following pieces featured line drawings by Loretta Vollmuth, an in-house *Newsday* editorial illustrator who, as Loretta V. Krupinski, had a successful career as an illustrator of children's books. This essay was paired with a sketch of a UH-D Huey helicopter flying over rice paddies.

75 "I wrote you about the teeming": *Newsday* #53. This piece included a drawing by Vollmuth of a street scene in Rach Kien, a small hamlet recently retaken from the Viet Cong. The pull quote read: "The hamlet chief and the school teacher had been early murdered, which is the V.C. method of eliminating traditional order and traditional culture . . ." A postscript directed readers toward "More Steinbeck on Following Page."

78 "It is easy to remember": No *Newsday* number. This piece appeared with a set of black and white illustrations by Vollmuth that included a folksinger, a go-go dancer, a peace march, an urban street, and football players. There were two pull quotes: "Is it any wonder that a smart and amazingly dedicated army falls back on satire?" and "The newspapers they receive . . . tell a story amounting to treason in attitude, a population reeling under the heavy burden of prosperity."

79 "Although I am numbering this": This essay was not dated, not given a *Newsday* number, and not published in any form. Although, as Steinbeck mentions in the first sentence, he did give it a number, he addressed his note to Lou Schwartz, the *Weekend* section editor at *Newsday*, not "Dear Alicia," indicating his hesitancy about it running as a column.

87 "I guess everyone who has been here": *Newsday* #55. This column had the headline "A Plan for the Saigon Cowboys," and two photos credited to Associated Press Radiophoto. One was captioned "Vietnamese boy holds rock

while another takes refuge behind a cart," and the other "Knife-bearing youths post 'Do Not Enter' sign on a Da Nang street."

90 "You know how it is when large": *Newsday* #56. The second page had the pull quote "You soon get to dreaming of cool, tasty water."

92 "Students all over the world": *Newsday* #57. The piece had an AP photo captioned "Students in Saigon staged this anti-government demonstration in 1966," and the pull quote "Students . . . have become barometers of unrest."

96 "One of the most interesting and": *Newsday* #58. The *Newsday* headline read "John Steinbeck's Vietnam Letters to Alicia: The 'Clean Man's' Judo School." An AP wirephoto of Tam Giac was included with a paraphrase of Steinbeck's text as the caption: "Thich Tam Giac: He is called a 'clean man,' and that is a rare animal indeed."

99 "Before I started this journey": This column was not published and not given a *Newsday* number, although a transcribed copy titled "Letter No. 38" is in the Guggenheim files. Steinbeck sent the excerpts from *The Art of War* to *Newsday* apparently hoping they would publish the whole document. The excerpts conclude with the following paragraph, presumably written by General Westmoreland or one of his staff:

> It is hoped that a careful perusal of the foregoing will give an indication of how the Viet Cong and the North Vietnam Army can be expected to operate. For, knowingly or not, they are steeped in the philosophy of warfare enunciated by Sun Tzu. The Viet Cong emphasis on careful reconnaissance and detailed planning; their use of secret agents; their careful camouflage and the use of surprise; their unwillingness to engage except when all factors are in their favor, are all traits that are two and a half millennia old. May this paper help you to "Know your enemy and know yourself; in a hundred battles you will never be in peril."

100 "It is time for us to continue": *Newsday* #60. This column was written from notes in Bangkok, even though it ends "soon we will be in Bangkok"; Steinbeck uses the past tense up to that sentence. In Thailand, he lost access to the Pan American Airlines diplomatic pouch he had used up to that point, and had to resort to sending several columns at once by regular airmail, making determining their order more difficult. This dispatch appeared in *America and Americans and Selected Nonfiction* (307–10) under the title "Puff the Magic Dragon."

104 "I must tell you that it is a delayed": *Newsday* #61. *Newsday* editors cut the phrase "they have never been conquered nor colonized." The column included an AP photo of the grounds of the Royal Temple showing two

aspirants for the priesthood strolling by a large statue of Buddha. It also included the pull quote "No Gunfire, No Hollow Roar of Howitzers."

106 "This letter is not one of speculation": *Newsday* #59. This was published before the other Bangkok essays above, but was probably written later, since it is reflective and not based on field notes. *Newsday* changed "The U.S." to "we" in the sentence about bombing civilians.

108 "You remember how, when you are": *Newsday* #65. The headline for this column was "A Look at Corporal Chatterley's War"; also included was a Loretta Vollmuth drawing of Cpl. Chatterley sitting on a footlocker smoking a cigarette and drinking a Coca-Cola.

111 "I'm not going to give you": *Newsday* #68. The headline for this column, "No *Playboy* in Thailand," was followed by the *Playboy* bunny logo with a large *x* over it. The core of the essay is an exchange between Steinbeck and a Thai major general, indicating that Steinbeck received the same high level of military attention in Thailand that he did in Vietnam.

114 "This flitting about may make me": *Newsday* #62. *Newsday* editors deleted the phrase "and the taxes were so low, and hardly collectable, that the village was only vaguely conscious of the capital." There was a short quote serving as a headline, "A Strange Forgotten Country."

116 "I wonder whether I made it clear in": *Newsday* #63. The headline on the second page was "Touring in Thailand: Inside Terror Territory." There was an unattributed photo with the caption "Two Thai women prepare to board their small boat on river [*sic*] near their village." The last paragraph's mention of Sag Harbor shop owner Nada Barry gave a local Long Island touch to this column.

119 "In my last I started to tell": *Newsday* #64. Published directly after the previous column on the same date. Steinbeck's description of the decimated landscape brings the defoliant Agent Orange to mind. According to documents from the Department of Defense and the Veterans' Administration, the herbicide was sprayed extensively in the area around Udon Thani in the northeast of Thailand beginning in 1964.

121 "I've probably tried to tell you": *Newsday* #66. This piece was put together from impressions of field visits in Northern Thailand and ran on the same day as the next column. The second page had the pull quote "We can't look up precedents, procedures of the past."

124 "The year is running and it is time": *Newsday* #67. The mention of Edmunds Scientific by name was no doubt a way to thank the company for responding to his earlier column by sending a shipment of their alnico magnets to Col. Hyatt's unit in the Mekong Delta.

126 "A traveler is reported to have said": *Newsday* #69.

128 "As you may know, the subject": *Newsday* #70. *Newsday* deleted "North Vietnam, North Korea, Albania and Cuba," the countries besides China that Americans were not permitted to enter at the time. And after the reply in French to Steinbeck's request for a visa to visit Cambodia was received, *Newsday* deleted the sentence about waiting "for a change in Prince's liver and/or policy."

132 "I guess I learn slowly": *Newsday* #71. Note that Steinbeck wrote "us" in describing his rescue from a firefight in Houei Kong near the Cambodian border—his wife Elaine was with him on this dangerous visit. "Pop" Ewell's actual name was Edgar Buell. He was a farmer from Indiana who worked in Laos for the International Voluntary Services and later the Agency for International Development. According to Don Schanche's 1970 book *Mister Pop*, Buell was notorious as a fearless supporter of the Hmong tribesmen's efforts in fighting the Pathet Lao.

134 "By now I know some things about Vietnam": *Newsday* #72. The first paragraph given here was deleted by *Newsday* due to its potentially libelous remarks about the *New York Post*. The edited version begins at the second paragraph, "Before the whole world sinks . . ." This opening is usually the sentence that gives the column its name in the various archival collections. The new chief editor Bill Moyers's memo on the subject, typed on *Newsday* notepaper, reads as follows:

> Bill D. Moyers, Publisher
>
> Captain Guggenheim,
> This is something we need to talk about. The lawyers say this first paragraph is close to libelous, and would be deemed so by them if it were not John Steinbeck in question. For that reason, and also because I think it grants the New York Post more recognition than the Post deserves, I recommend we change it. Or just begin with the second paragraph. I understand how angry John feels about something like the Post's position, but it doesn't do any good to take them on like this. Outside New York, who cares about the Post?
>
> BILL MOYERS

138 "This is a place": *Newsday* #73. The single word "Steinbeck" was the headline on the second page. Steinbeck's call for other American writers to come to Vietnam and see things for themselves gave *Newsday* reporter Mike McGrady the occasion to request, and receive, permission from Moyers to go to and present the "Dove's View" to *Newsday* and syndicated readers. His antiwar columns ran for several months in the spring and summer of 1967. His memo requesting the assignment read as follows:

To: Captain Harry Guggenheim/Bill Moyers/Bill McIlwain
Re: Vietnam Coverage
From: Mike McGrady

It seems to me that John Steinbeck makes an excellent point in the attached column. Though I don't pretend to the stature of the writers mentioned, I do think that the newspaper might well obtain a fresh— or at least different—viewpoint by sending me over to cover it for a while.

I find myself in substantial disagreement with the Administration and with this newspaper's editorial policy. And so that there would be no doubts on the matter, I would suggest that the series of columns be entitled "A Dove in Vietnam." Running such a series would, I feel, demonstrate once again *Newsday*'s tradition of fair play and editorial independence.

142 "I recently was present at": *Newsday* #74. The Steinbecks arrived in the Indonesian capital in time to witness the deposing of President Sukarno. The Johnson administration saw this as a big step in stemming the Communist tide, and quickly recognized General Suharto's government. Steinbeck didn't know the coup that put Suharto in power took between 80,000 and 100,000 lives and he did not live to see the corruption and repression that marked Suharto's thirty-two-year reign.

146 "I guess you can call this": *Newsday* #75. This piece continued the arch tone of the previous column and pointed out Sukarno's excesses and personal quirks. Though the column does not mention Vietnam, the domino theory obviously linked the Indonesian regime change to its northern neighbor in Steinbeck's mind.

150 "I remember promising": *Newsday* #76. Again, the word "Steinbeck" was the headline on the second page. Cynthia Wallsten, whose name Steinbeck misspelled here, was the wife of Robert Wallsten, an actor John and Elaine had known since the Broadway staging of his play *Burning Bright*. The two couples were close friends and often traveled together. Mao Tse-tung was in fact alive when the column was written; he died on September 9, 1976.

154 "Our time is nearly up": *Newsday* #77. The *Newsday* printing of this final column did not include the editor's note, but it was sent to the syndicate newspapers and many placed it with the essay. This column was the last written work of John Steinbeck's published in his lifetime.

BIBLIOGRAPHY

Anderson, Raymond H. "Moscow Reports Steinbeck Reply." *New York Times*, July 17, 1966, p. 5.
———. "Soviet Poet Bids Steinbeck Speak." *New York Times*, July 8, 1966, p. 6.
Barden, Thomas. "John Steinbeck and the Vietnam War." *Steinbeck Review* 5, no. 1 (Spring 2008): 10–24.
Benintendi, Tim. "Steinbeck in Vietnam, Spring 1966." *Steinbeck Studies* 16, nos. 1 and 2 (Spring 2005): 127–31.
Benson, Jackson. *John Steinbeck, Writer*. New York: Viking Press, 1994.
Brinkley, Douglas. "The Other Vietnam Generation." *New York Times Book Review*, February 2, 1999, Section VII, p. 27.
Buell, Hal, ed. *We Were There: Vietnam*. New York: Tess Press, 2007.
Butwin, David. "Steinbeck Here on Way to Vietnam." *Honolulu Advertiser*, December 6, 1966.
Collier, Peter. "The Winter of John Steinbeck." *Ramparts*, July 1967, p. 59.
D'Amour, Dominic. *John Steinbeck dans les Annes 1960: Un Intellectual Americain Liberal de Gauche?* MA thesis, University of Quebec at Montreal, 2006.
Department of Defense. *"Suggestions": transcription of tape by John Steinbeck*. Memoranda on Vietnam to Secretary McNamara.
Federal Bureau of Investigation. *Dossier #100-106224 [Steinbeck, John]*.
Fensch, Thomas, ed. *Conversations with John Steinbeck*. Jackson: University Press of Mississippi, 1998.
Galbraith, John Kenneth. "John Steinbeck: Footnote for a Memoir." *Atlantic*, November 1969, pp. 65–67.
Garfinkle, Adam H. *Telltale Hearts: The Origins and Impact of the Vietnam Antiwar Movement*. New York: St. Martin's Press, 1995.
Guggenheim, Harry F., Papers. Library of Congress. Boxes 275–77.
Harmon, Robert B. *John Steinbeck & Newsday with a Focus on "Letters to Alicia": An Annotated and Documented Reference Guide*. San Jose, California: Privately printed, 1999.
Hayashi, Tetsumaro, ed. *Steinbeck and the Arthurian Theme*. Steinbeck Monograph Series. Muncie, Indiana: Ball State University Department of English, 1975.
———. *John Steinbeck and the Vietnam War (Part 1)*. Steinbeck Monograph Series. Muncie, Indiana: Ball State University Department of English, 1986.

Hayes, Sarah H. *The Quotable Lyndon B. Johnson.* Anderson, South Carolina: Droke House, 1968.

Hellman, John. *American Myth and the Legacy of Vietnam.* New York: Columbia University Press, 1986.

Herring, George C. "The War in Vietnam." In *Exploring the Johnson Years,* ed. Robert A. Divine. Austin: University Press of Texas, 1981.

James, Doug. *Walter Cronkite: A Reporter's Life.* New York: Alfred A. Knopf, 1996.

Keeler, Robert F. *Newsday: A Candid History of the Respectable Tabloid.* New York: William Morrow, 1990.

Leary, William M. "CIA Air Operations in Laos, 1955–1974: Supporting the 'Secret War.'" CIA publications website. https://www.cia.gov/library/center-for-the-study-of-intelligence/csi-publications/csi-studies/studies/winter99-00/art7 .html.

Lisca, Peter. *John Steinbeck: Nature and Myth.* New York: Thomas Y. Crowell, 1978.

McGrady, Mike. *A Dove in Vietnam.* New York: Funk & Wagnalls, 1968.

O'Nan, Stewart. *The Vietnam Reader: The Definitive Collection of Fiction and Non-fiction on the War.* New York: Anchor Books, 1998.

Parini, Jay. *John Steinbeck: A Biography.* New York: Henry Holt and Company, 1995.

Roberts, Chalmers H. *First Rough Draft: A Journalist's Journal of Our Times.* New York: Praeger, 1973.

Schanche, Don A. *Mister Pop.* New York: David McKay, 1970.

Schulberg, Budd. "John Steinbeck: A Lion in Winter." In *The Four Seasons of Success.* New York: Doubleday, 1972.

Steinbeck, Elaine A. "Half a World from Home." *McCall's Magazine,* June 1967, pp. 42 and 137.

Steinbeck, John. *America and Americans and Selected Nonfiction.* Edited by Susan Shillinglaw and Jackson J. Benson. New York: Penguin, 2002.

———. Foreword to *The Speeches of Adlai Stevenson,* 5–8. New York: Random House, 1952.

———. Letters to Alicia. *Newsday,* November 20, 1965–May 20, 1967.

———. Letters to Alicia manuscripts. Pierpont Morgan Library, New York.

———. "One American in Paris." *Le Figaro Litteraire,* June 12 and September 18, 1954.

———. "Open Letter to Poet Yevtushenko." *Newsday,* July 11, 1966, p. 3.

———. Preston Beyer Collection. Princeton University Library.

———. *Steinbeck: A Life in Letters.* Edited by Elaine Steinbeck and Robert Wallsten. New York: Viking Press, 1975.

———. "What's Happening to America?" *Reader's Digest,* October 1966, pp. 175–84. Condensed from *Saturday Evening Post.*

Steinbeck, John, IV. *In Touch*. New York: Dell, 1970.

Steinbeck, John, IV, and Nancy Steinbeck. *The Other Side of Eden: Life with John Steinbeck*. Amherst, New York: Prometheus Books, 2001.

U.S. Army Intelligence. *(G-2) investigative report (IX-O/S-1403c) [Steinbeck, John]*. 1943.

Valenti, Jack J. *A Very Human President*. New York: Norton, 1976.

INDEX